Tangible Things

TANGIBLE THINGS

January 24 to May 29, 2011
Collection of Historical Scientific Instruments
Monday - Thursday, 9am to 5pm; Friday 9am to 4pm

Tangible Things

MAKING HISTORY THROUGH OBJECTS

Laurel Thatcher Ulrich
Ivan Gaskell
Sara J. Schechner
Sarah Anne Carter

with photographs by
Samantha S. B. van Gerbig

OXFORD
UNIVERSITY PRESS

OXFORD
UNIVERSITY PRESS

Oxford University Press is a department of the University of Oxford.
It furthers the University's objective of excellence in research, scholarship,
and education by publishing worldwide.

Oxford   New York
Auckland   Cape Town   Dar es Salaam   Hong Kong   Karachi
Kuala Lumpur   Madrid   Melbourne   Mexico City   Nairobi
New Delhi   Shanghai   Taipei   Toronto

With offices in
Argentina   Austria   Brazil   Chile   Czech Republic   France   Greece
Guatemala   Hungary   Italy   Japan   Poland   Portugal   Singapore
South Korea   Switzerland   Thailand   Turkey   Ukraine   Vietnam

Published in the United States of America by
Oxford University Press
198 Madison Avenue, New York, NY 10016

Library of Congress Cataloging-in-Publication Data
Ulrich, Laurel Thatcher.
Tangible things : making history through objects / Laurel Thatcher Ulrich, Ivan Gaskell,
Sara J. Schechner, Sarah Anne Carter with photographs by Samantha S. B. van Gerbig.
pages cm
Includes index.
ISBN 978–0–19–938228–6 (pbk.; alk. paper)—ISBN 978–0–19–938227–9 (hardback; alk. paper)
1. Material culture.   2. Material culture—Philosophy.   3. Civilization—History.
4. Social evolution.   I. Title.
GN406.U57 2015
303.4—dc23
2014028717

For all the people who care for and preserve tangible things:
museum curators, conservators, conservation scientists,
collection managers, registrars, administrators, and volunteers.

Why do precisely these objects which we behold make a world?
—Henry David Thoreau, *Walden*, 1854

Contents

About the Companion Website

www.oup.com/us/tangiblethings

Tangible Things is both an introduction to the range and scope of Harvard's remarkable collections and an invitation to reassess collections of all sorts, including those that reside in the bottom drawers or attics of people's houses. It questions the nineteenth-century categories that still divide art museums from science museums and historical collections from anthropological displays and assume that history is made only from written documents. The 406 images presented on the companion website give readers access to items that were part of this project but are not shown in this book, as well as alternative views of the items that are included here. Explore these varied things and ask: What can these objects reveal about history, about the people who made or collected them, and about the museums that have kept and preserved them? How might an examination of these tangible things change the way we think about the things that surround us every day?

Log in to the companion website using username: **Tangible5** and password: **Objects1636**.

Preface and Acknowledgments

As a collaboration among four authors and one photographer, this is an unusual publication. It began with an exhibition called *Tangible Things* that we created together at Harvard University in the spring of 2011. We learned so much from that project that we decided to write what we thought would be a retrospective catalog. Instead, it became this book. All of us had a hand in the general chapters. We composed the case studies individually although they were built on shared ideas.

The exhibition grew out of a much longer collaboration between Laurel Ulrich and Ivan Gaskell. Since 2002, they had been teaching small research seminars using material things as entry points into history. Laurel Ulrich has taught and published on American colonial history at the University of New Hampshire and, since 1995, at Harvard, often focusing on material culture. Ivan Gaskell spent twenty years as a curator at Harvard's Fogg Art Museum, also teaching history, before joining the faculty of the Bard Graduate Center in 2012.

Over the years, students who took these courses produced seminar papers on everything from textile fragments from the fifteenth-century Spiro Mounds in Oklahoma to a nineteenth-century folding toothbrush. Some went on to write undergraduate honors theses on topics as diverse as a Rubens painting and Vietnamese noodles. Others entered Ph.D. programs in art history, material culture, history, or American studies; or they carried their newfound interest in tangible things into elementary and secondary school teaching. The work they did on the items they chose to research individually for their final papers contributed to shaping this book, for as many of these things as possible were incorporated into the

Tangible Things exhibition. As is acknowledged in the notes, some of those student papers inform the case studies presented here.

The *Tangible Things* exhibition developed out of an attempt to "scale-up" the seminar course for a wider range and greater number of undergraduates. It took more than two years to plan it and the general education course taught alongside it. Among the 250 students in that course were roughly equal numbers of freshmen, sophomores, juniors, and seniors representing the full range of undergraduate concentrations (majors) in the humanities, social sciences, and sciences. There were two lectures per week, plus interactive sections conducted by advanced graduate students. The weekly section exercises and course assignments all required visits to the exhibition, and to other Harvard galleries in which individual, extra items had been introduced into existing displays. Comprising 280 items drawn from seventeen Harvard collections, the exhibition was an integral part of the course, as well as a research vehicle in its own right.

Organizing so ambitious a project as the *Tangible Things* exhibition was the work of many minds and hands. In the first place, the support of the Harvard University Collection of Historical Scientific Instruments was vital in furnishing the project not only with exhibition space in its Special Exhibitions Gallery, but also with the organizational infrastructure that only experienced museum professionals can provide. Working to absorb what could be learned from the exhibition itself, it became clear that the project could only be fittingly extended into the publication phase by expanding the authorial team. Sara Schechner, Sarah Anne Carter, and Samantha van Gerbig therefore joined Laurel Ulrich and Ivan Gaskell. As curator of the Collection of Historical Scientific Instruments, Sara Schechner had taken responsibility for planning the installation of *Tangible Things*. Sarah Anne Carter, who was then teaching in the History and Literature program at Harvard, was project manager for the exhibition. Samantha van Gerbig, who designed the exhibition, contributed a sense of what it is to look attentively at any given thing through her photographs of the items included. Even though looking alone scarcely exhausts examination, the close visual attention exemplified by these photographs was fundamental to the approach shared by the authors in their study.

In realizing such a complex project, comprising both the exhibition and this publication, the curators and authors incurred many debts. They would like to thank the directors, curators, and staffs of the following Harvard University collections for loans, invaluable help in research, and permission to photograph: the Arnold Arboretum, Baker Library of the Harvard Business School, the Collection of Historical Scientific Instruments, Harvard Art Museums, Harvard University Archives, the Harvard Botanical Museum and Harvard University Herbaria, Houghton Library, the Harvard Mineralogical and Geological Museum, the Museum of Comparative Zoology, the Peabody Museum of Archaeology and Ethnology, the Arthur and Elizabeth Schlesinger Library on the History of Women in America and the Radcliffe Archives of the Radcliffe Institute for Advanced Study, the Semitic Museum, the Horatio Storer Memorial Collection of Medical Medals of the Boston Medical Library in the Francis A. Countway Library of Medicine, the General Artemas Ward House Museum, and the Warren Anatomical Museum in the Francis A. Countway Library of Medicine. The curators and authors also thank the directors, curators, and staffs of the following Harvard University collections for accommodating guest objects: the Collection of Historical Scientific Instruments, Harvard Art Museums, the Harvard Museum of Natural History, Houghton Library, the Arthur and Elizabeth Schlesinger Library on the History of Women in America of the Radcliffe Institute for Advanced Study, the Peabody Museum of Archaeology and Ethnology, and the Semitic Museum.

The exhibition was made possible by funds from the Harvard Arts Initiative, Harvard College Program in General Education, the Office of the Dean of the Graduate School of Arts and Sciences, the Office of the Provost, and the Harvard Art Museums' Gurel Student Exhibition Fund.

At Harvard, the curators and authors would like to thank Allan M. Brandt, Peter Galison, Lori Gross, Jay M. Harris, Steven E. Hyman, Stephanie Kenen, Judith A. Lajoie (retired), Martha R. Richardson, and Elizabeth A. Werby (now of the American Museum of Natural History) for their generous, imaginative, and unstinting support.

This publication would not exist without Nancy Toff, the editor at Oxford University Press who took on the project. The authors are grateful for her cracks of the whip no less than for her enthusiastic advocacy, as well as for the support of her colleagues.

With Ivan Gaskell, Laurel Ulrich thanks the many students, graduate and undergraduate, who have made teaching with objects such a pleasure, and the curators, registrars, and conservators who have gently guided her explorations into little-known topics and places. She also acknowledges the support of Janet Hatch and other staff members in the Harvard Department of History who met her sometimes-odd requests with such grace. A special thanks for finding a way to hang the *Tangible Things* banner outside her office.

Ivan Gaskell gratefully acknowledges the award of the Beinecke Fellowship at the Sterling and Francine Clark Art Institute, Williamstown, Massachusetts for the fall semester, 2011. This enabled the writing of three of the case studies presented here. He wishes to express his gratitude to the (now retired) director of the Research and Academic Program, Michael Ann Holly, and her colleagues, the other fellows at the Clark, and his research assistant, Jesse Feiman. His case study in chapter 1, "A Limestone Mold: Set in Stone," is excerpted and adapted from "After art, beyond beauty," in *Inspiration and Technique: Ancient to Modern Views on Beauty and Art*, edited by John Roe and Michele Stanco (Oxford, UK, and New York: Peter Lang, 2007), and is reprinted with the permission of the publisher. Among the many colleagues at Harvard to whom Ivan Gaskell is indebted, he particularly wishes to thank those at the Peabody Museum of Archaeology and Ethnology where he remains research associate in North American ethnology. At the Bard Graduate Center, he developed some of the ideas explored herein with the graduate students in his fall semester seminar, 2012, which resulted in an offspring pop-up exhibition with a digital version: http://bgcdml.net/making-a-world-with-a-hundred-things/. He wishes to express his gratitude to the dean, Peter Miller, exhibition designer Ian Sullivan, and director of the Digital Media Lab Kimon Keramidas. In his fellow *Tangible Things* authors, Ivan Gaskell knows that he had the very best collaborators—and friends—that any scholar could ever wish for. He is indebted to his son, Leo Gaskell, for producing a vivid video of the *Tangible Things* exhibition, and to Jane Whitehead, for being not only his life companion but also his best editor.

Back in the late 1970s and early 1980s, Sara J. Schechner pioneered both a new method of and new purpose for "reading" historical scientific instruments and material culture. Drawing upon her training in physics, philosophy, and history of science, she accepted the instability of categories, the permeability of boundaries, and the tenet that there were no unvarnished facts. She also believed—and her research confirmed—that "like the dyer's hand," human endeavors, including scientific thought and experiments, were colored by the philosophical, religious, political, economic, popular, and social predilections of their human agents. If this were true for scientific thought and practice, why not for its material things? So in an age of antiquarianism in instrument studies, and to the chagrin of certain leaders in the field who told her publicly that she should confine herself to documenting the who-what-when-and-where of particular museum specimens, Sara Schechner set out to determine how the tangible tools of science could embody theories, beliefs, social needs, and human values. And finding that they could and did, she advocated for historians to appreciate them as portals into our understanding of past human experience. The starting point for these studies was a close physical analysis of particular instruments in juxtaposition with many similar examples and with dissimilar things from other disciplines. So when Laurel Ulrich and Ivan Gaskell approached her with their project, she both "got it" and "was all in." Sara Schechner would like to thank Jean-François Gauvin, administrative director of the Collection of Historical Scientific Instruments, for his encouragement of the book. She would also like to express her gratitude to the Harvard faculty and students from widespread disciplines for whom she has led museum-object–based seminars since 2000. These classes have refined her appreciation of the multivalent nature of scientific things. She acknowledges the loving support of her husband, Kenneth Launie, who appreciates a good tangible thing and has brought many into their home, and her daughters, Miriam and Naomi Genuth, who grew up among their mother's assemblages of museum objects. Naomi enrolled in the *Tangible Things* course, giving her mother more occasions to take her out for hot chocolate and see the experiment from a student's perspective. Lastly, Sara Schechner wishes to acknowledge the friendship and admiration she has for her fellow collaborators—Laurel Ulrich, Ivan Gaskell, Sarah Carter, and Samantha van Gerbig. *Tangible Things* was the most fun project ever!

In 2002, Sarah Anne Carter, then a senior in Harvard College, enrolled in an undergraduate seminar taught by Laurel Ulrich and Ivan Gaskell on Harvard's collections. Something must have stuck. Nearly a decade later, she had the true pleasure and privilege of collaborating with them, as well as with Sara Schechner and Samantha van Gerbig on the exhibition that developed into this book. She is grateful to these brilliant and kind teammates and to her caring mentors at Harvard and Winterthur who taught her how to study the material world and why it matters. She appreciatively acknowledges the Chipstone Foundation, a private foundation devoted to the study of material culture, and its director Jon Prown for their unflagging support. Finally, she thanks her family, especially her husband, Simon and her son, Paul.

Since knocking on the door of the Collection of Historical Scientific Instruments in 1997 to see if they offered part-time jobs for undergraduate students, Samantha van Gerbig has worked in the museum world. During this time, she has had the pleasure of working with a large number of very talented and giving people. To begin, she would like to thank both Jim Bennett and Stephen Johnston of the Museum of the History of Science in Oxford, UK, for giving her the chance to do her first large-scale museum-based photographic project (*Universal Geometry*: http://www.mhs.ox.ac.uk/astrolabe/). She would also very much like to thank Jean-François Gauvin, administrative director of the Collection of Historical Scientific Instruments, for his tireless support of her work on *Tangible Things*, as well as the many registrars and conservators with whom she's had the pleasure to work over the last decade and a half. Most importantly, she would like to express tremendous gratitude to her partner, Joy Snow, for her sweet-natured, ever-present patience and support.

Work by students in Laurel Ulrich and Ivan Gaskell's graduate and undergraduate seminars between 2002 and 2010 forms the basis of the entire project—both course and exhibition. They researched many of the objects selected, developed the source archives for individual objects on the general education course website, and wrote and recorded cell phone commentaries. The organizers are indebted to seminar teaching fellows Emily Conroy-Krutz, Caitlin Hopkins, and Kristen Keerma, and to all 83 students: Naomi Ages, Krystal Appiah, Mia Bagneris, Nicole Bass, Richard Bell, Emma Benintende, Rachel Bennett, Audrey Boguchwal, Julia Bonnheim, Katherine Bringsjord, Tri Chiem, Meaghan Cain, Maggie Cao, Sarah Anne Carter, Nicholas Castañeda, Danielle Charlap, Sakura Christmas, Robert Collier, Eduardo Contreras, John Dixon, Lauren Dunwoody, Claire Eager, Barbara Elfman, Miranda Featherstone, Maggie Gates, Melissa Gniadek, Rosario Inéz Granados Salinas, Lindsay Grant, Spring Greeney, Alexandra Harwin, Kyle Hawkins, Nathan Heller, Caitlin Hopkins, Catherine Jampel, Sarah Johnson, Alexandra Jumper, Suk Young Kang, Shawonipinesiik Kinew, Kendall Kulper, Shoshona Lew, Joy Lin, Lindsey McCormack, Joyce McIntyre, Marcella Marsala, Whitney Martinko, Lisa May, Brittney Moraski, Shannon Morrow, Jen Morse, Rachel Nearnberg, Garrett Nelson, Jane Newbold, Katherine O'Leary, Sigurd Østrem, Eva Payne, Sophie Pitman, Christopher Platt, Clare Ploucha, Brian Polk, Anne Porter, David Pullins, Stephen Chartey Quarcoo, Julia Renaud, Andrew

Rothman, Meg Rotzel, Charlie Ryland, Claire Saffitz, Adam Scheffler, Jake Segal, Jared Small, Jennifer Stolper, Sam Stupak, Victoria Sung, Edward Styles, Michaela Thompson, Vanessa Torres, Nicolas Trépanier, Kirby Tyrell, Jeff Wannop, Thomas Weisman, Gloria Whiting, Nicholas Woo, and Jessica Zdeb.

Thinking with Things

How can we approach aspects of the past that written words do not record? How can we mobilize not just a few kinds of things that have survived from earlier times, but many, to create history? If we acknowledge that material things of many kinds are traces of the past, how can we make use of them to understand the past? What are the circumstances that shape our encounters with them, and how do those circumstances affect—perhaps even determine—how we might use them? As historians working with material things, these are among the puzzles we face. These are our concerns in this book.

We did not write this book in isolation. It represents the culmination to date of a long-term investigation. It reports on an experiment we conducted at Harvard University in the spring of 2011 involving the use of material things of many kinds—from medical specimens to artworks. The fact that we did it at Harvard does not mean that others cannot try their own experiments with less extensive collections. The issues involved are certainly not confined to one institution, nor do we believe that one need have access to a world-class collection in order to employ the strategies it adapted.

We have discovered through our own experiences as writers, researchers, museum curators, college professors, and leaders of workshops for museum professionals, public school teachers, and the general public that focusing on a single object can generate excitement, prompt historical curiosity, and produce understanding. Of course, having access to a dazzling set of material things is a great advantage, but as television programs like *Antiques Roadshow* or the *History Detectives* remind us, dazzling things sometimes show up in ordinary places, and, as good poets know, common objects when looked at anew have a dazzle of their own.

Tangible Things builds upon a rich tradition of practice and theory in material culture, as well as on our own experiences as scholars and teachers. Specialists will recognize in these pages a number of issues that have been debated in universities and museums in recent years. Although we have entered into these arguments by offering some philosophical speculations in general terms, we have chosen to focus our efforts in this book primarily through case studies, believing that in many circumstances example really is the best teacher. In contrast to more traditional works, our topic is not the evolution of particular objects or forms over time, but rather a method of investigation that begins with a specific artwork, artifact, or specimen and then moves outward in an ever-widening circle.

The things we discuss are not the unbounded things of recent "thing theory," but rather definite physical entities. To call something a "thing" rather than an "object" in certain disciplines indicates that it may have inanimate or numinous qualities. For these practitioners and philosophers, we recognize that the word "things" evokes resonances that "objects" does not. Although we pay close attention to the nuanced meanings of the material world, we have chosen to adhere to widespread convention and use the terms "object" and "thing" interchangeably.

Because we are historians, our primary approach is historical. But our engagement with tangible things has led us beyond the boundaries of our own discipline and our own specialized knowledge. We want to argue here that just about any tangible thing can be pressed into service as primary historical evidence. Our purpose is not to offer comprehensive accounts of each field to which these sources might relate, but to demonstrate that attention to singular, physical things can reveal connections among people, processes, and forms of inquiry that might otherwise remain unnoticed. Our engagement with Harvard's collections has led us to question the very categories through which we understand history. It has also led us to imagine a university in which museum specialists and librarians might work more closely with faculty to create more engaging and lively exhibits and courses.

There has been a great deal of emphasis lately on the supposed overspecialization of the academy, on the need for university teachers to teach broadly and for meaning, and for specialists to find a way to address the general public. Although it may seem counterintuitive, we actually think that a good way to broaden knowledge is to narrow the focus. This is one of the secrets of micro-history. Asking students to study an object—any object—almost always leads them in unexpected directions. To take just two examples, a Harvard undergraduate who had never before shown any interest in biology found herself reading treatises on the foraging habits of mice in order to understand the curious presence of a mouse skeleton in a patent medicine bottle from the American Civil War; and a student in the history of science who wanted only to understand the anatomical theories behind a model of the human body suddenly found that she needed to know something about Greek art.

Teaching with tangible things challenges teachers as much as it challenges their students. None of us is simultaneously an expert in Civil War history and mice. But good teachers know how to use libraries, websites, and their colleagues to guide students into areas they do not know. In our case, that meant working closely with the curators, archivists, conservators, and registrars that care for Harvard's many collections. Teaching in this manner becomes collaborative at many levels. The kind of open-ended inquiry we model here is much easier today that it would have been in the past. The growing willingness of major institutions, including Harvard, to share texts and images electronically makes it easier to connect written and material sources, and to connect objects housed in one collection with another or with the seemingly ordinary things found in people's bureau drawers and attics. This is not to claim, though, that electronic versions of texts and other objects are invariably adequate substitutes for the things themselves; many puzzles demand attention to those very things—exalted or commonplace—as well as to their virtual representations.

Our description so far might imply that the *Tangible Things* project is no more than elaborate antiquarianism: an inspection of individually fascinating items in which anyone might take an interest for their own sake, but of little or no relevance to the big picture of historical inquiry. Can *Tangible Things* fulfill a truly historical purpose by helping anyone who wants to know about the past in order to live critically in the present? Yes it can. We believe that the mobilization of material things can enhance any comprehensive historical inquiry and that the procedures we advocate will enhance knowledge of the past that is too often constrained by reliance on written materials alone.

Historians generally rely on text-based sources, but these are severely limited. Only a minority of human societies has used writing systems.

Even within those that have, many people left few traces, if any, in written form. Oral traditions can be documented and interviews made, but except in the case of various indigenous societies, these verbal records are of recent memory and do not take us very far back. Historians can extend the range and depth of their inquiries by learning to use not just written and oral accounts, but all traces of the past. With appropriate skills to exploit a wider range of sources—material and visual, as well as word-based culture—historians may uncover what would otherwise be undetectable lives, often of the socially disadvantaged; they will also enrich knowledge of those who have been known to a greater or lesser extent solely from written texts.

What are these material records of the past? They range from portable personal possessions to entire landscapes. They encompass things that are human-made—a medieval ceramic container from Syria—and natural things modified by human behavior, such as a conifer cone from New Guinea bound with straw to retain its integrity. While there may be considerable overlap in the skills historians need to interpret such a wide range of things, each also requires a particular, appropriate mode of address. A taxidermy specimen of a mounted duck-billed platypus actually has much in common with an oil painting on canvas—both are crafted through the artifice of a skilled maker. But, in order to use them as sources, historians must take into account the differences between them, both ontological and in terms of human cognition and use. Even then, such things are scarcely self-sufficient individually. Humans have always dealt with such things in terms of the perceived relationships among them. These relationships often involve using language, whether oral or textual. Material things, then, do not exist entirely independently

1. What can be learned from a water bottle representing a woman with a young child of the Moche people of Peru, ca. 150–800? Pottery portraits in Moche culture appear to represent actual individuals and their social activities. Artworks like this portrait jug frequently depict the flow of water through human bodies, thereby embodying the Moche society's dependence on irrigation. Peabody Museum of Archaeology and Ethnology, Harvard University.

2. Made in Syria ca. 1200, this medieval ceramic pharmacy jar—an *albarello*—held ointments or dry medicines prepared by an apothecary. Harvard Art Museums/Arthur M. Sackler Museum.

3. This specimen cone of the tree *Agathis labillardieri* was artfully bound with plant material, making it more durable and beautiful, by Richard Archbold, who financed and led three biological expeditions to New Guinea in the 1930s. Arnold Arboretum Herbarium, Harvard University Herbaria.

4. A mounted platypus, *Ornithorhynchus anatinus*, is more than a scientific specimen of Australian fauna. It is an engaging example of the taxidermist's art of stretching skin on a frame to create the appearance of motion and life. Museum of Comparative Zoology.

of texts, spoken or inscribed; but neither can such things be reduced to texts.

How do material things function in human use? Humans gather them, nurture them, walk across them, climb them, kill them, eat them, make them, wear them, tell stories about them, bury them, revere them, destroy them, claim descent from them, forbid them to one another, give them to one another, exchange them, and much more. By manipulating them, humans articulate their own relationships with

5. A tintype photograph of botanists Merritt Lyndon Fernald and George Golding Kennedy posing with their essential field gear for plant collecting in front of a painted backdrop of the outdoors, ca. 1890. Each man holds a trowel, a vasculum (a tin case for carrying fresh specimens), and a portable plant press. Gray Herbarium, Harvard University Herbaria.

6. This cross-section of submarine telegraph cable celebrated the laying of the first permanent telegraph line across the Atlantic Ocean by the British ship *Great Eastern* in 1866. The little trophy captured people's excitement that new technologies had made the world smaller. A message that once had taken ten days to deliver by ship between Europe and America now took just minutes. Telegraph companies, however, reputedly made greater profits from selling souvenir sections of cable than from transmission fees. General Artemas Ward House Museum.

one another. Various human societies perform all these actions—and more—differently from each other, often in mutually incomprehensible ways. In order to perform all these actions in a repeatable manner, humans distinguish things from one another, name them, and group them. For the most part, however, things are radically unstable. They change physically over time, in their uses by successive human groups, and in their significance to various peoples. A telegraph cable designed to carry messages beneath the Atlantic Ocean can be cut into innumerable slices for souvenirs. To trace an original use or significance is to account for only one period in the life of a thing, a period not necessarily more important than others it might subsequently have had. To ascribe precedence to a maker's intentions or to an object's first use is to fall into a trap of oversimplification. This has happened to many people who have studied material things historically. We do not dismiss intention or first use—far from it—but propose that, even if intention and first use can be reliably established, they constitute just a part of the story.

Although we can sample some of what humans do and have done in relation to the things they choose, make, and use, this project as a whole—and this book in particular—clearly cannot hope to be comprehensive in its examination of these phenomena. Yet we can confidently offer a chart for future navigation and instances (case studies), each one of which may initially appear to be an island, but that in unexpected or even scarcely perceptible ways are all a piece of the continent, a part of the main.

Tangible Things examines a core group of concerns in the study and use of material things: how Westerners have distinguished, named, sorted, grouped, gathered, and subsequently deployed material things in order

7. "Great objects make great minds" is among the quotations that Sarah Henshaw Ward Putnam penned on the pieced quilt, dated 1881, which she sewed for her spinster nieces in Shrewsbury, Massachusetts. Her source was "Night Thoughts" by the eighteenth-century English poet Edward Young. Widowed three months after her wedding, Putnam spent her remaining seventy years shuttling between relatives' homes. The potholder, piecework style of this quilt suited her mobility, but the quotation is poignant as Putnam had few objects of her own. General Artemas Ward House Museum.

to make knowledge claims about both them and the emergent concepts their users have associated with them. These activities are the basis of much Western methodical thinking. Distinguished thinkers have considered them since classical antiquity. Although a great deal of ink has been expended on museums and other collections of things as constitutive of the social order, comparatively little consideration has been given to them as instruments of thought. Our project approaches that topic by exploring how museums aggregate particular selections of material things for the purpose of thinking.

In the nineteenth century, scholars in museums tended to regard the things in their collections as transparent, reliable indicators of reality independent of human cognition. Those who distinguished, gathered, sorted, and named all kinds of tangible things assumed that they were uncovering identities and relationships that existed regardless of what anyone might think about them. Their arrangement constituted actuality. They were, in short, object lessons. From the late nineteenth century and onward, scholars like William James questioned such assumptions and

8. A survey of established facts: Master basket maker Clara Darden wove this basket using river cane from the homelands of the Chitimacha people in southeastern Louisiana between 1900 and 1910. The complex double-weave basket is one basket woven inside another. The interior of the basket is woven from natural cane, and the exterior has the up, across, and down pattern woven in red, black, and undyed cane. The basket's strength, water resistance, and glossy finish derive from silica in the river grass woven into it. Peabody Museum of Archaeology and Ethnology, Harvard University.

9. When one thinks of Harvard's august Houghton Library, one thinks of rare books and manuscripts, not works of modern art made of jumbled metal kitchen utensils. Resembling a junk drawer, the piece was described by the artist as a metaphor for a fast-paced, disorganized life. Shouldn't this work be in a museum of contemporary art? Houghton Library's curators did not think so. They added it to the library holdings because it was art realized in the form of a book. Artist's book, *Little Chaos*, by Deborah Phillips Chodoff, 1996 (detail), Houghton Library.

introduced the idea that things and human minds are mutually dependent: Things do not function or even exist independently of the way
humans think of them. This undercut the intellectual authority of collecting institutions, which formed their collections on the assumption that
the ordering they employed conformed to an actuality beyond human
contrivance. Additional developments in the twentieth century further
undermined the authority of museums. Here the works of French philosophers Michel Foucault (1926–84) and Jean Baudrillard (1929–2007)
(who, with their numerous followers and in different ways, examined
the contingencies and artifice of human knowledge claims, subordinat-
ing all human activity to the conditions of language) are of particular
importance. While it remains important to take such works into account,
we resist the tendency to confine analysis of tangible things to consider-
ations of language, and the reduction of the institutions that deal with
them—museums—to instruments of social control alone. Museums led
the way in the development of still-significant fields of inquiry before
being superseded by emergent research universities that addressed pure
intangibles unconstrained by the relative unwieldiness of material things.
However, collections of tangible things—museums—remain not only
as scholarly institutions in their own right, however compromised their
claims to intellectual authority may be, but also as parts of larger scholarly
institutions that are less directly engaged with the public, such as colleges
and universities.

Our own work in universities drives us to ask: What place can university
and college museums play in the ever-developing research and teaching
endeavors of the institutions of which they form parts? Museums bring
many challenges, among them the need for the continuing physical care
of their collections and physical plants, the difficulty of access, the seeming irrelevance to many active areas of inquiry, and the expense. Most of
all, their physical nature and often their scale—Harvard's Museum of
Comparative Zoology alone holds an unfathomable twenty-one million
things—render them unavoidably cumbersome. The individual collections at Harvard, like other collections elsewhere, continue to contain—
and constrain—these various things in collections that sometimes appear
to impede creative inquiry. This state of affairs arose because collections
were formed in relation to particular disciplines and academic departments. In recent years, new areas of research and teaching have emerged
that challenge traditional disciplinary boundaries. At Harvard and elsewhere, the structures of collections have not kept pace with these changes.

10. Before the invention of typewriters and mechanical writing machines, inventors looked to musical instruments for keyboard designs. An example of blurred boundaries is this French state-of-the-art printing telegraph, ca. 1870–85. The operator did not need to know Morse code to send a text message, just how to play the piano. Collection of Historical Scientific Instruments.

The 2011 *Tangible Things* exhibition at Harvard was the most far-reaching intellectual and practical challenge yet attempted to the relative isolation of the university's collections. It queried the very rationale that continues to structure Harvard's—and many other—methodical collections. The future of academic research and teaching in many fields will depend on far greater permeability among collections than is the case at present. In our own teaching, for example, we needed to bring a Native American riding whip handle from Harvard's General Artemas Ward House Museum into physical conjunction with bison ribs in the Museum of Comparative Zoology and with artifacts made by the nineteenth-century Indigenous inhabitants of Nebraska in the Peabody Museum of Archaeology and Ethnology. With such materials, we were able to explore the story of westward expansion of peoples of European origin across North America in the years following the Civil War in a fresh and precise way. If these things—and others both like and very different from them—remain isolated in their disciplinary collections, never

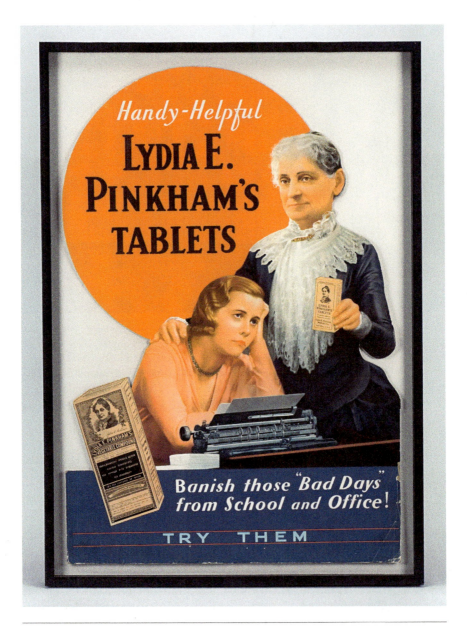

11. One way to overcome the problem of dated categories is to consider new uses for material things and redefinitions of their purposes. For instance, Lydia E. Pinkham's patent medicine remained popular long after her death in 1883 because of clever advertising that appealed to the changing needs of American women. Here Mrs. Pinkham, in a dowdy black dress complete with a bustle and froth of white lace on her bosom, counsels a young office worker, with bobbed hair and finger waves of the 1920s, sitting at her typewriter. Arthur and Elizabeth Schlesinger Library on the History of Women in America.

crossing boundaries, our opportunities to conceive new ideas about the material world in all its richness and variety in a whole host of fields will be curtailed.

Although *Tangible Things* is a history project—the authors are, after all, historians—it is also a plea for and a demonstration of the need for far greater flexibility in the management and deployment of collections of all kinds on behalf of all disciplines that make use of such materials. New ways of sorting and describing these tangible things will facilitate their application to new areas of inquiry. Could new modes of grouping and gathering allow these things to be compatible with new and future requirements of universities and scholarship more generally? Can we overcome the inertia of collections, despite numerical growth, or are they doomed to be just so many expensive and increasingly irrelevant encumbrances? How did organized Western inquiry reach this seeming impasse in respect to tangible things?

Whatever other purposes they may serve, these things and their modes of organization are magnificent sources for historians—when they take the trouble to learn to work with them. Does this use alone justify their

12. In late March 1965, the Rev. Dr. Martin Luther King Jr. led thousands of civil rights demonstrators on a fifty-four-mile march from Selma, Alabama, to the state capital, Montgomery, to petition for the voting rights of black people. This photograph by Matt Herron—documenting what was hailed as the greatest demonstration in the history of the civil rights movement—is treated today not simply as a historical record but also as fine art. Harvard Art Museums/Fogg Museum.

13. Mundane objects can tell remarkable stories. The toes of these slippers sport the coat of arms of Radcliffe College in needlepoint. The extra-large shoes belonged to Wilbur Kitchener Jordan, the male president of the women's college from 1943 to 1960. Radcliffe Archives.

retention and cultivation? Probably not. Yet historians, with their particular charge to translate the ever-changing past into the ever-emerging present, are especially well placed to argue for the potential of collections of tangible things in scholarly inquiry. Worthwhile future uses may not resemble past or even present uses. A photograph made to record a contemporary newsworthy event might be redeployed as a historical document recording the particularities of a significant past moment, or as an artwork in recognition of its aesthetic qualities. If collecting institutions are to become more useful as instruments of inquiry, they will have to be more flexible and less exclusionary in both the development of their collections and the uses to which they put them.

We developed the *Tangible Things* project in order to address these large-scale, consequential puzzles. We used Harvard's collections as a convenient case study. These particular tangible things, and the collections into which they have been formed, were readily accessible to our students and to us, as well as to visitors interested in exploring our puzzles. Yet there is nothing deferential or celebratory in our choice of the Harvard collections as our focus. Just as much can be done with commonplace or "found" objects treated as traces of the past, wherever they may be. Nonetheless, our use of Harvard's collections did lend our project an additional dimension. If, for much of its existence, Harvard was an obscure regional school for local gentry and clergy, it emerged in the course of the nineteenth and twentieth centuries as a place of scholarly competence, renown, and influence, both nationally and internationally. Its patterns of organization, however idiosyncratically formed in individual institutional instances, came to carry weight beyond

14. This homely travel toothbrush folds up into its metal case and is crafted from repurposed implements. It is witness to the growth of dental hygiene in the mid-nineteenth century that led many travelers to carry their own homemade toothbrushes. General Artemas Ward House Museum.

15. The Harvard undergraduate portrayed in these vintage wax candles wears "plus fours," baggy breeches that were characteristic of Ivy League fashion in the 1930s, when the candles were made. Harvard University Archives.

Cambridge, Massachusetts, and in at least some cases, reflect and affect developments elsewhere.

Tangible Things therefore both reflects, and reflects upon, institutional collecting developments consolidated by the late nineteenth century at Harvard and in Western thought and practice more widely. In the Special Exhibition Gallery of the Collection of Historical Scientific Instruments, we placed a wide variety of things within each of the six fundamental categories into which tangible things have frequently been sorted since full-scale institutionalization in the nineteenth century. These correspond not only to Harvard's division of collection labor, but—broadly speaking—to that of Western societies generally (though, obviously, there are some variations among them both regionally and nationally). Each of these six fundamental categories contains a vast diversity of materials within it, but those materials all exhibit characteristics that make their placement in each category appear plausible, or in many instances, even natural. The categories are *anthropology and archaeology, art, books and*

16. Engraved with a long and wordy tale and mounted as a trophy, this silver teapot no longer brews the hot beverage its owner, Samuel Johnson, so relished. The English lexicographer bequeathed the teapot to his Jamaican companion and valet, Francis Barber, in 1784, but it was purloined by Johnson's executor and sold, as the inscription relates, "at the very Minute" when Dr. Johnson's body was being autopsied in the next room. Houghton Library.

17. An ear of corn is as commonplace as can be, but close examination may reveal beauty in its beaded structure. This cob, harvested in Brazil in 1918, reminds us that corn has been cultivated for more than 6,000 years in the Americas, where it remains the preeminent grain crop. Economic Botany Herbarium of Oakes Ames, Harvard University Herbaria.

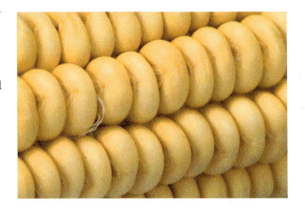

manuscripts, history, natural history, and *science and medicine*. The things we exhibited in these categories are what we describe in the next chapter as "Things in Place."

In the same gallery, clearly marked to differentiate them from the cases containing the "Things in Place," we arranged further cases containing arrays of things exhibited without discernible order. In these cases, we created a miscellany that we informally termed our "muddle." We put a tiger skull near an ancient tortilla, an Australian Aborigine message stick, a Japanese sword and scabbard, an Indonesian accordion-bound manuscript, a Native American quirt (whip) handle, samples of fabric for enslaved African Americans' clothing, and a contemporary artist's book made from kitchen implements.

These things—and others—seemed to have nothing to do with one another beyond the fact of their physicality. Their arrangement issued a friendly, quizzical challenge to the viewer—and to ourselves—that we made explicit by text panels urging visitors to "SORT THEM!" These are the objects we discuss as "Things Unplaced."

A third feature of the *Tangible Things* project involved exploring the galleries of seven Harvard collections after interlopers from one collection were inserted into the preexisting display of another collection. The seventeen "guest objects" were hidden in plain sight, revealing new aspects of themselves by virtue of being seen in unfamiliar surroundings. The guest objects also exposed and encouraged scrutiny of the basic

18. This French dagger, ca. 1840s, was exhibited under the category of art and interpreted as an art critic might: To hold this weapon is to take envy into one's hand, for the figure (on the handle) personifies this emotion. Harvard Art Museums/Fogg Museum.

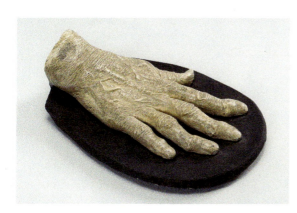

19. A plaster cast of an arthritic hand, made in the United States between 1904 and 1906, is at home among objects of science and medicine. Warren Anatomical Museum in the Francis A. Countway Library of Medicine.

20. An item in the "muddle": A tiger cranium and jaw is a specimen of *Felis tigris tigris*, but a note inked on the skull—telling us that on the day after Christmas, 1849, this tiger was shot in the head in Hyderabad, India—makes it something more. Museum of Comparative Zoology.

21. How does one classify an unidentified text written on fan-folded sheets of palm leaves bound in wood? As a herbarium specimen of economic botany, an Indonesian ethnographic object, or a book illustrating the widespread use of accordion bindings from India to China and Southeast Asia? Houghton Library.

22. A tiger skull, a Japanese sword, a book made of palm leaves, an artist's book of metal kitchen tools, a riding-whip handle, a hundred-year-old tortilla, and the tapeworm of a Boston Brahmin are some of the items clustered in this "muddled" case in the 2011 exhibition *Tangible Things* at the Collection of Historical Scientific Instruments, Harvard University.

23. Although this armillary ring sundial made in Lucca, Italy, in 1764 was displayed as a "thing out of place" to be sorted, it belonged to a rich traveler who could use it to find true north, his location, and the time at any latitude. Collection of Historical Scientific Instruments.

assumptions underlying each host display. We examine this aspect of the project in "Things out of Place."

"Things in Stories—Stories in Things" examines the way the undergraduate general education course *Tangible Things: Harvard's Collections in World History* employed objects to tell stories about Harvard's relation to the wider world. We also look at some of the stories habitually told in Western society—especially in America—about these things and the people associated with them, and show how new stories emerge. These objects and their entangled stories offer proof that the study of particular things can lead to far-reaching historical discoveries by revealing patterns, relationships, and complexities that would otherwise remain hidden.

In the chapters that follow, we explore the structure of the *Tangible Things* exhibition in further detail, looking at the categories we identified, the "muddle" of things we chose and assembled, the interventions we contrived with guest objects at their various locations, and the stories told through and from things. We undertook this exhibition not to produce a tidy, finished product—as is usually the case with museum exhibitions—but rather to extend a process of investigation pursuable only by means of the assembly of the objects concerned. The exhibition was truly an experiment, the results of which we could not possibly foretell. Therefore, rather than produce an anticipatory catalog, the common museum practice, we chose to write about it—here—only after we had had the opportunity to take our observations of the many juxtapositions and interventions in the exhibition itself into account. We offer case studies of tangible things, each of which opens a portal to the past, but each of which also carries a promise for the future as we explore how the radical instability of tangible things transcends the collections that have sought to contain them. We seek to do all this confident that these things will present us, and our successors, with fresh opportunities to develop both historical understanding and innovation in a wide variety of fields.

CHAPTER ONE

Things in Place

By the end of the nineteenth century, collecting institutions had defined the categories into which they conventionally sorted all kinds of tangible things. The assistant secretary of the Smithsonian in charge of the United States National Museum, George Brown Goode, laid them out methodically in his 1895 publication *Principles of Museum Administration*. Goode's categories were as follows: "A. Museums of Art; B. Historical Museums; C. Anthropological Museums; D. Natural History Museums; E. Technological Museums; F. Commercial Museums."[1] With the exception of the last category—commercial museums—this schema still applies to the majority of Western collecting institutions, including those at Harvard.

The Harvard Art Museums (comprising the Fogg Museum, the Busch-Reisinger Museum, and the Arthur M. Sackler Museum) correspond precisely to Goode's category A. (The Fogg contains European and American art; the Busch-Reisinger deals with art of the German-speaking lands; and the Sackler holds art from classical antiquity and Asia.) The Harvard University Archives, the Radcliffe Archives, the Arthur and Elizabeth Schlesinger Library on the History of Women in America, and the General Artemas Ward House Museum conform to category B, though the latter is the one history museum at Harvard that addresses only issues beyond Harvard and Radcliffe. Together the Peabody Museum of Archaeology and Ethnology and the Semitic Museum encompass anthropology and archaeology, Goode's category C. The Museum of Comparative Zoology, the Mineralogical and Geological Museum, and the Harvard University Herbaria clearly correspond to category D.

Goode defined his category E, technological museums, as those devoted to industries and their tools, raw materials, manufactured products and commercial interconnections, as well as to various technical professions, which included engineering, medicine, the art of war, and engraving. Harvard has no technology museums as such devoted to mining or the textile industry, or chock a block with steam engines, but it does have two specialized historical museums that focus on science, engineering, medicine, and the tools of these trades—the Collection of Historical Scientific Instruments and the Warren Anatomical Museum of the Center for the History of Medicine. For our purposes, we have put these institutions under Goode's category E.

Goode excluded books and manuscripts from his schema, treating libraries as a different kind of collection entirely. Yet books and manuscripts include a vast variety of materials from many societies and time periods with different traditions of writing and inscription, so we regard them as artifacts no less than any other human-made things, assigning them to their own category, however uncertain its boundaries may be.

It is worth noting that Goode himself recognized that there were overlaps between his categories, and that some objects could rightfully find a place in multiple types of museums, but the categories still feel robust to us, perhaps at first glance even obvious. As the *Tangible Things* project divided up Harvard's collections, each category contained a considerable variety of things differing materially, geographically, and chronologically. We did not assign any given thing to any given category according to necessary and sufficient conditions, but by discerning what the philosopher Ludwig Wittgenstein termed "family resemblances."[2] The boundaries of these categories are as indeterminate as those of the light cast by his reading lamp, as Wittgenstein explained in the *Blue Book*[3]; yet, like that beam, each category coheres nonetheless.

Let's look in turn at each of the systematic categories into which we divided our tangible things.

Natural history contained things from its three constituent classes: zoology, botany, and mineralogy. Harvard's Museum of Comparative Zoology is divided into ten collections: entomology (insects), herpetology (amphibians and reptiles), ichthyology (fishes), invertebrate paleontology (fossil animals without backbones), invertebrate zoology (animals without backbones like sponges, spiders, and protozoa), malacology (mollusks), mammalogy (mammals), marine invertebrates (aquatic creatures without backbones like starfish), ornithology (birds), and vertebrate paleontology (fossil animals with backbones). The Harvard University Herbaria is similarly subdivided into six specialized collections of pressed, dried plant specimens plus separate wood and paleobotany collections. And the Mineralogical and Geological Museum is systematically arranged into minerals and gems, rocks and ores, and meteorites.

Each specimen is a portal not only into natural history but also human history. For instance, the herpetology specimen of Blanding's turtle (*Emydoidea blandingi*) was fished out of Walden Pond in Concord, Massachusetts, by philosopher Henry David Thoreau, who donated it to Harvard in 1847.[4] Louis Agassiz, the founder of the Museum of Comparative Zoology, collected the pink fairy armadillo (*Chlamyphorus truncatus*) that is now in the mammalogy collection during the 1871–72 *Hassler* Expedition to South America in which he traveled with his wife, Elizabeth Cary Agassiz, also a naturalist, and the first president of Radcliffe College.[5] The botanical specimens from the University Herbaria are similarly rich in associations. An orchid specimen (*Epidendrum*

24. More than nature is represented in the prepared skin of a pink fairy armadillo (*Chlamyphorus truncatus*) collected by the naturalist Louis Agassiz in Mendoza, Argentina, in 1872. It recalls a deep-sea dredging expedition around South America on the steamship *Hassler* in 1871–72. Led by Agassiz and chronicled by his wife in newspapers, the expedition sampled life at the sea bottom and onshore, looking in part for evidence that Agassiz hoped would refute Darwin's theory of evolution. Museum of Comparative Zoology.

25. Harvard chemistry professor John White Webster stored this prized specimen of vesuvianite with other minerals in a large tea chest. In 1849, police investigators discovered something more gruesome in the chest: the dismembered torso of George Parkman, a Boston businessman whom Webster had murdered in order to avoid repaying a debt. Mineralogical and Geological Museum at Harvard University.

lorifolium) received by Oakes Ames from a collector in Panama was fixed to the same paper sheet as a watercolor drawing of it by Blanche Ames Ames in 1923, thereby married together for posterity like the husband-wife team that created it.[6] Among the minerals, a specimen of vesuvianite came from the mineral collection of the antebellum Harvard chemistry professor John White Webster.[7] Webster pledged his collection twice over to different creditors as collateral against loans, leading to a deadly conflict with one of them. The vesuvianite was stored with other minerals in Webster's tea chest, the grisly spot where investigators found some of the remains of Boston businessman George Parkman, whom Webster was convicted of having murdered and dismembered in 1849.[8]

The natural world and the subjects of anthropology are divided by a permeable boundary. Since the mid-nineteenth century, Westerners have treated humans then thought to be primitive—allegedly without sophisticated culture—and their artifacts as akin to the natural world, so in the exhibition, we installed the category *anthropology and archaeology* beside *natural history*. Many collecting institutions embody this association, among them the American Museum of Natural History in New York City. Anthropology and archaeology emerged as disciplines in the mid-nineteenth century. Anthropology developed to account for humans increasingly seen as being beyond the bounds of history. Archaeology addressed American so-called pre-history, as well as the Mediterranean classical and West Asian biblical civilizations.

At Harvard, the archaeology of the Americas is studied in the Peabody Museum of Archaeology and Ethnology together with that of parts of East Asia and Europe. The Semitic Museum focuses on West Asian archaeology in particular. These collections provided many provocative, tangible things for our exhibition. Cultural objects belonging to Indigenous peoples and dating from a period before Europeans arrived in North America included textile fragments from the Spiro Mounds, the major ceremonial site of the Mississippian mound-building culture, located in present-day Spiro, Oklahoma. These fragments were woven before 1450.[9] Another curious object was a stone pestle carved into the likeness of a bird's head. It belonged to Henry David Thoreau, who amassed a collection of some 900 early Indian artifacts during his lifetime, most of them found as he walked near Concord, Massachusetts.[10] The site of the Hurrian city of Nuzi in

26. Surviving only as fragments, these textiles were woven before 1450 by the Muscogee people, who were part of the Mississippian culture that built earthwork mounds. The fragments were found at a major ceremonial site, Spiro Mounds in Oklahoma, which has suffered from looters. Peabody Museum of Archaeology and Ethnology, Harvard University.

27. Two cuneiform tablets with clay envelopes are grain receipts from 1500 BCE. They illustrate a Mesopotamian method of preventing fraud: The same text is written on both the tablet and its enclosing envelope. They come from the city of Nuzi (today Yorghan Tepe, Iraq). Semitic Museum.

Mesopotamia provided us with two clay cuneiform tablets complete with their envelopes of the same material from about 1500 BCE.[11] These were tamper-resistant grain receipts. An identical text had been written in the wet clay of both the tablet and the envelope, so that if the exterior were altered or destroyed, one could break the envelope and read the duplicate within.

Anthropology and archaeology included other examples of writing or pictographic systems, which in the exhibition we placed on the boundary between this section and the adjacent one devoted to *books and manuscripts*. One was an old Babylonian cylinder seal of an administrative official, another a first-century clay tile stamped "LEXFR" for *Legio decima Fretensis* (Tenth Legion of the Sea Strait), one of the four Roman legions that besieged and destroyed Jerusalem in CE 70.[12] Fragments of two oracle bones from Henan Province, China, exemplified a practice dating back as far as 1600 BCE: predicting the future from cracks in heated bones.[13] These were inscribed with some of the earliest known Chinese characters.

In the neighboring *books and manuscripts* section, we included another fragment with written characters: a ragged sliver of papyrus from the third century with some lines in Greek from Plato's *Republic*.[14] Other things categorized as manuscripts were less familiar to many people, even when dating from more recent times and well-known locations. An example is an 1855 letter addressed to "my dear sister Bessie," from the Huntting-Rudd Family Papers in the Schlesinger Library.[15] The recipient was Bessie Huntting, a mid–nineteenth-century schoolteacher from a prosperous whaling family in Sag Harbor, Long Island, New York. She assumed responsibility for her family's affairs after the

28. As far back as 1600 BCE, people predicted the future from cracks in heated bones like these from the Henan Province, China. The fragments of oracle bones are also inscribed with some of the earliest known Chinese characters. As evidence of an ancient divination practice, they are classified as *anthropology and archaeology*, but as writing samples, they could have been grouped with *books and manuscripts*. Peabody Museum of Archaeology and Ethnology, Harvard University.

29. By using cross-hatching, the writer of this 1855 letter saved paper and postage and prevented a busybody from reading over her shoulder as she wrote. Arthur and Elizabeth Schlesinger Library on the History of Women in America.

death of her father, Gilbert Huntting.[16] Confusing to modern readers, the letter is cross-hatched: The filled page of script was overwritten with another at right angles to it. Filling a page in both directions saved paper and postage, and discouraged the casual reading of private communications.

Printing is a relatively recent innovation in the inscription and diffusion of language, and printed books are conventionally grouped with manuscripts in Western collections. Among such items in the *books and manuscripts* section of the exhibition was the first-known, widely published cookbook by an African American, Abby Fisher: *What Mrs. Fisher Knows About Old Southern Cooking* (San Francisco, 1881).[17] After the Civil War, Fisher set up a pickling business that caught the attention of the San Francisco elite, who arranged for the publication of this cookbook. It was a transcription of Fisher's oral instructions, for, like many formerly enslaved people, she could neither read nor write.

Books and manuscripts have long had an affinity with prints and drawings. We included a silkscreen poster, *Women Are Not Chicks*, produced in 1972 by the Chicago Women's Graphics Collective, in the *books* section.[18] We also placed prints and drawings in the category of *art*. All but one of the items in the *art* section of *Tangible Things* came from the Harvard Art Museums. Western people today tend to think of the archetypal artwork as a painting, yet in spite of having been given more exhibition space than any other single art form in the Harvard Art Museums for many decades, paintings do not predominate numerically in that collection. The same can be said of many art museums, with the exception of those institutions devoted exclusively to paintings, such as the National Gallery in London. We purposely included just one Western oil painting in the *art* section, *The Message* (1893), by the American artist Edward Lamson Henry.[19] It depicts a young woman in a buggy giving a note to an African American boy. It would seem to evoke a romantic anecdote in which the boy acts as the intermediary between the young woman and a suitor. The painting was given to the Harvard Art Museums anonymously in 2003.

30. *Women Are Not Chicks* is a silkscreen poster produced by the Chicago Women's Graphics Collective in 1972. Working collaboratively, members of the collective promoted women's liberation through art and refused to sign individual names on their work. Arthur and Elizabeth Schlesinger Library on the History of Women in America.

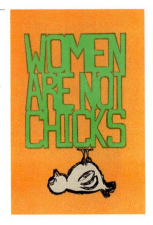

Sculpture in the classical tradition is often paired with painting to form the twin pillars of Western art. Three works that span nearly 4,500 years of three-dimensional figurative carving represented sculpture in the exhibition. One was the head of a female figure from the Greek islands of the Cyclades, made in about 2500–2400 BCE.[20] The second was a marble torso of the goddess Aphrodite, created in Greater Greece between about 250 and 100 BCE.[21] The third was by Hiram Powers, an American sculptor working in Florence in the mid-nineteenth century. Called *Loulie's Hand*, the marble carving depicted his infant daughter's hand emerging from a sunflower and was derived from a plaster cast made in 1839.[22]

Since the nineteenth century, Western art institutions have expanded their aesthetic appreciation to include decorative, as well as fine, arts. In the *Tangible Things* exhibition, we represented the new appreciation for European and Euro-American decorative arts with a silver cann made between 1750 and 1760 by the New York Jewish silversmith Myer Myers.[23] Art institutions have also featured the arts of certain Asian societies—in particular, China, Korea, and Japan—that in nineteenth-century terms Europeans considered civilized. A conical tea bowl with a *Yōhen*-type glaze by the contemporary Japanese ceramicist Kimura Moriyasu was one such item now found in the Harvard Art Museums and included in *Tangible Things*. Made in 1999 but embodying a long ceramics tradition, the tea bowl exemplifies a technically challenging style brought to Japan from China in the fourteenth century.[24] In recognition of the art status of certain things made in the Islamic world, our exhibition included a seventeenth-century silk lampas textile cover for a coffin or cenotaph from the Ottoman Empire.[25]

31. In *Loulie's Hand*, the nineteenth-century American sculptor Hiram Powers depicted his one-year-old daughter's hand emerging from a sunflower, symbolizing devotion. Harvard Art Museums/ Fogg Museum.

32. Exemplifying a technically challenging style brought to Japan from China in the fourteenth century, Kimura Moriyasu's conical tea bowl (1999) demonstrates the persistence of tradition in Japanese ceramics. It is classified as Asian decorative art. Harvard Art Museums/Arthur M. Sackler Museum.

33. A lampas is a luxurious silk fabric combining two weaves, each having its own warps and wefts. The intricate pattern created by layering the supplemental weave on top of the ground weave can be seen in this detail of a seventeenth-century Ottoman lampas. Serving as a cover for a coffin or cenotaph, it emulates the ceremonial covering of Islam's most holy site, the Kaaba in Mecca. Harvard Art Museums/Arthur M. Sackler Museum.

By the early twentieth century, collectors and curators forming Western collections were beginning to recognize certain cultural products of pre-contact American societies as art, such as a limestone ritual mask from Teotihuacán, Mexico, made between the third and seventh centuries.[26] Similarly, thanks to the attention given them by Western artists like Pablo Picasso and theorists like Roger Fry, institutions began to define carvings from sub-Saharan Africa as art, an example being a figure of a spirit spouse, or *Blolo Bla*, from the Baule peoples of Côte d'Ivoire.[27] Such works were incorporated within a twentieth-century Western Modernist aesthetic that encompassed clean-lined early sculpture from classical antiquity and contemporary art. The Baule *Blolo Bla*, the Cycladic head, and the Aphrodite marble torso were all part of a gift from Lois Orswell to the Harvard Art Museums in the year of her death. Orswell was a patron of the American abstract expressionist sculptor David Smith, whose works formed the bulk of the gift.[28] The abstract turn in

34. In Côte d'Ivoire in West Africa, the Baule people believe that before birth, a man weds a wife in the spirit world—the *Blolo Bla*—who, when properly honored through the medium of a carved wooden figure, brings good fortune to him and his family. Once transported from Africa to an art museum, however, the figure of the spirit spouse is treated as sculpture. Harvard Art Museums/Fogg Museum.

twentieth-century Western art also helped, beginning in the 1930s, to encourage Western art museums' incorporation of photography into their collections, such as the *Cabbage Leaf* (1931) by the American photographer Edward Weston.[29] His work demonstrated that a photograph of an actual thing in the world can be made to seem a contrived abstraction.

Photography is a practice used for making art that is rooted in early nineteenth-century scientific discovery. Although our exhibition category *science and medicine* did not include any scientific photographs or darkroom supplies, it did include Civil War–era bottles of chemicals[30] and an instrument used in the 1970s by Edwin Land, the inventor of Polaroid film. Land dubbed his colorful instrument a "mondrian" because of its resemblance to the work of artist Piet Mondrian, and used it to develop a new theory of color vision.[31] *Science and medicine* also included several examples of pre-photographic, direct representations, among them three plaster casts of heads made before 1835.[32] Donated to Harvard by the Boston Phrenological Society and now in the Warren Anatomical Museum, two of the heads—those of French philosopher René Descartes and the reputedly insane French Revolutionary Anne-Josèphe Théroigne de Méricourt—had belonged to the German physician Johann Gaspar Spurzheim, one of the founders of phrenology, the study of the human

35. Edward Weston's photograph *Cabbage Leaf* (1931) transforms a dinner ingredient into abstract art. Harvard Art Museums/ Fogg Museum.

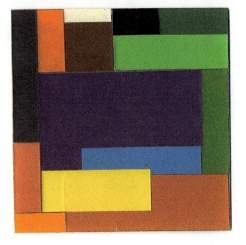

36. Where art and science mix: The inventor of Polaroid, Edwin H. Land used color-blocked panels—dubbed "mondrians" because of their resemblance to the work of artist Piet Mondrian—as laboratory instruments in developing a new theory of color vision in the late 1970s. Collection of Historical Scientific Instruments.

skull as an index of a person's mental proclivities and capacities. The third was a cast of Spurzheim's own skull. During his only visit to America, Spurzheim died of typhoid fever in Boston, where, following a public autopsy, his brain, skull, and heart were exhibited to an admiring public.

The pursuit of scientific knowledge was far from being exclusively Western, and its use was not just the domain of specialists. The *Tangible Things* exhibition project included a pocket sundial made in Turkey between about 1675 and 1725 in the style of dials made in Augsburg, but with the addition of a *qibla* indicator to satisfy the need of its Muslim user to find the direction of Mecca and the correct times for prayers.[33] A Project Moonwatch telescope exemplified both the industrial production of scientific equipment in the mid-twentieth century and the role of citizen scientists.[34] Project Moonwatch was the brainchild of Harvard

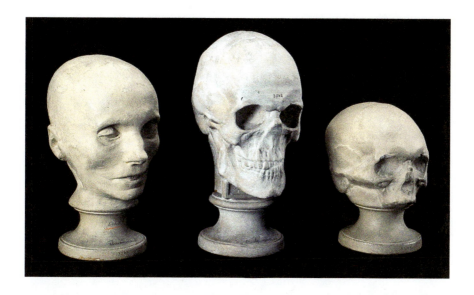

37. Plaster casts of the head of Anne-Josèphe Théroigne de Méricourt, a violent political fanatic during the French Revolution; the skull of Dr. Johann Gaspar Spurzheim, a founder of phrenology; and the skull of French philosopher René Descartes, giving new meaning to his line, "I think therefore I am." These casts were owned by the Boston Phrenological Society before 1835. Although similar to sculpture, these heads represent an episode in the history of medicine. Warren Anatomical Museum in the Francis A. Countway Library of Medicine.

astronomer Fred L. Whipple, who in 1957 established a network of volunteers to track the first artificial satellites—or moons—launched by the United States and the Soviet Union, which unexpectedly succeeded first with Sputnik in October of that year.

Interestingly, Harvard's relationship with the Soviet Union during the height of the Cold War was not quite as simple as Whipple's Project Moonwatch might imply. Situated on the border between the categories of *science and medicine* and *history*, which addressed Harvard and Radcliffe history, we placed an armillary sphere used in teaching astronomy.[35] Dating from about 1960, its form recalls Russian Revolutionary Constructivist sculpture of the 1920s. When Cold War politics halted Soviet imports to the United States, Harvard administrators, rather than relinquish this equipment, simply concealed the prominent "MADE IN U.S.S.R." sticker on the base with an adhesive label.

Such spheres were not the only manifestations of European Modernism embraced by Harvard following World War II. In 1948,

38. Used to teach astronomy since ancient times, the armillary sphere is a model of the heavens with rings representing the celestial equator, the tropics of Cancer and Capricorn, the path of the sun, and the sphere of fixed stars. This Soviet model was distributed in the United States in the late 1950s by the Ealing Corporation, until Cold War politics prevented its importation. Collection of Historical Scientific Instruments.

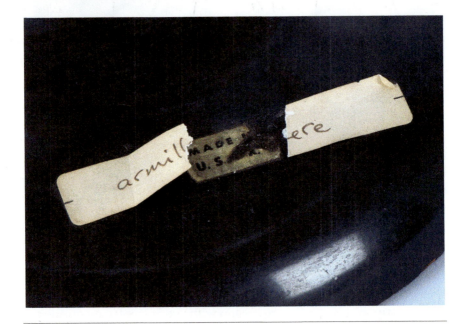

39. The "MADE IN U.S.S.R." sticker was covered over on the Soviet armillary spheres at Harvard when they became illegal in 1960. They remained in use for another forty years. Collection of Historical Scientific Instruments.

Harvard commissioned the first complex of buildings in the Modernist manner by any major American university: the Harvard Graduate Center (now part of the Harvard Law School). The Architects' Collaborative (TAC), a practice founded three years earlier by the exiled German head of the Graduate School of Design, Walter Gropius, designed the buildings. A fellow German exile and former teacher at the Bauhaus design school, Anni Albers, designed the furnishing textiles for the graduate

40. Harvard graduate students—curled up on their beds with stacks of books in the 1950s—may not have known that the woven-cotton bedspreads beneath them had been commissioned by Walter Gropius and designed by an exiled German woman, Anni Albers, a Bauhaus artist. The 1949 dormitory bedspread is now cherished as a modern art textile. Harvard Art Museums/Busch-Reisinger Museum.

41. Like the old joke, "George Washington Slept Here," this blue sash made the rounds. It is likely the sash denoting Washington's unique rank as commander-in-chief that appears in Charles Willson Peale's portrait of the general, and it was first put on exhibit in Peale's Museum in Philadelphia. After Peale's Museum went out of business in 1845, showmen Moses Kimball and P. T. Barnum bought and split the holdings for their separate museums. The sash came to the Boston Museum with Kimball's half. After a fire damaged the museum in 1899, the Kimball family gave Harvard's Peabody Museum the pick of ethnographic objects, including many from the Lewis and Clark expedition. Somehow, Washington's sash came with them. Peabody Museum of Archaeology and Ethnology, Harvard University.

student residences, including the plaid bedspreads that now form part of Harvard's history of involvement with both Modernism and the wave of immigration resulting from the rise of the Third Reich.[36]

Several items in the *history* category also suggested the troubled relations between the sexes at Harvard and Radcliffe. A crimson field-hockey dress from about 1925 illustrated the progressive development of a vibrant collegiate culture at Radcliffe separate from male-dominated Harvard.[37] Such uniforms not only freed Radcliffe athletes from the heavy wool "bloomers" worn by earlier participants in women's sports; they also helped define Radcliffe as an institution.

A cluster of objects associated with American military history reminded us that things did not always end up where one might have expected. Owing to the peculiarities of institutional succession in the nineteenth century, the Peabody Museum of Archaeology and Ethnology was the repository of the blue watered-silk sash worn by George Washington to denote his rank as commander-in-chief.[38] This was the very sash depicted by Charles Willson Peale in his various portraits of Washington. Badges of rank, however,

42. A historical conundrum: This framed military epaulet, possibly of French origin, ca. 1780, is said to have been captured by Major General Artemas Ward more than twenty years earlier at a battle in which he did not participate. General Artemas Ward House Museum.

43. Detail of the epaulet's fringe showing the complex construction. Each metallic thread is a long strip of silver wrapped around a fiber core in such a way as to reveal the core's taupe color, producing a light golden effect. Some metallic threads are twisted together to form two-ply ropes. Others are bundled with crinkled silver ribbons and sequins in order to form a chain of droopy bows. Clusters of metallic ropes alternate with cascades of bows along the length of the fringe. General Artemas Ward House Museum.

were not always what they seemed. Also on display was a framed military epaulet belonging to Major General Artemas Ward, Washington's immediate predecessor by virtue of being the ranking officer in the New England militias at the outbreak of hostilities with colonial authorities in 1775. This epaulet had long been closely associated with Ward at a property bequeathed to Harvard in 1925 by a descendant in Shrewsbury, Massachusetts, to be a "public and patriotic museum" in memory of the general. Tradition had it that the military epaulet had been taken by Ward from a captured French officer after the Battle of Ticonderoga in 1758 during the French and Indian War.[39] However, its origin is far from certain. Although Ward served as colonel of a militia regiment during the campaign, he was sick on the day of the battle and did not take part in it. Furthermore, the form of the epaulet suggests a date of origin in the 1780s rather than the 1750s, adding to the uncertainty surrounding its origin.

This brief description of our six long-established, standard Western categories of collection may suggest confidence in their capacity to accommodate all the things in the world unambiguously. Those who administer collections are obliged to be decisive, regardless of epistemological challenges. A glass jar containing a parasitic tapeworm preserved in alcohol belongs in the Museum of Comparative Zoology by both Linnaean and phylogenetic taxonomy criteria that place it uncontentiously in the collection of the invertebrate zoology department.[40] Human-made things—artifacts—may

44. Could this jar holding a parasitic tapeworm (*Taenia*) that was extracted from the intestinal tract of Bostonian Connie Lukewater in 1893 ever cross the boundary separating medical and zoological specimens from contemporary art? Museum of Comparative Zoology.

seem to rival creatures in the natural world numerically in their variety, but they cannot be sorted in quite the same way as living things. Curators in the Harvard Art Museums, even if they cannot define precisely what art actually is (no one has done so), nonetheless operate by a workable rule of thumb for accepting certain things—a sculpture by Hiram Powers, say—but not others, such as a jar containing a parasitic tapeworm. However, art being an open kind of category (things constantly move in and out of it), an artist might in the future designate a jar of tapeworms as an artwork making that particular jar eligible for accession to the Art Museums' collections of contemporary art. Even if criteria for categorization of the entire range of tangible things vary in their persuasiveness, all are variously unstable or open to ambiguity, however inconvenient this may be for those who form and maintain collections.

In the six case studies devoted to individual things that follow—one for each of our six categories—we implicitly acknowledge the confidence with which each has been assigned to its place by those responsible: a fourth- or fifth-century Roman glass to the Semitic Museum and *anthropology and archaeology*; a sixth- to ninth-century Avar metalworker's mold to the Art Museums and *art*; the third-century papyrus fragment of Plato's *Republic* to the Houghton Library and *books and manuscripts*; a Radcliffe College field-hockey dress from the 1920s to the Schlesinger Library on the History of Women in America and *history*; a 1923 orchid specimen mounted with a watercolor drawing to the University Herbaria and *natural history*; and a group of bottles of chemicals shipped from Paris to Alabama in 1862 to the Collection of Historical Scientific Instruments and *science and medicine*. Yet a moment's reflection leads to the realization that, for all the decisiveness underlying the institutional categorization of these things, uncertainty regarding the finality of placement remains the one constant throughout. We might find the same amenability to multiple classifications in any collection of things, however much it may appear to conform to common sense. As soon as one delves into the character of an item, ambiguities open up and common sense begins to break down.

Natural History

AN ORCHID: SAY IT WITH FLOWERS

The Harvard University Herbaria hold more than five million specimens. Exemplifying *natural history* is one of the approximately 131,000 pressed

45. A pressed orchid specimen, *Epidendrum lorifolium*, accompanied on the same sheet by a watercolor drawing of the live plant in flower is preserved in a traditional wooden herbarium tray. The sheet is a collaboration of the botanist Oakes Ames and his wife Blanche Ames Ames (1923). Orchid Herbarium of Oakes Ames, Harvard University Herbaria.

specimens from the Orchid Herbarium of Oakes Ames. Such pressed botanical specimens can be found in innumerable professional and amateur collections worldwide, large and small.

In this instance, pressed specimens are taped to either side of the watercolor drawing of the stem, leaves, and flowers, flanked by details drawn in pencil. Various stamps, labels, and inscriptions accompany them.

Although not unique to the Orchid Herbarium of Oakes Ames, the practice of combining a specimen and watercolor drawing on the same herbarium mount is unusual. The drawing is by Oakes Ames's wife, Blanche Ames Ames. The specimen is a faded remnant of *Epidendrum lorifolium*, whereas the drawing shows the thriving plant, its petals "pink-purple."[41] They are juxtaposed to provide the most accurate visual information possible, so that other plants might be compared with it and an accurate taxonomy of the genus *Epidendrum* constructed. Yet the contrast between

46. The real thing and its representation: A dried orchid married to a vibrant painting, like the husband and wife who together created the sheet, prompts the question: Which better captures the essence of the plant (if essence there is)? Orchid Herbarium of Oakes Ames, Harvard University Herbaria.

47. A pen-and-ink drawing of
Dendrochilum Foxworthyi Ames by
Blanche Ames Ames in the style
of the Arts and Crafts movement,
published in 1908 in a volume
of Oakes Ames's *Orchidaceae.*
Harvard University Herbaria.

real thing and representation—specimen and artifact—is inescapable,
even if both are interpretive in their respective ways.

The relationship between Western botanists and illustrators has long
been problematic.[42] Lorraine Daston and Peter Galison have described
the challenge of "four-eyed sight": the reconciliation of the views of the
naturalist and the illustrator, each of whom seeks to convey a different
combination of generalities and peculiarities for their own reasons.[43] This
tension has epistemological, as well as social, consequences. At one end
of the spectrum were the professional artists and illustrators who took
the credit for botanical publications they initiated.[44] At the other, male
naturalists kept control by employing their wives, sisters, and daughters
to provide illustrations to their precise specifications.[45]

At first glance, the relationship between Oakes Ames and his wife,
illustrator of numerous herbarium sheets and Ames's publications, might
seem to be one of domestic subordination in botanical inquiry. Yet the
case is more complicated. The illustrations by Blanche Ames Ames for
Oakes Ames's *Orchidaceae* (1905–20) derive from pen-and-ink drawings with distinctive hand lettering that are at once scientifically clear
and stylistically distinct.[46] They conform to the artist's own variant of
American Arts-and-Crafts-movement illustration. The assumption that

an appropriate artistic style clarified the appearance of things was the basis for the couple's partnership. Blanche Ames Ames's contribution was therefore far from subordinate, and this was widely acknowledged, even by Oakes Ames himself.[47] He dedicated the fifth fascicle of the *Orchidaceae* (1915) "To Blanche Ames Ames my wife colleague and playfellow."[48]

Blanche Ames was the daughter of Adelbert Ames, a general in the Civil War Union Army and the Reconstruction-era governor of Mississippi. She graduated from Smith College as president of her class in 1899, marrying Oakes Ames (no relation) in 1900. Far from being a retiring helpmeet, she was not only an accomplished artist, but also a women's suffrage campaigner and birth control advocate.[49] Her partnership with Oakes Ames extended to contributing decisively to the design of Borderland, the house they began constructing in North Easton in 1910, built to be fireproof to protect their library and Oakes Ames's ever-growing orchid herbarium.[50]

Oakes Ames, born in 1874, grew up in North Easton. His father, Oliver Ames, a former governor of Massachusetts, had an interest in botany. Ames graduated from Harvard in 1898, joining the faculty in 1899. Nathaniel Britton, director of the New York Botanical Garden, advised Ames that *Orchidaceae* presented a particular challenge, for it was among the most abundantly varied families of the plant kingdom, and its classification was especially confused.[51] Ames devoted his career at Harvard to *Orchidaceae*, first in the Botanic Garden (1899–1922), then as curator and later director of the Botanic Museum (1923–45). He simultaneously held faculty positions, rising to Arnold Professor of Botany in 1932. He retired from the faculty in 1941 and the Botanic Museum in 1945. He died in 1950, acknowledged as the foremost living orchidologist.[52]

The Western study of orchids had long been a field of jealously guarded knowledge and reputation. A succession of scholars claimed authority to adjudicate ever- more complex and profuse taxonomic puzzles by reference to the living collections and herbaria they formed or controlled. Publications of lavishly illustrated volumes bolstered their reputations. Envy and fear of contradiction and confusion meant that only one such scholar could reign at any given time. Much was at stake, for from the 1830s and onward, orchid collecting and cultivation became big business.[53] Among Ames's predecessors as orchid czars were John Lindley,[54] the first botanist to propose a substantial classification of *Orchidaceae*, Heinrich Gustav Reichenbach[55] of the University of Hamburg, and Robert Allen Rolfe[56] of the Royal Botanical Gardens, Kew. Conflicting decisions among these and other authorities led to a state of taxonomic confusion in the huge family of *Orchidaceae*. Such was Reichenbach's hostility to the younger Rolfe that on his death in 1889, he bequeathed his herbarium to the Naturhistorisches Hof-Museum in Vienna rather than to Kew, as had been expected, on condition that it should remain sealed for twenty-five years.

These were the circumstances in which the next great orchid arbiter, Rudolf Schlechter, rose to prominence. He became a curator at the Botanischer Garten und Botanisches Museum at Dahlem, near Berlin, in 1913. He developed his own orchid herbarium and proposed more than 1,000 new orchid species before his untimely death at the age of fifty-three.[57] It was to Schlechter that Charles W. Powell, the American orchid collector living in the Panama Canal Zone, sent specimens for identification after his appeal to Rolfe, who was unable to consult the Reichenbach Herbarium in Vienna, had failed.[58] A specimen of *Epidendrum lorifolium* was among them. Schlechter published it as a previously unrecognized species in 1922.[59] In that year, Ames and Schlechter met for the first time in Berlin, though they had been exchanging orchid specimens for some time.[60] Ames and Schlechter agreed to collaborate on a major study of *Orchidaceae*, a project aborted by the latter's early death just three years later. Powell supplied Ames with specimens of the same orchids he had submitted to Schlechter, symptomatic of a change in practice from competition to cooperation.[61] This turned out to be just as well, because duplicates and drawings of specimens in Schlechter's herbarium by Schlecter's wife Alexandra that were sent to Ames meant that Harvard had a record of at least some of what was lost when British bombs destroyed the Dahlem herbarium in March 1943.[62]

The change from competition to collaboration during the interwar period was not simply a matter of personality, but rather a consequence of progress toward the standardization of taxonomy in botany as a whole. Transmission of taxonomic information requires consistency of description. Achieving this involved turning basic Western assumptions regarding the character of individual taxa on their heads. Instead of conceiving of each taxon as an essential ideal, scholars had to accept a single specimen of an actual plant as unambiguously representing it, in spite of its inevitable peculiarities. Assigning an unchanging name to an individual representative of a taxon became the crucial act, putting an end to competition among synonyms proposed by competing scholars. Each taxon should have but one commonly agreed identity, priority going to the first scholar to publish. The specimen designated by that scholar would be the "type specimen" against which all other claimants to identity with it would have to be measured by firsthand comparison. This procedure comprises what Lorraine Daston describes as "an *art* of transmission."[63] It was not made formal internationally with real effect until it was resolved by the International Botanical Congress in Vienna in 1905.[64] Although this agreement was not universally adhered to for the following twenty-five years, it substantially ended the free-for-all that had vitiated the reliable transmission of taxonomic information. Ames and Schlechter were among the beneficiaries. Scholars became far more ready to submit and exchange specimens than previously. The newly identified species *Epidendrum lorifolium* Schltr. took its place in its genus without controversy, though it lost its status in 2008.[65]

Blanche Ames Ames's pencil inscription states that the specimen came from "Powell's Garden, Balboa" on the Panama Canal. Powell was an employee of the Panama Canal Zone Authority. As the water level of Lake Gatun, part of the canal, rose, Powell was able to collect epiphytic orchids from a boat rowed among the partly submerged trees.[66] In 1926, the Missouri Botanical Garden in St. Louis acquired the garden from Powell to become its tropical station.[67]

The fact that the Canal Zone was an American possession and Powell a colonial official reminds us that botany, like various other disciplines from anthropology to zoology, followed empire. In Ames's case, this is no more evident than in his long-term work on the *Orchidaceae* of the Philippines, ceded by Spain to the United States in 1898.[68] Unlike in Germany, no American botanical collection or herbarium was founded specifically to study the flora of its conquered territories and colonies. Yet even Oakes Ames's corner of Harvard, like the Missouri Botanical Garden in the case of Panama, embraced the extension of American interests. In his first year of employment at Harvard, 1899, Oakes Ames helped to establish the Harvard Botanic Station for Tropical Research and Sugar Cane Investigation in Cienfuegos in recently conquered Cuba. Harvard ran the station under various names and administrations—Ames was its supervisor between 1927 and 1935—until abandoning it in 1961 after the Cuban revolution.[69] Ames was deeply interested in the exploitation of plants for commercial ends. He formed a Collection of Economic Botany and an Economic Herbarium, and gave them to Harvard in 1918 after his wartime service on the Botanical Raw Products Committee of the National Research Council.[70] However, botany, while an element of colonial enterprise, could not be reduced to inventory and control alone. Orchids, in particular, carried associations well beyond the botanical.

Although there are numerous species of orchids indigenous to Europe and North America, their proliferation in the tropics led to an association with "tropic, dense, languid magnificence," as American poet George Sterling put it in his 1909 poem "House of Orchids."[71] Further, horticultural intervention to produce ever-more exotic varieties led to tension among orchid enthusiasts between the claims of naturally occurring species and the contrivances of the greenhouse. This division can be traced back to the study of orchids by horticulturalists, as well as by field botanists, since at least the early nineteenth century.

No one did more to promote the association of hothouse orchids with decadence than the Irish writer Oscar Wilde, the fin-de-siècle epitome of aestheticism and wit, who was undone by his conviction and imprisonment in 1895 for "gross indecency." In *The Picture of Dorian Gray*, his protagonist says: "Yesterday I cut an orchid for my button hole. It was a marvelous spotted thing, as effective as the seven deadly sins."[72] The basis of such associations may have been the exaggeratedly sensual appearance of certain species to attract pollinators. Even respectable orchidologists could be vulnerable to quizzical scrutiny. What might onlookers have thought when, on arriving in Berlin by train from Vienna in 1922, Ames recognized Schlechter on the crowded platform thanks to the German extending a spray of large white orchids?[73]

Orchidologists could not depend on institutional support because of the association of orchids with decadence. As Nathaniel Britton had mentioned to Oakes Ames when recommending *Orchidaceae* as a field of study, he did so in part because he knew that Ames had independent means. Oakes Ames was an heir to the Ames Shovel Company fortune. Ames shovels had dug for gold in California and Australia, had built the first transcontinental railroad, and had been issued to the U.S. Army in every conflict from the Civil War to Korea. Although the Ames Shovel Company ceased production in Easton in 1952, Oakes Ames had built his botanical career on its profits.[74] In consequence, an ironic connection unexpectedly unites the specimen and watercolor drawing of *Epidendrum lorifolium*. That specimen originated in the Panama Canal Zone. The canal, a vital American interest built with massive effort between 1910 and 1914, was dug with the very shovels—supplied by the Ames Shovel Company—that created the floods that allowed Charles Powell to collect his orchid specimens, and the sales of which furnished Oakes Ames with his means of study.

I. G.

Anthropology and Archaeology

A GLASS JAR: A SURFACE FIND IN THE SEMITIC MUSEUM

When the Ottoman Empire officially entered the Great War in August of 1914, a small, iridescent green-glass jar began its long journey from North Africa to the Semitic Museum at Harvard.[75] Maximilian Lindsay Kellner acquired this jar along with other antiquities when he conducted excavations in Palestine and Syria in the summers of 1913 and 1914. After his death, Kellner's collection of more than one hundred glass and ceramic items eventually passed to Harvard. Kellner was a professor of Old Testament languages and interpretation at the Episcopal Theological School (now the Episcopal Divinity School) and a lecturer at Harvard. His intellectual work was closely tied to that of the Semitic Museum. As an artifact of daily life in the Holy Land, the jar is at home in this museum. It offers archaeological evidence about craftsmanship, technology, the transmission of culture, and everyday experience. But it may offer more than that. The iridescent surfaces of glass items like this one inspired a range of new art objects around the turn of the twentieth century. The desire for things with a rich historical patina, a real or invented link to the

48. Excavated in 1914, this four-handled glass jar is archaeological evidence of daily life, technology, and culture in Syria and Palestine during the fourth and fifth centuries. Semitic Museum.

49. The iridescent surfaces of glass jars like this one—which were chemically caused by centuries of burial—inspired nineteenth-century glass artists like Louis Comfort Tiffany to reproduce this accidental effect in their works. Semitic Museum.

past, had deep literary, artistic, and historical resonance for Kellner, his wife, and their contemporaries.

At just over ten centimeters in height, the tiny jar was created during the fourth or fifth century CE in Syria or Palestine, then still in the eastern part of the Roman Empire. Its rounded, globular body sits on a concave base. Four curved handles connect the base to the rounded rim and echo the shape of the open, rounded roll near the opening. In the fourth century CE, the glassblowing industry in the eastern Roman Empire was thriving, perhaps because of the relative stability that the reigns of Diocletian and Constantine brought to the east.[76] Scholars have documented the technological innovation and wide variety of glass forms found in Syria and Palestine during this period through studies of applied ornament, diverse mold forms, and a variety of shapes and functions. This small jar was likely free-blown and then transferred to a pontil or rod, as indicated by the scar at its base. Using the pontil, the rough lip could be reheated to form the rounded rim and the projecting roll near the top before the four handles were applied. Looking closely, it is clear that it could not have been used for drinking, as liquid would have been trapped in the open, decorative roll. It may have been used as a small storage jar or as tableware.[77] The jar's most notable feature is its newest: an iridescent patina, variably opalescent greens, pinks, and yellows. Centuries of contact with the earth created this unintentional chemical reaction. Its corroded surface still retains some dirt.

The bits of dirt on the jar's surface are the only direct evidence of its place of origin. According to the records of the Semitic Museum, it was found in a Greek or Roman tomb.[78] However, there is no information about how Kellner acquired the collection of Roman glass from which this jar is drawn. In an article he published after his 1913 excavations, the biblical scholar proudly narrated his discovery of scores of flints. He noted even the theatrical detail of the names of the three horses, Abdullah, Abu Shaker, and Hamar, that carried heavy saddlebags weighed down with his Neolithic finds.[79] In June 1914, Charles Peabody, curator of European archaeology at the Peabody Museum at Harvard, joined Kellner's expedition. They focused on gathering items related to Neolithic and Paleolithic Palestine and Syria. Peabody published his notes from his six-week camping trip with Kellner and made no mention of the glass.[80]

Kellner does not seem to have published anything about his acquisition of the sixty pieces of pottery and forty works of glass that he collected on the same trip. Instead, another frustrated scholar wrote of the shaky provenance of some of the ceramic items Kellner procured in 1913, describing questionable dealers and noting of some objects, "nothing is known as to their provenance beyond the vague and valueless rumor that it was the Jordan valley." And later, "as usual, nothing definite could be learned as to the locality from which they came."[81] Most of Kellner's early research employed Assyrian texts, artifacts, and monuments to study the Old Testament to learn more about the connections among Israel-Judah, the Hebrews and other peoples.[82] His work with flints was similar: He believed that the artifacts of prehistoric people could shed light on some aspects of the Old Testament. The small glass jar appears to be millennia too late for his main research interests.

In addition to his scholarly credentials, in his mid-forties, Kellner married into Anglican aristocracy when he wed the widow of prominent Rev. Phillips Brooks's brother, Elisabeth Willard Brooks. Mrs. Kellner seemed to be as fascinated with the Mediterranean's ancient past as her new husband was. She accompanied her husband on his 1914 summer collecting trip and was there when he, "at great inconvenience," managed to bring artifacts back to the United States while the war in Europe raged.[83] She also seems to have had her own collection of antiquities and a deep interest in the meanings of the past.[84] In her novel *As the World Goes By* (1905), the power of Rome's antiquity directly transforms her main character into a submissive protestant saint.[85] While this romantic view of the past appears to be at odds with the archaeologically rooted Biblical history promoted by much of her husband's work, it fit squarely within the anti modernism that dominated American intellectual life at the turn of the twentieth century.

Artists, writers, and reformers viewed the past, both distant and near, as direct intellectual and spiritual inspiration. Cultural historian Jackson Lears identified the late-nineteenth to the early-twentieth century as an "antimodern" moment in American history, when the culture of the past seemed to offer vital lessons.[86] Antimodernism was not just about the ancient past, but encompassed visions of the early American past as well. Colonial revival projects like the transformation of the Artemas Ward House into a "Public Patriotic Museum" offered a specific vision of early American history as white, protestant, and rural. Such a vision aligned with nativist sympathies and offered a static, limited definition of "American" in the face of an influx of immigration. Artists and designers fed this movement through the development of objects that echoed, replicated, and transformed ideas about the past to fit present aesthetic and consumer needs—whether through the creation of faux Americana or the development of fine art objects inspired by Arthurian legends or the ancient world. The discovery and display of Roman glass, such as this jar, contributed to this trend.

In the last decade of the nineteenth century, Louis Comfort Tiffany began producing fine glassware. Among the techniques that would make Tiffany's Favrile glass famous, "Cypriote" glass was created in imitation of corroded ancient glass from Cyprus. It was inspired by objects in the collections of the Metropolitan Museum of Art. Glassmakers would roll a blown object in a layer of crushed glass and then apply an iridescent glaze, creating a variegated, colored surface that mimicked the oxidation caused by centuries of burial. Like this small glass jar, the surfaces of Tiffany's Cypriote glass glistened with a range and depth of colors. Other forms inspired by the ancient world—by Rome, Egypt, and Samos— joined Cypriote glass in the Tiffany stockroom. The glazes and techniques Tiffany pioneered took inspiration from ancient forms and created new artworks through technological innovation.[87] The new forms added a sense of history to the highly ornamented surfaces of Tiffany interiors.

Photographs of what may be Max Kellner's own study reflect this style.[88] They suggest the personal appeal that objects of the late Roman period may have held for him and his wife, more so than the scores of carefully studied flints he collected to trace the history behind the Old Testament. A vase of peacock feathers, small, decorative glass and ceramic vases, and religious art all rest atop his bookcase. Heavy drapes, a fringed desk lamp, and a wall tiled with photographs complete the scene

50. Likely the study of Maximilian Kellner, an Old Testament scholar and collector of Roman glass, this interior shows an appreciation for art objects that echoed the past but were transformed by contemporary aesthetics. Harvard University Archives.

and suggest an aesthetic sensibility.[89] Cypriote glass would have been as at home in this interior as the antiquities he collected.

Apart from the items on his study shelves, there is only one clue that suggests Kellner had a personal interest in glass, a pamphlet tipped inside his scrap album in the Harvard University Archives. The pamphlet is a visitor's guide to the Glass Flower exhibition at the Harvard Natural History Museum. Leopold and Rudolf Blaschka, father and son craftsmen in Dresden, Germany, created the glass flowers between 1887 and 1936 as teaching aids. The life-sized models combined technical virtuosity with artistic skill and scientific precision. Though the lamp work required to craft the delicate flowers may seem to be a world away from the fire-rounded rim of the four-handled jar, it is not. The Blaschkas, just like the fourth-century CE Syrian or Palestinian glass-maker who created this jar, and even Louis Comfort Tiffany's designers, transformed an ancient art through precise skill and a sophisticated awareness of the properties of glass.

In the *Tangible Things* exhibition, we placed an elegant floriform Tiffany glass vase from the collections of the Fogg Art Museum beside the Blaschkas' more scientific creations. Together in the Natural History Museum, they forced visitors to query the connections between art and science, artifice and nature. Perhaps Kellner would have understood this juxtaposition even more deeply. Consideration of his Roman glass collection, now in the Semitic Museum, raises additional questions about the distinctions between past and present, tradition and innovation, and inspiration and imitation. Housed in a museum devoted to archaeology and anthropology, artifacts like Kellner's glass jar may provide nearly as much evidence about the complex culture of collecting in the early twentieth century as they do about daily life in the ancient world.

S. A. C.

Books and Manuscripts

A PAPYRUS FRAGMENT: PLATO FROM THE SHARP-NOSED TRASH

Pressed lovingly between glass plates, the frayed papyrus barely contains eighteen incomplete lines of the third book of Plato's *Republic*.[90] The Greek letters appear to tumble and push their way off all the ragged edges. The papyrus is fragile, but the ink is strong and dark. It challenges our belief that the manuscript is nearly 1,800 years old.

Plato wrote the *Republic* between 386–367 BCE, but the oldest, complete Greek manuscript extant is a Byzantine copy from the ninth century

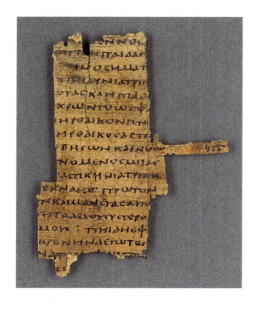

51. A fragment of Plato's *Republic* on papyrus, copied in Oxyrhynchus, Egypt (ca. 250–300). Houghton Library.

(the Codex Parisinus 1807).[91] Copied more than a millennium after the original was written, and unknown in Europe until about 1490, the late codex explains the care taken with this earlier fragment of a scroll. Dating from the middle to latter part of the third century CE, the glass-mounted papyrus is one of the earliest and precious few direct copies of Plato's work. It helps to establish the text.[92]

It is a passage about health, and Plato speaks through Socrates.[93] He has just been discussing education, which in his ideal city is to be grounded in music and gymnastics. Not just any music, or related poetry, he has said, but rhythms and topics designed to inculcate morality, bravery, honesty, and a sense of beauty. Physical education should be directed to keep both the soul and body healthy in order to avoid doctors. In contrast to his ideal, the prevailing "vicious and ugly system of education" had produced a world filled with self-aggrandizing lawyers and doctors who merely treated chronic problems arising from a dissolute populace and had never done society any good. In the passage on the fragment, Socrates goes on to warn that ongoing, coddling medical treatments are wrong-headed. They are no better for the soul than a love of litigation. As a case in point, he takes Herodicus, a fifth-century BCE physician, today revered as the father of sports medicine because he advocated a combination of diet and physical exercise as a way to combat disease. Socrates dismisses Herodicus as a dangerous fool for fussing away his life in cures, first on himself and then on others. A good working citizen has no time for long treatments. If he gets sick, he should be cured by drugs or surgery and return to his usual business. Otherwise, he should die and be done with it. This republic of Plato was a harsh place, indeed.

The stern passage was written in rounded capital (uncial) letters typical of the third century CE by a scribe with an irregular hand. We can only guess what the scribe thought about Plato, but we do have an inkling about the opinion of a later owner of the scroll. The reverse of the fragment contains nine lines of an unidentified document written in cursive. It has nothing to do with philosophy and dates from the late third or fourth century. Apparently, this copy of Plato's words had been recycled!

The fragment was found in a vast rubbish dump in Egypt at the site of the ancient city of Oxyrhynchus, the "city of the sharp-nosed fish." The city is named after a fish worshipped by Greek settlers who colonized a pharaonic town that dated back to the twelfth century BCE.[94] Today little meets the eye at the location a hundred miles south of Cairo and ten miles west of the Nile except a lone Greek column, a quiet village, and low hills on the

52. The reverse side of the papyrus fragment was written fifty to a hundred years later in a different hand than the Platonic text on the front and has nothing to do with philosophy. It reveals that the writing surface was recycled. Houghton Library.

edge of the desert. Gone are the ancient walls, public baths, temples, gymnasium, race course, town hall, theater, colonnades, and porticos of a thriving Greek city in Egypt under Greek and then Roman rule; gone are the thirty Christian churches, 10,000 monks, and 20,000 nuns of the Byzantine period. When two young British archaeologists, Bernard Pyne Grenfell and Arthur Surridge Hunt, began excavations on the site in the winter season of 1896–97, it did not look very promising. But those low hills, it turned out, were trash heaps on the outskirts of the settlement, and they yielded up surprises: a trove of papyri of Roman and Byzantine date, including the unknown *Logia* (or "Sayings of Jesus"), which later turned out to be the apocryphal *Gospel of Thomas*. A new field of study—papyrology—was born.

Grenfell and Hunt returned again and again in the winters of 1903–04 through 1906–07. From mounds thirty feet deep, the excavation yielded major Greek and early Christian works known only by reputation or not at all—the *Paeans* of Pindar, songs of Sappho, Euripides' *Hypsipyle*, a history of Greece, comedies of Sophocles and Menander—works lost in the Middle Ages and not read for more than a thousand years. There were also earlier versions of texts than the ones that had been previously available—mathematical diagrams from Euclid and fragments of Plato, for example. Even more of the wastepaper shed light on the society of Oxyrhynchus. There were government orders and tax returns, accounts of fishing and household affairs, shopping lists, wills, contracts, vulgar stories, medical prescriptions,

53. Excavation of Oxyrhynchus, Egypt (ca. 1905) showing hills of dusty trash to be painstakingly sifted. Egypt Exploration Society.

and many letters. There was a letter from a son to his father: "If you don't send for me, I won't eat I won't drink so there"; doodles of a schoolboy: "King Midas has ass's ears"; instructions to a policeman to produce two defendants in a legal case; censored town council minutes; amulets made of papyrus— one for a Christian containing the Epistle of Jude, and another for a pagan featuring the *ouroboros* (a snake biting its own tail) and a blank place for the user to fill in his own name. There were even menus: "For dinner on 5th: a Canopic cake, liver. For dinner on 6th: 10 oysters, 1 lettuce, 2 small loaves, 1 fatted bird from the water, 2 wings."[95] All in all, there were 500,000 fragments, a wealth of garbage taken back to Oxford to be preserved, sorted, and analyzed. Our Plato fragment had been keeping some unusual company. The dry sands of Egypt had preserved paper documents for millennia that the wet environs of Greece and Italy had consumed.

The dig was sponsored by the Egypt Exploration Fund, established in 1882 in London and today known by the name of the Egypt Exploration Society. Grenfell and Hunt published their first finds in six volumes of the *Oxyrhynchus Papyri* (London, 1898–1908). In exchange for contributions to the effort, the Egypt Exploration Fund distributed the finds among various research institutions on a pro-rata basis. In 1903, David Gordon Lyon, curator of Harvard's Semitic Museum, offered $500 to support the work of Grenfell and Hunt during the upcoming season. The museum received the Plato fragment and other papyri in return.[96] Although today it seems fitting that such an authoritative fragment of Greek philosophy would be housed at Harvard's Houghton Library among other rare books and manuscripts, this was not always the case. The Semitic Museum's cache of papyri was transferred to Houghton Library around 1959.

One of Plato's most famous passages in the *Republic* is the "Allegory of the Cave," in which he sets forth his view of knowledge and reality.[97] People are like prisoners in a cave who can never see the true forms of reality outside the cave, but only the shadows they cast on the back wall. Like these shadows, the material world of our senses is incomplete, corrupt, changing, and suspect. The goal of philosophy is to "leave the cave" and seek the ideal, abstract forms that constitute the truths of our world.

The irony here is that Plato's own philosophy would lead us to privilege the ideas contained in his writings over the medium that bears them. But without this ragged papyrus and materials like it, his ideas would have been lost to us entirely.

S. J. S.

Art

A LIMESTONE MOLD: SET IN STONE

A small, irregular oblong stone is one of the very many and varied things that can exemplify *art*. This stone has been extensively worked. Set at an angle to the rectangle of the mottled face is an incised rectangle enclosing a design. It also has two gouged depressions beside one another along one of the longer edges, outside the incised rectangle. Along a short side of the stone on this face, a section of the edge has been worked away to form part of a funnel. Within the rectangle, also incised, is a stylized animal. A similar, though less deeply carved design, is to be found on the opposite face. This stone is a mold.[98] An unfinished or rejected perforated bronze plaquette in a private collection representing an animal helps us to ascertain the purpose of the mold, for it was derived from one that must have been very similar.[99] The animal is what is generally described as a griffin. Griffins are characteristic of the metalwork of the Avar people from at

54. Carved out of limestone and taking the form of a griffin, this mold is for casting openwork metal ornaments, perhaps for a belt. It belonged to an Avar metalworker living in the Balkans in the mid- to late seventh century. Harvard Art Museums/Arthur M. Sackler Museum.

least the second half of the seventh century and onward. Our stone is an Avar metalworker's mold, probably from the mid- to late seventh century.

Who were the Avars? What was the griffin-embellished metal plaquette used for? It is in the collection of the Harvard Art Museums, but is such a thing properly an artwork? Even if the bronze piece might be art, what about our mold? Is it not merely an antiquarian curiosity, not even to be dignified with archaeological status, having been severed from the context of its site, which remains unidentified? Yet it exhibits aesthetic qualities resulting from human action: a complex set of grooves and indentations to form not only the matrix from which another object could be made, but a representation. That carving is an ambitious attempt to convey the likeness of a creature forming part of an unknown mythology, suggesting an entire life of the imagination and a narration far beyond the bare function of whatever the object might be.

The mold might serve as an example of metallurgy, so it would be fitting for categorization in *science and medicine*, or *anthropology and archaeology*. Yet if its aesthetic qualities command attention, the stone might be thought to belong in an art museum. This is when philosopher Nelson Goodman's terms come into play, as he asks the question "When is art?" as opposed to "What is art?"[100] Whether it is art or not in an ontological sense, it functions as art. In practical, even if not in philosophical terms, we can acknowledge it to be art.

More than 5,000 graves at Avar sites have been excavated in Hungary and neighboring countries. Among the most conspicuous finds have been belt fittings. Wealthy Avars wore elaborate belts, sometimes more than one, adorned with bronze, gilded bronze, or gold fixtures. Some of these fixtures were in large part decorative, but some also allowed useful objects, such as an arrow quiver, to be attached.[101] Who were the people who made and wore such things?

Little is known about the Avars in comparison with other migrating peoples of late antiquity and the early Middle Ages in Europe.[102] In 558, Avar envoys caused a stir in Constantinople. They were a Mongol horse-riding, nomadic people who had come from the eastern steppes. The men wore their hair in long, beribboned plaits. A late seventh- or early eighth-century gold flask in the Kunsthistorisches Museum, Vienna, derived from Persian Sassanian silver prototypes, gives some idea of their idealized self-image.[103] It depicts a mounted, spear-bearing warrior clutching a prisoner who is on foot by the head. It also indicates the skill in goldsmiths' work fostered in a society that had acquired various provincial Byzantine characteristics. As warriors, the Avars were not only spear-bearers, but mounted archers, like the Huns who had first so troubled Europe some 150 years previously. They introduced an innovation that was to make a huge difference to mounted warfare, giving them an immediate advantage over their adversaries: iron stirrups. A pair of iron stirrups in the Balatoni Múzeum, Keszthely, Hungary, is inlaid with silver wire, once again giving an indication of the Avars' metalworking skills and love of embellishment.[104] Their dedication to their horses and their perceived need for them in the afterlife are suggested by the burials of wealthy men with their mounts.[105] Unlike most other migrant peoples, they never adopted Christianity, either Catholic or Arian, and only a few inscriptions of indecipherable characters on various objects indicate fragments of a (still unknown) written language. We are dependent on Byzantine, Lombard, and Frankish chronicles, and on archaeological evidence for our knowledge of the Avars.

In 567, they allied with the Lombards to destroy the Gepids, a people then inhabiting the central Carpathian basin in the northern Balkans. Successive Byzantine emperors had tried to play the three groups off against one another while paying them subsidies in gold. Justin II (r. 565–578) cut off subsidies to the Avars and prepared to support the Gepids against the Lombards. The Gepids' center was the old Roman city of Sirmium.[106] When the Avars and the Lombards attacked the Gepids, Justin intervened to retain control of Sirmium. After the Gepid defeat, the Germanic Lombards, notionally Arian Christians, perceived the danger they were now in from their recent allies, and in 568, moved into northern Italy, leaving Norricum and western Pannonia deliberately devastated to deter Avar pursuit.

Between 573 and 626, Constantinople sent no fewer than four-and-a-half million *solidi* (about 44,000 pounds) of gold to the Avars as subsidies and ransoms. In 626, the Avars attacked the city. Their siege failed, and they retreated into chaos as Slavs and Bulgars revolted in the rear. This was the end of Byzantine gold tributes, and any mention in Byzantine chronicles. The Avars retained the ability to intervene periodically in western European affairs until the future Holy Roman Emperor Charlemagne (r. 768–814), then king of the Franks, invaded their lands along both banks of the Danube in 791. Within five years, the Franks had destroyed the internally fragmenting Avar realm, and, as the phrase has it, they "disappeared from history."

Of course, the Avars did not disappear physically. They disappeared in a political and cultural sense. Yet what might ever have been authentically Avar? Was the maker of our mold undoubtedly a descendent of a Mongol people who had ridden down from the steppes to cross the Danube in the middle of the sixth century? The physical anthropologist Pál Lipták has collated an analysis of the skulls from innumerable Avar period gravesites and found that only 17 percent can be described as Mongol. The Carpathian basin was inhabited by a considerable variety of ethnic types during the 230 years of Avar ascendancy. Even if the people Lipták describes as Mongol were prevalent, though far from exclusively so, among the skeletons identifiable by grave objects as belonging to the top ranks of Avar society, the population as a whole included what must have been peoples of Mediterranean, Germanic, Slav, and Bulgar origin at least.[107] The maker and user of our stone mold might have been from any of these groups.

In the wake of recent conflicts in the Balkans that involved appeals to notions of "nation" and "people," the historian Susan Reynolds has cautioned us that such gatherings are not finally racially determined, but may exemplify what the social anthropologist Benedict Anderson has termed "imagined communities": communities that are principally politically defined and united, first, by shared laws and customs, and, second, by myths of common descent.[108] Such groups were not necessarily stable and, as Reynolds remarks, "groups that are now perceived as the founders of modern nations were not always more cohesive than those whose names have disappeared."[109] The name of the Avars has not disappeared, but much of what distinguished them—including language—has.

Even exemplary Avar forms, such as our mold, must be regarded as the product of what the Martiniquan literary theorist Édouard Glissant calls *métissage*: cultural intermixture that stresses the value of reticulation—a network of relationships—rather than filiation or lines of descent.[110] Our stone, itself literally a matrix, becomes the matrix in another sense, not of cultural authenticity as it is understood to pertain to a classical ethnic social entity—the Avars narrowly construed—but of an ever-shifting network of cultural processes that exists only in terms of ever-shifting relations among people over both space and time. What Glissant terms *relation* is the key to the aesthetic and historical comprehensibility of this matrix, indeed, of this stone. This stone, so superficially negligible, becomes the mode of entry into an entire world of cross-cultural and cross-temporal *relation*, taking us from the Balkans in late antiquity to the Harvard Art Museums and to *Tangible Things*, by means of a poetics that is the very stuff of historical understanding.[111]

I. G.

Science and Medicine

A COLLECTION OF POWDERS: POLITICAL CHEMISTRY

The seven bottles of chemicals from the Collection of Historical Scientific Instruments are of differing sizes, all with ground glass stoppers and many still sealed with string and parchment.[112] The bottles have long necks with rims, for ease in handling. One is of blue glass indicating that it holds a poison. The others hold colorful powders, woodsy looking stuff, and lumps of resin. They are labeled in French: Brômure de Sodium, Sulfure d'Argent, Oxide de Chrôme, Lac-dye, Chrômate de

55. Glass jars with stoppers sealed by parchment and string hold colorful chemicals that were imported from France around 1862. The stockroom numbers on the bottom edges of the bottles show that they were part of a large set. Collection of Historical Scientific Instruments.

56. The label on this bottle of chromic oxide indicates that the Medical College of Alabama placed a large custom order with the overseas manufacturer Rousseau Frères, which was located down the street from the Faculty of Medicine in Paris. The current physical location of the bottle—on a Cambridge shelf with many others like it—reveals that the bottle never made it to Mobile. A blockade of the South during the Civil War caused the chemicals to be redirected to the North. Collection of Historical Scientific Instruments.

Plomb, Opopanax, and Rocou. Someone has penciled chemical formulas alongside the names, perhaps to facilitate translation of the foreign words. There are stockroom numbers near the base of each bottle. The numbers run into the thousands, suggesting that these bottles were part of a large set. Indeed, more than a hundred such bottles survive at Harvard, where they have sat on laboratory shelves since the mid-nineteenth century. They were prepared and sold by Rousseau Frères of Paris. And here's a surprise: All are labeled "Medical College of Alabama."

The bottles tell us many things beyond how chemicals were packaged. First, there are simple things such as when and where and for whom they were made. The firm on the label—Rousseau Frères—was in business from about 1820 until 1870. When these chemicals were bottled, the firm was at number 9, Rue d'Ecole de Medicine, Paris. The earliest year that they could have been made was 1859, since that was the year in which the intended owner—the Medical College of Alabama—was established in Mobile, Alabama, largely through the efforts of Josiah Clark Nott, an accomplished surgeon who wanted to raise medical standards in the South. The bottles also point out some social and economic facts. Serious money was spent overseas to equip the new school. Indeed, the state of Alabama gave $50,000, which was more than matched by private donors. Dr. Nott's first act was to go on a long shopping trip to Europe to purchase books, anatomical models and specimens, chemical apparatus, surgical tools, microscopes, and instructional materials. These bottles were part of a large custom order filled in Paris sometime between 1859 and 1862 for use in the school's chemical and pharmaceutical laboratories.[113]

Nott's need to go overseas "to purchase the complicated apparatus necessary to put such an institution in motion" is a story repeated at many institutions of higher learning in the United States in the nineteenth century.[114] Chemistry was slow to get a foothold in the United States, and serious students went abroad to London, Edinburgh, Paris, and Munich to study the subject.[115] Chemical supplies and apparatus also had to be imported from Europe. There were no manufacturers here. The bottles confirm this.

In 1672, Harvard president Leonard Hoar wrote to the English natural philosopher Robert Boyle, author of *The Sceptical Chymist*, about his dream to set up a "laboratory chemical" for the students since "readings or notions only are but husky provender."[116] However, it was not until the end of the eighteenth century that Harvard students had the opportunity to witness demonstration lectures on the chemistry of gases delivered by the professor of natural philosophy.[117] For the most part, learning in chemistry was by reading and recitation until the founding of Harvard's Medical School in 1782 and the appointment of a professor of chemistry and *materia medica*, Aaron Dexter. Dexter at first had to borrow his apparatus from the professor of natural philosophy, Samuel Williams, but he and his successors were given leave to purchase apparatus from London or Paris to set up and maintain a chemical laboratory in one college basement or another. Chemical glassware often broke, and reagents were consumed. Few items could be replaced in Boston. Harvard sent a number of faculty members on study and buying trips to Europe to train with the leading chemists and to purchase state-of-the-art equipment. At other times, the university expected the faculty to replenish chemical supplies out of their own pockets.[118]

When the Rousseau Frères chemicals were bottled in Paris, Harvard had several chemists on the faculty. Teaching at the college and medical school, Josiah P. Cooke was the Erving Professor of Chemistry and Mineralogy, succeeding John White Webster in 1850 at the age of twenty-three after Webster was hanged for murder.[119] Cooke spent the first six months in Europe studying the subject and visiting chemical laboratories before returning to Harvard to establish a teaching laboratory for undergraduates in University Hall and later in 1857, a bigger and better chemical laboratory in Boylston Hall.[120] Charles W. Eliot was an assistant professor of chemistry (1858–63) before becoming president of the university in 1869. He conducted research with Frank A. Storer, who from 1865–70 was MIT's Professor of General, Industrial and Analytical Chemistry before he took up the Professorship of Agricultural Chemistry at the Bussey Institution, Harvard's School of Agriculture and Horticulture. Oliver Wolcott Gibbs, MD, was yet another chemist on campus, serving as the Rumford Professor of the Application of Science to the Useful Arts (from 1863), dean of the Lawrence Scientific School (1863–71), and dean of the School of Mining and Practical Geology (1865–68).[121]

Any of these scholars would have welcomed a large set of Rousseau Frères chemicals, especially if they did not have to pay for them out of pocket. Three cite chemicals supplied by Rousseau Frères in their publications.[122] Moreover, the range of chemicals in the bottles coincides well with the interests of the chemical faculty and Harvard's various schools— namely, natural philosophy, medicine, chemistry, mineralogy, geology, horticulture, and applied sciences. Sodium bromide, for instance, was employed as a hypnotic agent, anticonvulsant, and sedative in their day. Chromic oxide had uses in metallurgy and as a paint pigment. Lead chromate was another pigment. Two organic dyes were the brilliant red lac obtained from secretions of an insect and the orange rocou (or annatto) derived from achiote trees found in tropical South America, Central America, and the Caribbean. Rocou was used as food coloring and flavoring, body paint and lipstick, a treatment for heartburn and stomach distress, a sunscreen, and insect repellent. Opopanax resin (better known as sweet myrrh) was a highly flammable resin that could be burned as incense or used in perfume. In medicine, it was used to treat spasms, asthma, chronic infections, hysteria, and hypochondria, and to promote menstruation. In nature, silver sulfide is a mineral and presents itself as different silver ores. It is also the corrosion found on silverware. The substances in these bottles were suitable for quite a range of experiments, courses, and demonstrations at the university.

But how did bottles destined for the Medical College of Alabama come to be at a Yankee institution like Harvard? The answer is found in the Anaconda Plan to strangle the Confederacy in the Civil War and the unlucky timing of Alabama's orders for apparatus. In 1859, Josiah Nott had gone on his shopping spree to Europe and presumably had placed the order with Rousseau Frères. The custom labels prepared by the firm for the college indicate that this was a large, expensive order. It would have taken some time to fill. In the interim, Nott returned to Mobile as part of the new medical faculty. They taught the first course of lectures in the winter of 1859–60 and the second in 1860–61. In April 1861, soon after the fall of Fort Sumter, President Lincoln issued a proclamation calling for a blockade of southern seaports from Virginia to Texas in order to prevent export of cotton and import of goods and military supplies. Mobile, Alabama, home to the new medical college, had been a top cotton-exporting port before the war. Vessels caught running the blockade were captured and sent to the nearest Union port where their cargo was seized. It may have been that a prized cargo of French chemicals destined for Mobile was redirected to Boston, where a northern institution, Harvard, took advantage of the booty. This is the lore at Harvard, and it is a reasonable story.

Another possibility is that Rousseau Frères found itself holding the bag when the Medical College of Alabama closed its doors in 1861 as its students and faculty rushed to the lines of battle. Nott himself was famous for his racial theories on the biological inferiority of Africans and Native Americans, and an ardent supporter of secession and slavery. In the autumn of 1861, he jumped at the chance to serve in the medical department of the Confederate Army. With the medical college shut until 1868, Rousseau Frères would have looked for another buyer.[123] The problem with this version is that there are no records of correspondence or invoices between Harvard and Rousseau Frères. In either case, Harvard took advantage of the war to stock its chemistry cabinets.

The capture of scientific equipment was not an isolated incident during the hostilities. In 1860, the University of Mississippi had plans to build the world's largest refracting telescope, and ordered an 18½-inch lens to be custom-made by Alvan Clark and Sons of Cambridgeport, Massachusetts. When Ole Miss was unable to take possession of the superlative glass, the Harvard College Observatory tried to raise the funds—$11,187—only to be outwitted in 1863 when some businessmen from Chicago swooped into Cambridgeport with ready cash and purchased the lens for an observatory not yet built.[124] The cash-strapped Harvard director was very bitter since his observatory had a ready-made mount and dome perfect for installing the 18½-inch lens. He called the Chicago project "another of those stupendous humbugs—an American Observatory of the first class—Europe is to be dazzled and America enlightened on quite an extensive scale. The harm thus far accomplished is that they have by paying down a small sum to Clark secured the large object glass which we should certainly have soon had in our dome doing good service."[125]

Harvard's disappointment in having the world's best lens "stolen" out from under it (while the school was trying to do the same to the University of Mississippi) may have strengthened its efforts not to let the Alabama-bound chemicals slip away when they became available. Or if it had been first the case that the chemicals were easily "captured," the later loss of the lens would have been maddening.

The Rousseau Frères chemicals certainly belong in the category of *science and medicine*, first as useful chemical-laboratory equipment, and later as obsolete supplies stored in a laboratory corner or closet. Very often such things get tossed when the room is needed for current research or teaching. In this case, however, the chemicals were preserved as material evidence of Harvard's scientific heritage. But these seven bottles, closely examined, reveal much about the world beyond Cambridge, Massachusetts. We value them for what they tell us about scientific research and education, politics, and economics in mid-nineteenth-century America. The bottles bear witness to the slow development of chemistry and instrument-making in the United States. They show America's dependence on foreign trade to supply its chemical needs for industry, medicine, agriculture, research, and education, and the efforts of some scientists to overcome this challenge—even to the point of seizing goods intended for their colleagues.

S. J. S.

History

A FIELD-HOCKEY DRESS: FIT FOR A KNOCKABOUT SPORT

Elizabeth Wright Plimpton wore this soft red dress when she played field hockey at Radcliffe in the 1920s.[126] In 1987, she gave it to the Radcliffe Archives along with two bulging scrapbooks tied with black string. The dress is a more powerful record of her undergraduate days than the scrapbooks. The crumbling newspaper clippings stuffed into the scrapbooks contain little that is personal. Even her dance card from the "Radcliffe Promenade" is empty. In contrast, the hand-printed letters "PLIMPTON" on the inside of the back neck of the dress connect her

57. A lightweight cotton field-hockey dress worn by Elizabeth Wright Plimpton at Radcliffe College, around 1925, gave its owner freedom of motion. Arthur and Elizabeth Schlesinger Library on the History of Women in America.

to the college and the sport. The bright "R" with the little "H" beneath it affirms that she won her letter in hockey.

Plimpton's red dress is not only a marker of her own lifelong commitment to sports; it is a document in the history of Radcliffe. Chartered by the commonwealth of Massachusetts in 1894, Radcliffe College was a hybrid institution, a compromise between decades-long efforts of women to secure admission to Harvard and the intransigence of Harvard overseers who believed that co-education was an untried and dangerous experiment. Its students secured access to Harvard faculty, who were paid extra for repeating their lectures at the college, but were segregated in all other ways from the parent university.[127] Radcliffe secured its own identity as a college primarily through extracurricular activities. Initially the emphasis on physical activity at Radcliffe was a response to the arguments of Edward H. Clarke, a Harvard Medical School professor who warned that serious study might damage young women's reproductive capacities. Advocates of female education retorted with campaigns for health and fitness. They were determined to "hold students as strictly accountable for avoidable illness, faulty development, and crooked spines, as for failure in the academic branches."[128]

By 1898, Radcliffe had its own gymnasium where students engaged in gymnastics, fencing, aesthetic dancing, and basketball.[129] Basketball led to field hockey, then little known in the United States. As Elizabeth Wright, an early director of the gymnasium explained, "One day a graduate brought to me a young English woman who was anxious to learn the American game of basket ball. In talking over out-door sports with her, I learned that she was an enthusiastic field hockey player. . . . We agreed to teach her basket ball if she would teach us hockey." The students cleared off an open space near one of the college buildings, laid out lines, and began to play. "This little field, too narrow, too short, and far too full of hummocks and hollows" served until 1913, when a better field was created.[130] By then field hockey had become part of extracurricular life in other women's colleges in the region. (The strong association of field hockey with women's colleges may explain why a sport that is played competitively by men in other parts of the world is considered appropriate only for women and girls in the United States.)[131]

There is no information on why Libby Plimpton's parents named her Elizabeth Wright Plimpton. The surname "Wright" does not appear in any easily accessible family records. It is tempting to think that Plimpton's full name reflects a friendship between her mother and Radcliffe's early gym director, Elizabeth Wright. Wright arrived at Radcliffe while Libby's mother was a student there. That Edith Hall Plimpton was involved in sports is evident from the gymnasium suit that her daughter gave to Radcliffe along with her own field-hockey dress. The contrast between the two garments adds another layer to the history of Radcliffe and the history of women's sports in general. Libby's lightweight cotton uniform, meant to be worn with a short-sleeved white blouse and long stockings or knee socks was designed for maximum freedom. Her mother's costume emphasized coverage. With a little help from stockings, the gymnasium dress completely encompassed the body. Small buttons reached from chin to waist. Full puffed sleeves ended in tight cuffs at the wrist. A voluminous "divided skirt," what we today would call "bloomers," disguised every possible contour of buttocks and thighs. Furthermore, the entire costume was made of wool. Waistbands on a separate bodice and skirt overlapped and were buttoned together, producing four layers of fabric around the waistline, perhaps compensation for the lack of a corset.

58. The heavy wool gym suit worn by Plimpton's mother twenty years earlier had voluminous bloomers to conceal the wearer's body during sports. Radcliffe College Archives, Arthur and Elizabeth Schlesinger Library on the History of Women in America.

The contrast between Edith Plimpton's gymnasium suit and her daughter's hockey dress exemplifies a crucial transition in women's clothing and education in the early decades of the twentieth century. Contemporary instructions for cutting out a gymnasium suit make clear that the lower half of the garment was considered a "skirt." Certainly it competed with many skirts in width, since the instructions called for joining two lengths of fabric—"more if you wish"—extending from waist to knees plus 9 inches. With fabric measuring from 36 to 42 inches in width, the circumference of the skirt would have ranged from 72 to 84 inches. In fact, the lower half of Edith Plimpton's gym suit measures roughly 80 inches. Pleated to a waistband, it falls 18 inches, just as the instructions specified, and then divides into two legs. The transition between skirt and pants was marked by a gusset created by turning one point of a 9-inch square toward the front of the garment and the other toward the back. The "legs to the skirt" were then gathered at the bottom with an elastic casing.[132]

Despite its apparent modesty, this garment, when first introduced, was considered too risqué for public view. Before dressing rooms were introduced into women's gymnasiums, students at respectable colleges were warned to wear additional skirts over their gym costumes when walking to their rooms.[133] Gymnasium bloomers exemplified Radcliffe's ambivalence. They supported female education, but wanted to maintain visible boundaries between the sexes. An outraged dean supposedly chastised the captain of the basketball team for allowing students to be photographed in their uniforms on the steps of the gymnasium. It was one thing to play in such garb, another to be seen wearing it outside.[134]

In the earliest photographs of field hockey at Radcliffe, taken around 1910, players wear full-length skirts and shirtwaists, sometimes with a long sweater or blazer. They might as well have been playing croquet.[135] Libby Plimpton's field-hockey dress with its loose pleats and casual sash marked a new bravado and pride in being at Radcliffe. Women who participated in competitive sports helped to define the college as a school with spirit. A Radcliffe song, one of the few documents in Plimpton's own handwriting in her college scrapbooks, makes that point:

> Radcliffe girls they say are very busy
> People seem to think we all are grinds
> Folks believe that we have come to Radcliffe
> Simply to cultivate our minds....
> Now we'll admit that we're acquiring knowledge
> As everyone of us improves her mind
> Altho we are at Radcliffe we have much besides our classes
> And we've much to do besides becoming grinds
> Yes, we've much to do besides becoming grinds.[136]

The song, filled with the spirit of the 1920s, asserted the importance of extracurricular activities in shaping college life.

But could girls engage in competitive sports and remain girls? Promoters of female education insisted that they could. As LeBaron Russell Briggs, president of Radcliffe College from 1903 to 1925, wrote, "The notion that a woman is at her best a sort of pretty fool with smelling salts is one of the first false notions that the girls' college has dispelled." He insisted that education actually made women better companions for their husbands and better guides and guardians for their children. Alluding to controversy over the place of athletics in the curriculum, he assured skeptics that "a slight athletic swagger in a young woman with a basketball halo does not mean that she will be mannish for life. It subsides, like the puffed cheeks of mumps—rather grotesque while it lasts, but not at all prophetic."[137] His defense of sports was earnest but condescending. He seemed to believe that participation in physically demanding activities was a temporary stage in a girl's life, a "mannish" phase before she succumbed to romance and marriage.

Libby Plimpton's life story challenges that assumption. After graduating from Radcliffe in 1929 with a degree in biology, she went to Wellesley College for a teaching credential in hygiene and physical education. Then, in the midst of the Depression, she took a teaching position at Alice Deal Junior High School in Washington, D.C., where she remained for thirty-six years, eventually becoming department head. She was not content simply to coach young girls. On her Radcliffe 25th-year reunion questionnaire, she proudly noted her own continuing involvement in competitive sports as a member of a number of women's field-hockey teams in the southeast. She played in national tournaments in 1946, 1947, 1949, 1950, 1952, and 1953. "My position is goalie now," she added.[138]

She remained physically active long after retirement. The March 1971 *Radcliffe Quarterly* noted that "Elizabeth Plimpton upheld our record on the ice with the Radcliffe Club of Boston at Watson Rink." More intriguing was a full-page feature story in a local newspaper reporting on her roller skating activities, noting that her family had been "rolling along for more than 100 years" and that at the age of seventy-five, she had decided to take up the sport again. Her grandfather, James Leonard Plimpton, invented what is now considered to be the first modern roller skate, and her own father helped improve the design. She eventually donated some of their skates to the Smithsonian and others to the National Museum of Roller Skating in Lincoln, Nebraska. Long past the age of retirement, she

59. The sporty bow of the cloth belt of the knockabout field-hockey dress challenges the assertion made by contemporary male educators that female athletes were mannish and even grotesque. Arthur and Elizabeth Schlesinger Library on the History of Women in America.

began skating every Tuesday at a rink in Waltham, Massachusetts. "I'm probably a little old for this," she told the reporter, but, ever the teacher, added that it was certainly good exercise.[139]

Historians sometimes emphasize the importance of sports in developing self-confidence and a competitive spirit in women. Eleanor Roosevelt once claimed that the happiest day of her life was when she made the first team in field hockey at Allenswood School in England. Her biographer believes that reveals something essential about Roosevelt's character. She "was a very competitive woman, a team player who delighted in the knockabout field of sport." Eventually she carried those attributes into politics.[140] Libby Plimpton did not share Roosevelt's political views. She was proud of having attended a Girl Scout reception at the White House hosted by Mrs. Herbert Hoover, and in one of her reports to the Radcliffe Alumni, she admitted to being "impatient with young liberals."[141] But to the end of her life, she retained her passion for "knockabout" sports. Her college yearbook described her as "Erect, Practical, and Willing."[142] She was surely that. Like many women of her generation, she devoted herself to public education, community, and family. Although she did not marry, she cared for her eighty-five-year-old father after her mother died.[143] She was a modest woman who never lost her athletic swagger.

L. T. U.

CHAPTER TWO

Things Unplaced

In floor-to-ceiling cases around the walls of our exhibition, we bowed to tradition and installed objects according to the customary categories. We used the rest of our gallery space to challenge and confound those categories. We filled four large cases in the middle of the room with an unpredictable miscellany of objects. A bronze cast of Abraham Lincoln's life mask competed for attention with Samuel Johnson's teapot, an ornate Japanese sword, and a carved spoon from Angola. A plaster cast of the clasped hands of the English poets Robert and Elizabeth Barrett Browning was near an Indian necklace made from real beetles, a hanging sundial from Lucca, and a traveling toothbrush from rural Massachusetts. We had suspected that the traditional categories were somewhat unstable, and things could not be tied down within them. In this part of our exhibition, we had the chance to test this hypothesis. We invited gallery visitors to participate in the experiment with signs near this jumble of things exhorting viewers to "Sort Them!"

Everywhere visitors turned, they saw unexpected juxtapositions. To the right of the gallery entrance, we displayed an early printing telegraph whose input device was a black-and-white piano keyboard. To the left in its own vitrine was a frilly cotton "toga" that most visitors assumed had belonged to a woman but that, in fact, was worn at Harvard in the 1830s by a male undergraduate who wanted to make a fashion statement.[1] A giant tortoiseshell from the Galapagos Islands sat near *Norma* and *Normman*, a pair of statues depicting "the average U.S. girl" at the age of eighteen and her brother.[2] The statues were commissioned in the 1940s by an American

60. A bronze cast of Abraham Lincoln's life mask and hands, three suffragette pins, Samuel Johnson's teapot, and a potholder-style quilt are some of the things to be sorted in a "muddled" case in the *Tangible Things* exhibition at the Collection of Historical Scientific Instruments, Harvard University, spring 2011.

sexologist, Robert Latou Dickinson, and were based on his collection of anatomical measurements of thousands of college-age white Americans. Except for the Harvard affiliation, nothing in these displays seemed to belong together, and in the greater scheme of our inquiry, even that affiliation was in an important sense incidental. It would be perfectly feasible to create similar groupings of disparate things from a myriad of other sources.

These "muddled" exhibits were an attempt to render explicit the uncertainty regarding categorization that we found ourselves discovering in the course of the project, and for which the exhibition itself served as a research tool.

The central case in the gallery, for example, contained fourteen objects taken from eight different Harvard collections. On one side was a 1940s American board game called "Blondie Goes to Leisureland,"[3] on another the cranium and jaw of a tiger shot in India a hundred years earlier.[4] There was no apparent reason why these two objects should appear together. The same case held several tapeworms preserved in a jar of alcohol,[5] an Indonesian accordion-bound sutra written on palm leaves,[6] the engraved bison-rib handle of a quirt, or riding whip, from the Omaha or Ponca peoples of Nebraska,[7] and a sixteenth-century Japanese sword and scabbard.[8] There was no overarching narrative and no sequence of explanatory labels. The seeming chaos forced viewers—no less than the exhibit's researchers—to confront each object on its own or find plausible connections among them.

There were a few unexpected linkages. A cross-section of a transatlantic telegraph cable[9] sat near an aboriginal "letter stick" from Australia; this was purely accidental.[10] No one intended to create a story about changing modes of communication. An imaginative visitor might have linked a nineteenth-century corn tortilla from Mexico[11] and a twentieth-century artwork made from kitchen implements,[12] but that relationship, though interesting, was unintended. We deliberately avoided coherence.

Labels included the name of the collection to which each object belonged, but in assigning categories, that information was often more mystifying than helpful. What was a silver teapot, a first-century piece of broken pottery, or an embroidered pocketbook doing in Houghton Library, Harvard's repository of rare books and manuscripts? Obviously, things that came from the same collection had to conform in some sense to the defining categories of that institution. Thus the tiger skull and the tapeworm both qualified as zoological specimens and were held by the Museum of Comparative Zoology, while the telegraph cable cross-section and the quirt handle, which had both been collected by descendants of General Artemas Ward, had come from the museum that bears his name. But even though the repositories for these objects made sense, their destinies were not inevitable. Had the tapeworm been extracted from an unfortunate member of the general's family, it might have ended up in his museum, or if it ever were to be part of an art installation, it might well end up in a museum of modern art. Equally possible would have been a home in a medical museum. Under different circumstances, the quirt handle, which was constructed from a bison rib, might have been designated a zoological specimen or—given its engraving—been part of an ethnographic or indigenous art collection.

This "muddle" confounded easy assumptions about what belonged where. Seemingly close connections, such as the board game "Blondie Goes to Leisureland" and the dice made of sheep or goat knucklebones, both ostensibly made for play, did not guarantee their being in the same Harvard collection. "Blondie" was from the Baker Library of the Harvard Business School; the Iron-Age knucklebones were from the Semitic Museum, an archaeological collection. We also borrowed from the Baker Library so-called "Negro cloth" swatches.[13] The connection between them and "Blondie Goes to Leisureland" was commercial: The swatches were merchandise samples used to sell Rhode Island fabric to slave-owners in the

South; the board game was an advertising gimmick used by Westinghouse to promote a line of domestic electric appliances.

Although it was perfectly possible to find connections among items in this apparently randomly selected group, as a whole it was indeed a cabinet of curiosities meant to evoke wonder, as well as raise questions. To most visitors, it soon became apparent that each of the things we placed in this section of the exhibit could quite readily be incorporated into more than one of the six categories exemplified by the cases around the walls.

The sixteenth-century Japanese sword and scabbard provided a good example. The artistry involved in making such a thing—including the forging of the blade and crafting of the mounts—was formidable. As many as half a dozen specialists created it and invested it with an extraordinary degree of aesthetic and instrumental worth. It was therefore not surprising to find it in the collection of the Harvard Art Museums. And yet, the sword was also a showpiece of scientific and technical prowess. Its blade was forged from as many as five different pieces of steel, the combination of which gave it the scarcely compatible qualities of hardness, ductility, and the capacity to take a razor-sharp edge. It could

61. The handle (*tsuka*) of the Enju School short sword from Higo Province, Kyushu, Japan, ca. 1530, is a mixed-media delight. Black silk braid artfully wraps the handle, revealing the glittering and rough white ray skin (shagreen) beneath. Tucked into the wrapping is a silver ornament of a dragon, which fits neatly into the sword user's palm, giving it additional grip. Harvard Art Museums/Arthur M. Sackler Museum.

have readily found a place in a museum of technology and industry. But looked at in another way, the sword was also a part of Harvard history, and beyond that, the history of American-Japanese relations.

Albert Bushnell Hart, the Harvard professor who donated the sword to the Art Museums in 1936, probably acquired it while traveling in Japan in 1908. In essays he wrote on his return, he described Asia as "the great wonderland of the world," arguing that "[f]or the historian, the ethnologist, the student of civilization, the philologist, Asia is still the matrix of mankind," suggesting that without a knowledge of Asia, Americans could not understand "their own being."[14] Although Hart's specialty was American history, he helped to establish the so-called imperial school in American history, an approach that not only emphasized the nation's roots in the first British Empire, but also its own imperial history, beginning with its conquest of Indigenous peoples. Hart was a hardheaded "scientific" historian, trained in Germany, and famous for carrying a bag of documents into each lecture he gave. But he also had a bit of romance in his character, and as a military historian, he must have been intrigued by the aesthetic, as well as the technical, qualities of his Japanese sword. In a Harvard lecture in November 1918, he challenged stereotypes about Asian cultures, including the notion that "all other continents are to be subordinated to Europe and North America." But in 1921, he resigned from Boston's Japanese Society because, in his view, its purpose was not just to promote good relations between nations but to promote immigration. He thought the presence of large numbers of Chinese and Japanese immigrants would "interfere with the unity and success of the American republic."[15] Cherishing a Japanese artifact did not mean for him the acceptance of Japanese immigrants as neighbors.

Such reflections on the deliberately unsorted items prompt a return to reconsider those we consigned firmly to one of the six defined categories. What if any of the confidently categorized things had been placed in the "muddle" instead? Each might similarly be amenable to alternative or even multiple categorizations. The color photograph of Earth taken from the capsule of *Apollo 10* on May 18, 1969,[16] was treated as art in both the exhibition category and the Art Museums, but it could equally find a place under *science and medicine* as an artifact of scientific endeavor. So could the medal of Livio I Odescalchi designed by Giovanni Martino Hamerani in Rome in 1689.[17] Not only is it an example of a metallurgical technology, thus qualifying it as an engineering specimen, but it is also an artifact that offers a glimpse into a system of mythology, for Livio, a nephew of Pope Innocent XI, fought against the Turks and was

62. Should this medal, minted in Rome in 1689, be interpreted as art, history, technology, or something else? It tells the story of Livio Odescalchi, an Italian nobleman who fought against the Turks at the Battle of Vienna in 1683. In recognition, his uncle, Pope Innocent XI, appointed him *gonfaloniere* (standard-bearer) of the Church, and Leopold I made him a prince of the Holy Roman Empire. On the obverse, the man is in profile encircled by the words "LIVIVS ODESC[alchius]. S[anctae]. R[omanae]. E[cclesiae]. G[onfanonarius]." On the reverse is Livio's emblem (the sun in splendor rising above the Earth at Vienna with Italy in the foreground) and his motto, "NON NOVVS SED NOVITER" (Not a new world, but newly run). Harvard Art Museums/Fogg Museum.

symbolized by the rising sun. It could therefore find a place in the *anthropology and archaeology* category.

Indeed, all of the objects in *Tangible Things* could be viewed as technological and as parts of systems of making and preparing things that gave them enriched and complex meanings. The relationship of technology to culture was present everywhere: in textile technologies evidenced by an ostracon quoting prices paid for cloth along the Nile in the second century,[18] in a so-called potholder-style pieced American quilt made in 1881,[19] in George Washington's grosgrain-ribbon sash from the late eighteenth century,[20] in a woven Harvard dormitory bedspread commissioned by the Bauhaus architect Walter Gropius soon after World War II,[21] and in late–nineteenth-century Chinese silk mercantile samples.[22] It was also present in writing and communication technologies evidenced by a Babylonian cylinder seal,[23] in a papyrus with a Greek fragment of Plato's *Republic*,[24] in playing cards lampooning the South Sea Bubble in 1721,[25] in a manuscript of a Hebrew-English dictionary,[26] in a pencil that belonged to Thoreau that was made with his graphite-clay lead invention,[27] in a

63. Imagine taking notes on a pottery shard—in this case, scribbling in Greek a list of textiles, including purple cloth, and sums of money, perhaps representing prices paid. This ostracon was found in the vicinity of the First Cataract of the Nile, Egypt, and dates from the second century. Houghton Library.

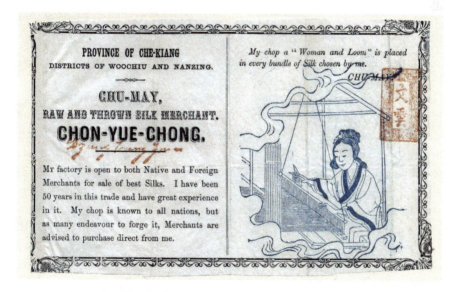

64. Chinese silk merchants used stamps—colloquially known as "chops"—to identify and authenticate their wares in the late nineteenth century. This merchant's chop artfully depicts a woman weaving silk on a loom. It is printed on a sample of the fabric. Baker Library, Harvard Business School.

ninth-century Egyptian tombstone inscribed in Arabic,[28] in a submarine telegraph cable section,[29] and in a slate with chalked "spirit writing."[30] Optical technologies evidenced in the quizzing glass (or handheld eyeglass) of a Harvard treasurer, circa 1800,[31] a camera lucida,[32] Louis Agassiz's and Mark Twain's personal microscopes,[33] a crystal ball,[34] and a telescope for tracking *Sputnik* also represented the relationship of technology to culture.[35]

Viewed from this angle, the *Tangible Things* exhibition restored the importance of "art" in its original technological sense in the "arts and letters" of knowledge production in the university. The visitor could even have seen the university as a technological system, a cultural power grid in which ideas and objects were gathered, exchanged, shared, and debated by different centers within the bureaucracy. The syllabus of a general education course based on the exhibition took this idea further, showing that a close study of the flow of objects and ideas could be used to trace back the history of the Harvard system and the university's place in world culture.

Do the possibilities of a one-to-many mapping of objects to categories indicate that all six of our categories are merely arbitrary, reflecting conventions of human thought rather than inherent characteristics of the things categorized? Insofar as things might be said to exist independent of human consideration and to exhibit characteristics amenable to human discernment, groupings of such things are not necessarily arbitrary. Yet even those things that appear on inspection to be physically identical need not be conceptually identical because of the varying intangible qualities that humans might associate with them. Furthermore, the categorizations of things—whatever their inherent characteristics may be, should they have any—are the result of their uses by humans. Those uses (even if one of them should be nothing more than classification itself) vary from group to group, time to time, and even from individual to individual. Not only do things change in and of themselves, human relations with them change. We are confronted with the way *technê* (craft or art) and *epistêmê* (knowledge) are interdependent and mutually reinforcing, as understanding gained from concrete experience (tangible things) must be. When considering categorization, we are on stronger grounds if we think in terms of contingent family resemblances as a means of grouping like things at any given time. We should do so in the knowledge that such groupings are inherently unstable, just as humans' relationships with the things that constitute these unstable groups or categories are themselves ever-changing. As such, they are subject to historical as much as philosophical investigation.

In *Walden* (1854), Henry David Thoreau asked, "Why do precisely these objects which we behold make a world?"[36] His question was profound. Objects make up our world and are mediated through the grasp of human hands and minds. We both hold and behold things. Whether Thoreau was collecting Native American tools on his walks in Concord, Massachusetts, preserving a turtle that he caught in Walden Pond and gave to Harvard in 1847, or devising a new method of making pencils in his father's factory, he was demonstrating the centrality of tangible things to his intellectual and material life. And when we look at an ancient bird-head pestle, a turtle, or a graphite pencil picked up, prepared, or made by Thoreau—as we did in this exhibition—do we consider these objects simply as archaeological, natural, or engineering specimens? Or are they markers of the long history of Concord, Massachusetts? Perhaps they are historical or aesthetic objects that gave impulse to a writer and philosopher, or (as Thoreau called himself), a civil engineer.

In the case studies that follow, we explore these instabilities further by investigating the characters, uses, and associations of several things that were included in our "muddle." Our starting points are the "Blondie Goes to Leisureland" board game, a shell of a Galapagos giant tortoise (*Chelonoidis nigra*), a hundred-year-old Mexican tortilla, an Angolan spoon carved in the form of a human hand,[37] an iridescent beetle ornament from northeast India or northwest Myanmar,[38] and a small, sewn package of drawings and a letter from eighteenth-century Britain.[39] In

65. This Native-American pestle with a carved bird's head was picked up by Henry David Thoreau on a walk near Concord, Massachusetts. During a lifetime of walks, Thoreau amassed a collection of some 900 artifacts, some up to 8,000 years old. Peabody Museum of Archaeology and Ethnology, Harvard University.

66. Henry David Thoreau collected this specimen of a Blanding's turtle (*Emydoidea blandingi*) at Walden Pond in Concord. He preserved it and donated it to Harvard in 1847. Museum of Comparative Zoology.

these case studies, the instability and ambiguities already apparent in tangible things proliferate, intensify, and cast further doubt on the entire project of classification.

A Gift from the Ladies of Llangollen: Memorandums of a Cottage

It has all the elements of a book—a cover, a title, a table of contents, and a succession of pages that include both words and illustrations.[40] Some words are in French, others in English. The illustrations portray a cottage in a rural landscape with a carefully drawn plan of its first floor. But this strange assemblage is both more and less than a book. It has only six pages. The words are elegantly printed by hand, the pen-and-ink drawings washed with subtle shades of green and rose that pick up the colors of the embroidered silk portfolio that contains the book in one pocket and a tiny reticule or purse netted from silver thread in the other. Entitled *Memorandums of a Cottage*, it was created in 1788 as a gift from two Irish women, Eleanor Butler and Sarah Ponsonby, to a Scottish friend and patron, Frances Lady Douglas, who had helped them secure the promise of a pension from King George III of England. The portfolio bears the initials "FD" in golden letters surrounded by a chain of green leaves and rose spangles on quilted satin. The tiny reticule tucked into the pocket was perhaps a symbol of Lady Douglas's efforts to fill Ponsonby's and Butler's own quite empty purses.[41] It is a book, a work of art, a thank-you note, a memento, a specimen of eighteenth-century embroidery, and a document in social and cultural history.

Ponsonby and Butler were poor because in 1778, they defied their families by fleeing Ireland and the prospect of marriage or life in a convent to establish a home together near the village of Llangollen in North Wales. They lived there in happy harmony until Butler's death in 1829, becoming known then and ever since as "the Ladies of Llangollen." The gift they created for Lady Douglas links their own histories to the age of romanticism and the history of sexuality.[42] Through careful management of their own stories, Butler and Ponsonby became the "most celebrated Virgins in Europe," appropriating an ethos of romantic friendship that had earlier been associated with men and celebrating their own withdrawal from conventional family life as virtue. Yet they puzzled their contemporaries, who did not know how to fit them into familiar categories.

67. A 1788 gift from the "Ladies of Llangollen" in Wales to their patron, Frances Lady Douglas (clockwise from lower right): a tiny netted purse of silver thread, a vellum booklet bound in quilted satin (shown closed), and the embroidered silk portfolio that held both. Houghton Library.

A journalist once described Butler as "tall and masculine" and as appearing "in all respect a young man, if we except the petticoats she retains." Yet at the time, she was short, plump, and well beyond middle age.[43] As they grew older, their reputation for eccentricity increased. One man said that at a distance, he might have taken them for "a couple of hazy or crazy old sailors," adding somewhat sardonically that they had picked a "charming spot for the repose of their now time-honoured virginity."[44] Another, seeing them at the theater dressed in men's coats, neck cloths, and beaver hats, told his wife that they looked "exactly like two respectable superannuated old clergymen."[45]

Yet while disrupting the heterosexual foundation of the bourgeois family, Butler and Ponsonby nevertheless modeled bourgeois values. Their

68. Detail of the corkscrew fringe on the handmade purse. Houghton Library.

69. The delicate embroidery on the silk portfolio featuring the recipient's initials. Houghton Library.

letters and diaries are filled with terms of affection usually reserved for married couples. Each of them spoke of the other as "My Beloved," a term Butler sometimes abbreviated to "M.B." To their admirers, they exemplified rural repose, enduring love, and selfless affection. On a mild night in 1785, they sent their servants to bed and sat by the kitchen fire talking of their poverty, a conversation that provoked Ponsonby to reaffirm her affection. Their withdrawal from polite society was both geographic and psychological. On a winter day in 1785, Butler who suffered from intense headaches (perhaps migraines) took to her bed, writing later that "My Sweet Love lay beside me holding and Supporting My Head 'til one o'clock when I by Much entreaty prevail'd with her to rise and get her Breakfast." On another stormy night, she reported, "Violent Squalls of Wind at times a perfect Hurricane—inexpressibly Comfortable in the Library—from one 'til Three reading Rousseau to the Joy of my life. She drawing."[46]

Ponsonby was the visual artist, Butler the literary connoisseur and writer. The gift they created for Lady Douglas reflects this division of labor. Ponsonby produced the watercolors, house plan, and needlework, Butler the text. This was neither the first nor the last project they shared. On January 1, 1788, Butler described "reading Sterne to My beloved while she worked on her Purse." The embroidery she did for Lady Douglas was probably very similar to the letter case she made for another of her friends of white satin with a gold monogram or cipher in the middle.[47] Butler no doubt selected the French verses that Ponsonby neatly inscribed on the last page of Lady Douglas's book. They came from a French translation of a German treatise on gardening that also borrowed from other works. She made it her own by rearranging three stanzas from a long poem and then adding an inscription appropriate to their own situation.[48] In English translation, the verses begin:

> Within this place, many a storm
> Has shaken heaven and loving hearts.
> The river, overflowing its banks
> Covered our orchards and our flowers.
> Oh, blessed Gods, repair these wrongs!
> And let those of this modest grove
> Find, by your favors, under this branch
> Some shelter for a warm repose.
> The lowly poor need little shade![49]

This affectation of poverty, modesty, and simplicity sustained their partnership and their withdrawal.

The watercolors Ponsonby created for Lady Douglas enlarged their cottage in relation to the surrounding Eglwyseg Mountains, contrasting

70. The cottage in Llangollen, Wales, nestled in the hills below the ruins of a castle, as painted on vellum by Sarah Ponsonby and bound in the booklet given to Lady Douglas in 1788. Houghton Library.

its apparent simplicity with the ruins of the crumbling castle on a nearby peak, and situating their dwelling within a picturesque aesthetic promoted by the books on landscape that Butler collected. The cottage, their supposed poverty, and the story of their undying love made them famous. Although they refused to open their home to strangers, they welcomed anyone with "a name." Among their visitors were Sir Walter Scott (a friend of Lady Douglas), the abolitionist William Wilberforce, the duke of Wellington, the manufacturer Josiah Wedgewood, and a whole succession of writers and poets.[50]

After a visit, William Wordsworth described their house as a "low-roofed Cot," even though it was a substantial stone dwelling as the house plan in their little book shows. Over the years, they transformed it into a "heavily ornamented, artfully contrived spectacle, a *cottage ornée*."[51] Their friend Anna Seward was especially entranced by the Gothic ornamentation of the library, which had a curious glass lamp in the elliptical arch of a door that when lit reminded her of the glow of a volcano. In one of the windows was a "large Eolian harp" that on windy days, when the sashes were opened, breathed "deep tunes to the gale, swelling and softening as that rises and falls."

The practical appointments were just as impressive. In the cow house, a mechanical churn produced just enough butter each day for the ladies' breakfast.[52] They lavished special attention on their cows, writing about them as though they were almost human. Butler wrote of the "loveliest of all lovely cows, called Beauty," and when their "lovely little Primrose" calved, noted that she had delivered "A son."[53] They had special affection for a cow named "Margaret," whom they allowed to wander around the grounds. When forced to put Margaret into the stable for winter, Butler provided her with a bovine companion "as it was known she could not exist without society."[54]

The ladies showed less compassion for other human beings. As their biographer observed, they expected their gardeners to sleep on the grounds six days out of seven and were "exceedingly conservative" in what they paid. Noting the "rapine and plunder" of a friend's servants, Butler was determined not to indulge her own. Even after being visited by Wilberforce, she concluded that West Indian slavery was probably better than life in benighted Africa. Within bounds, they were capable of compassion. They cast out a maid when she became pregnant, but when her father refused to keep her, they talked a local weaver into taking her on.[55] Llangollen was far from the rural paradise some visitors imagined. When a local cotton manufactory went bankrupt in 1819, the ladies were grateful they had not invested in it. In a letter to a friend, Ponsonby noted that "[s]cores of poor little creatures are to be dismissed from that odious employ." Unfortunately, she concluded, these child laborers were unfit for any other occupation, and their parents were "as incompetent of finding them a maintenance as we are in finding the Longitude."[56] Some people were worthy of a royal pension. Some were not.

Wordsworth was as confused as anyone else about what to make of these entrancing but disturbing women. At a distance, he almost mistook one of them (he did not name names) for a Roman Catholic priest. She was "oddly attired" and without a cap, with hair "bushy and white as snow." But in the poem he wrote after his visit, he idealized them as "Sisters in love, a love allowed to climb, / Even on this earth, above the reach of Time."[57] Sarah Ponsonby had a more sardonic view about time. She asked to have a passage from the book of Job carved on her tombstone: "But they shall no more return to their house, neither shall their place know them any more."[58]

Today that house has become a museum open to the public from Easter through October. It is perhaps fitting that their *Memorandums of a Cottage* came to Harvard through an endowment named for the poet Amy Lowell, another woman who defied convention and confused her contemporaries.[59]

L. T. U.

A Galapagos Tortoiseshell: "Ship Abigail"

The empty shell commands our attention immediately. Belonging to a giant Galapagos tortoise of the species *Chelonoidis nigra*, the burnished black shell looks like a huge boulder. It is about 41 inches long, 33 inches wide, and 23 inches tall, but the bulk is perhaps best expressed by the curved lengths over the dome of the carapace: 52 by 59 inches. The original owner must have been magnificent before sailors scrawled "SHIP ABIGAIL / 1835 Bj Clark / MASTER" on her back. Now she belongs to Harvard's Museum of Comparative Zoology.[60]

She came from the archipelago of volcanic islands situated along the equator in the eastern Pacific, six degrees west of Ecuador. First reconnoitered by the Spanish in 1535, the islands were soon named after the great numbers of gigantic, saddle-backed, land tortoises found there: Galapagos.[61] The islands had little to recommend them in their withering desolation and "emphatic uninhabitableness."[62] Mariners called them the *Encantadas*, or bewitched isles, because varying currents and misty winds made the islands appear to shift.[63] The islands were both spellbound and cursed, Herman Melville wrote in 1854, in "that to them

71. The dome-shaped shell, blistered and scarred, of a giant tortoise caught in the Galapagos Islands in 1834. This tortoise is the holotype—the specimen used by scientists to define a species—for *Testudo nigra*. Galapagos tortoises like this one led Darwin to think about the relationships of species to their environments. Museum of Comparative Zoology.

change never comes; neither the change of the seasons nor of sorrows." He described their wretchedness in vivid words:

> Take five-and-twenty heaps of cinders dumped here and there in an outside city lot; imagine some of them magnified into mountains and the vacant lot the sea; and you will have a fit idea of the general aspect of the Encantadas, or Enchanted Isles. . . . Man and wolf alike disown them. Little but reptile life is here found: —tortoises, lizards, immense spiders, snakes, and that strangest anomaly of outlandish nature, the *aguano* [iguana]. No voice, no low, no howl is heard; the chief sound of life here is a hiss.[64]

English pirates were the first Europeans to gain a footing in this dreary place, using the islands as bases from which to attack passing Spanish galleons loaded with treasure. In 1684, William Ambrose Cowley, a pirate onboard the *Bachelor's Delight* with William Dampier, mapped the islands and named them in honor of English aristocracy and royalty. Dampier's journals described some of the flora and fauna, and he noted how tasty the tortoises were: "They are extraordinary large and fat; and so sweet, that

72. Crude graffiti cut into the shell of the Galapagos giant tortoise reads "SHIP ABIGAIL / 1835 B[en]j[amin] Clark / MASTER." The *Abigail* was a whaling vessel out of New Bedford, Massachusetts. Museum of Comparative Zoology.

no Pullet eats more pleasantly." The oil saved from them was kept in jars and "served instead of Butter, to eat with Dough-boys or Dumplins."[65] A favored pirate hideout where tortoises and freshwater could be had in season was Buccaneer Cove on James Island (today Isla Santiago).[66]

Pirates made way for whalers by the end of the eighteenth century. James Colnett was sent to survey the Galapagos as a potential whaling station for the British South Seas fishery in the 1790s and reported at length in his book, *A Voyage to the South Atlantic and Round Cape Horn into the Pacific Ocean* (1798). Not only were sperm whales and fur seals plentiful in the vicinity, but "this place is, in every respect, calculated for refreshment or relief for crews after a long and tedious voyage."[67] The news spread quickly, opening up floodgates to seal and whale hunters from all over the world. At first it was the British whalers who dominated the waters, but after the War of 1812, American whalers had the upper hand. Between 1811 and 1844, more than 700 American vessels sailed among the Galapagos Islands along with another 1,000 ships from other countries.[68]

One of these ships was the *Abigail* of New Bedford, Massachusetts—a 97-foot, 310-ton ship built in Amesbury in 1810. Her captain on two voyages to the Pacific whaling grounds was Benjamin Clark. He sailed from New Bedford in May 1829 with a crew of twenty-five, returning in June 1831 with about 2,500 barrels of sperm whale oil. After some months ashore, he sailed off again in November 1831, this time as part owner of the vessel. He returned in June 1835 with 2,254 barrels of oil.[69]

Refreshment in the Galapagos came packaged in giant shells. Captain Colnett gave voice to the sentiments of sailors away from land for many months: "But all the luxuries of the sea, yielded to that which the island afforded us in the land tortoise, which in whatever way it was dressed, was considered by all of us as the most delicious food we had ever tasted."[70]

Charles Darwin also ate his share of tortoise meat when the *Beagle* visited the Galapagos in 1835, but he described it as "indifferent."[71]

Having no fear of humans, the creatures were easy to catch, if not so easy to find among the lava or so easy to lift. The small ones weighing fifty to seventy-five pounds were carried knapsack-style, one to a man. Larger ones weighing hundreds of pounds were turned on their backs and dragged by ropes or slung over oars borne by two or more men. New England sailors called the hunting "turpining"—from the Algonquin word "terrapin." It was hard work among the volcanic rock and uplands, but a whale boat of twenty to thirty feet in length could haul a large catch back to the main vessel, and a single tortoise could feed many men. On board, the creatures provided fresh meat to the crew for many months, surviving without food or water for as long as a year. They were piled among the casks in the hold or allowed to roam the decks. They "did not seem to care whether they stood on their head or heels," a sailor recalled. "It mattered little to us, and apparently less to them, what their accommodations were, so long as they kept out from under foot."[72]

GIGANTIC LAND TORTOISE.—A PRESENT FOR HER MAJESTY.

73. An image of a giant tortoise hunted in the Galapagos Islands by an English whaler conveys both the trusting nature of the creature and the size disparity between captor and captive. *Illustrated London News*, July 13, 1850. Widener Library.

Melville was fascinated by them and tried to interest his publisher, Harper and Brothers, in 1853 with "300 pages, say—partly of nautical adventure, and partly—or, rather, chiefly, of Tortoise Hunting Adventure."[73] That book is lost, but Melville sold his story twice, and Harper's rival, George P. Putnam, published a shortened version as "The Encantadas" in *Putnam's Magazine* in 1854.[74] The work is semi autobiographical, drawing on Melville's own time in the Pacific. After five months at sea, his whaling vessel anchored in the Galapagos, and a crew sent ashore returned to the ship with three "really wondrous tortoises—none of your schoolboy mud-turtles—but black as widower's weeds, heavy as chests of plate, with vast shells medallioned and orbed like shields, and dented and blistered like shields that have breasted a battle."[75] Melville could just as well have been describing the ship *Abigail's* tortoise. "As I lay in my hammock that night," Melville continued, "overhead I heard the slow weary dragging of the three ponderous strangers along the encumbered deck. Their stupidity or their resolution was so great, that they never went aside for any impediment. One ceased his movements altogether just before the mid-watch. At sunrise I found him butted like a battering-ram against the immovable foot of the foremast, and sill striving, tooth and nail, to force the impossible passage.... Their crowning curse is their drudging impulse to straightforwardness in a belittered world."[76]

The giant tortoises provided entertainment, as well as food. The crew often kept one or two as pets for the entire voyage, feeding them bananas, potato sprouts, and peels.[77] Two Hood Island tortoises were given to Captain Robert FitzRoy as gifts and roamed the *Beagle*.[78] During dull parts of a voyage, all hands were employed in contests of strength demonstrated by efforts to lift a large tortoise.[79] Then after "a merry repast from tortoise steaks and tortoise stews," out came the knife to "convert the...mighty concave shells into...fanciful soup-tureens, and...the calapees [lower shells] into...gorgeous salvers."[80] Sailors told ghost stories about the brutes: "Concerning the tortoises found here," Melville recounted, "most mariners have long cherished a superstition, not more frightful than grotesque...that all wrecked sea-officers, more especially commodores and captains, are at death (and in some cases, before death) transformed into tortoises; thenceforth dwelling upon these hot aridities, sole solitary Lords of Asphaltum."[81] Seamen also carved the backs with graffiti, as the *Abigail* specimen bears witness. Huge tortoises too big to haul off the islands also became walking signboards. On Albemarle

74. Logbook of the ship *Abigail*, open to May 1834. The sailors hunted tortoises in the Galapagos to stow alive on their ship to consume as fresh meat during future months of whaling. Courtesy of the Trustees of the New Bedford Free Public Library.

Island in 1881, a famously large tortoise known as Port Royal Tom had ship names and dates going back to 1791.[82] A James Island tortoise caught in 1830 had the date 1786 carved on its shell. It took six men to lift it into the boat.[83]

The logbook of the *Abigail* records a two-week visit to the Galapagos Islands in May 1834, where the sailors enjoyed fresh trade winds and fine weather as they stopped to repair their ship, cut wood, and catch tortoises:

> May 14: 9 PM: Pilot comes on Board to take us down to Porters Island for turpin...5 AM got underweigh and steered for Porters Island
> May 15: all sail set steering for Porters Island 4 PM Came to Anchor in Downes Bay in 7 fathoms hard bottom and healed the ship...4 AM sent 3 Boats after turpin about 5 miles
> May 16: 7 PM Boats came on Board with 21 large turpin—...4 AM 3 Boats went after turpin
> May 17: 7 PM the Boats came on Board with 31 turpin—
> May 18: 3 AM 3 Boats went after turpin
> May 19: 7 PM Boats came on Board with 40 laiv [live] turpin—Latter parts much the same Employed getting turpin and cutting wood
> May 21: 3 AM 3 Boats sent after terrapin
> May 22: 6 PM the Boats Returned with 40 laiv [live] terpin—...8 AM got underweigh...we got here 140 Terepin and 10 Boats Loads of wood.

The restocking done, the *Abigail* resumed its "Cruising for Sperm Whales All Round the Coast."[84]

These log entries suggest that the *Abigail* tortoise specimen now in the Museum of Comparative Zoology was caught in May 1834 on Porter's Island (then also known as Indefatigable and today as Santa Cruz). It was likely not eaten until 1835, the date inscribed on the shell. The voyage ended in June 1835, so it is perhaps not surprising that the shell made it back to Massachusetts, possibly as a parting gift to Benjamin Clark, the captain.

The scale of the *Abigail*'s catch is mind-boggling but not uncommon for the time. Analysis of the logbooks of seventy-nine whaling vessels (mostly from Massachusetts) between the years 1831 and 1868 offers evidence of 189 visits to the Galapagos with as many as 350 tortoises taken by a vessel in a single visit. The collective catch has been estimated conservatively at 13,013 tortoises for the seventy-nine vessels. If one considers all the other vessels in the Galapagos at the same time, the yearly tally could have been as many as 9,000 tortoises, and even more before 1830 when the populations were more plentiful. Given that most of the tortoises caught were females, since they were smaller, easier to carry, and often ventured toward the lower country to dig holes for their eggs, and that a young tortoise took twenty years to reach maturity, it is clear that hunting decimated the animals before they could reproduce.[85] The pirates and men-of-war had certainly taken their share of tortoises in the two previous centuries before Colnett's book, but the next fifty years saw them hunted to virtual extinction.

When Charles Darwin visited the islands in 1835, he noted that the tortoises were being consumed for food at a staggering rate. The acting governor, Nicholas Lawson, concurred and told Darwin an interesting fact: From "the form of the body, shape of scales & general size," the locals could "pronounce from which Island any Tortoise may have been brought."[86] It was not until nine months later that Darwin realized the significance of this remark. Thinking back on the assertions about tortoises, and considering the distribution of mockingbirds in the Galapagos and foxes in the Falkland Islands, Darwin wrote, "If there is the slightest foundation for the remarks, the zoology of Archipelagoes—will be well worth examining; for such facts would undermine the stability of Species."[87] Today the giant tortoises of the Galapagos archipelago are celebrated for their contribution to Darwin's thinking about the influence of geological history on the diversification of organisms and the development of his theory of evolution through natural selection.

Initially the tortoises throughout the archipelago were described by zoologists as a single type, *Testudo nigra*, beginning in 1824 with naturalists Jean René Constant Quoy and Joseph Paul Gaimard, who prepared a zoological report of their scientific voyage around the world onboard the *Uranie* and the *Physicienne*, captained by Louis de Freycinet.[88] But as scientists observed that tortoise populations found on the different islands were morphologically distinct from each other—each lineage shaped by its interaction with its environment according to Darwin's theory—they began to classify these populations as different species or subspecies.[89] Although there has been some debate about the taxonomic ranking of the populations, the use of modern DNA techniques has led to the conclusion that there are ten known species (*Chelonoides* spp.), four of which are extinct.[90]

The ship *Abigail* specimen (R-11064) is identified as the holotype of the species *Testudo nigra*—that is, the specimen used by scientists to define this species. The Museum of Comparative Zoology received it from the Boston Society of Natural History "in exchange" on November 17, 1914, and a scientific description of it was published in 1917.[91] Early museum records indicated that the specimen was likely collected from Charles Island, which is known today as Floreana. But there was a puzzle. Tortoises from Floreana are saddle backed, whereas R-11064 has a domed shape; it does not seem to belong to *Chelonoidis nigra*, the species native to Floreana. Recent mitochondrial DNA analysis has confirmed that R-11064 is genetically related to the species on Santa Cruz (*C. porteri*). Researchers concluded that the presence of non-native tortoise R-11064 on Floreana was probably "the result of human-mediated transport"[92] by whalers, or tortoises floating over to the island after being cast overboard by buccaneers clearing their decks before doing battle.

Historical research confirms the scientific conclusion that the *Abigail* tortoise did not originate on Floreana, but not the suggestion that human activity put it on the island. We know from the *Abigail*'s logbook that R-11064 was caught in 1834 on Porter's Island (Santa Cruz)—just as the DNA tells us.

The giant tortoises haunted Melville long after his whaling days:

> Sometimes, even now, when leaving the crowded city to wander out July and August among the Adirondack Mountains, far from the influences of towns and proportionally nigh to the mysterious ones of nature; . . . I sit me down in the mossy head of some deep-wooded gorge, surrounded by prostrate trunks of blasted pines, and recall, as in a dream, my other and far-distant rovings in the baked heart of the charmed isles; and remember the sudden glimpses of dusky shells, and the long languid necks

protruded from the leafless thickets; and again have beheld the
vitreous inland rocks worn down and grooved into deep ruts by
ages and ages of the slow dragging of tortoises in quest of pools
of scanty water....

Nay, such is the vividness of my memory, or the magic of my
fancy, that...often in scenes of social merriment, and especially at
revels held by candle-light in old-fashioned mansions, so that shadows are thrown into the further recesses of an angular and spacious
room, making them put on a look of haunted undergrowth of lonely
woods, I have drawn the attention of my comrades by my fixed gaze
and sudden change of air, as I have seemed to see, slowly emerging
from those imagined solitudes, and heavily crawling along the floor,
the ghost of a gigantic tortoise, with "Memento * * * * *" burning in
live letters upon his back.[93]

So what is this tortoise marked "SHIP ABIGAIL / 1835 Bj Clark /
MASTER" to us? The most fundamental of scientific specimens, an
antique food remnant from the world of whaling ships, a message written
large on an Ecuadorian reptile, or an enchanted muse for our time?

S. J. S.

A Carved Spoon: Pointing a Finger

This wooden spoon has a pointing and purposeful finial: a small, naturalistic hand deftly carved into its tip.[94] Three curved fingers are held in
check by the bent thumb as the index finger points in the opposite direction from the spoon's bowl. It makes a decisive gesture, similar to the
letter "D" in American Sign Language. The hand is concave and appears
taut. The figure in the wood creates a lined, realistic surface for the palm.
It appears to be a hand according to Western conventions of representation. It does not simply suggest a hand but copies one, with realistic
joints and creases. The carved hand is attached to an elongated wrist that
morphs into a curved handle and links to the ovoid bowl of the spoon.
The skilled carver used the grain of the wood to emphasize the hand's
connection to a lean forearm. The carved wrist is resolved into the handle
through a simple incision. Its color, a rich reddish brown, could be that of
flesh. The spoon is about twelve inches long, and the entire carved hand
could fit inside of the large semicircular spoon bowl at the opposite end.

This object does not easily fall within any of George Browne Goode's six categories. In *Tangible Things*, it is an unplaced object.

Formally, the carving seems equally divided between function and representation: a serviceable spoon bowl on one end and a carved, pointing appendage at the other. These two aspects make it easy to consider it as an anthropological and art-historical object, one with a clear cultural context and function, as well as an aesthetic. It could as easily be housed in the Fogg Art Museum as it is in the Peabody Museum of Archaeology and Ethnology. A Western user, thinking of its potential culinary use, would hold this spoon at the slight crook in the handle, where the human form becomes a utensil. The wooden index finger would point above and behind the user, in the opposite direction from the spoon's bowl.

The precise anthropological context of the spoon is unclear. It was collected in sub-Saharan West Africa in the mid-nineteenth century. Its tribal affiliation and maker remain unknown, and it does not seem to have a clear iconographic link to an existing cultural group. The naturalistic carved hand may have more in common with Western art than with African forms of representation and could suggest a hybrid style. It may be a variation on the ceremonial spoon form, perhaps reflecting a combination of colonial Portuguese and West African traditions. Though it appears to be scaled for domestic use, the carefully carved hand may have had a spiritual function. Ceremonial spoons are objects that convey title, respect, and power in a range of African communities. Such spoons were part of the accruements of office for high-status women, and were

75. Collected in sub-Saharan West Africa in 1857, this wooden spoon has a handle that morphs into a carving of a human hand with a pointing finger. It is hard to categorize, appearing more ceremonial than functional. Peabody Museum of Archaeology and Ethnology, Harvard University.

76. The human hand carved on the spoon has elements more in common with Western than African art; perhaps it is an intercultural object. Peabody Museum of Archaeology and Ethnology, Harvard University.

used in ceremonies or in displays outside of homes rather than for cooking. The object may be related to a specific individual or title, giving it a social identity.[95] This potential anthropological context was not carried with this object to the United States, where it was cataloged simply as a "spoon." It remained a curio in private hands until it was donated to Harvard three decades after it was collected.

In *Tangible Things*, the spoon is an unplaced object precisely because it is equally uncomfortable as art and anthropology. As history, the spoon points to an even deeper discomfort, as a trace of the transatlantic slave trade.

The spoon was acquired on the southwest coast of Luanda, the present-day capital of the nation of Angola, in 1857. Mary Willis Sparhawk donated the spoon along with more than sixty other objects to Harvard's Peabody Museum of Archaeology and Ethnology in 1883. Her son, Clement Willis Sparhawk, was a medical student at Harvard at the time and graduated the following year. The objects she donated were from both Africa (the Congo) and South America (Brazil). Her husband, John Bertram Sparhawk, had collected them on his travels. He had been a Massachusetts merchant and traveler, with substantial interests in the Brazilian rubber industry, and had owned a plantation on Fernando Pó, now Bioko, an island off the coast of Cameroon that is part of Equatorial Guinea.[96] He was not just a trader and a merchant but also a farmer, who required substantial labor to produce rubber, coffee, rice, and cocoa for U.S. markets. In the 1850s, Sparhawk had sailed on ships owned by his wealthy uncle and namesake John Bertram, making trips across the Atlantic to Angola and Pará, Brazil. Objects like this spoon and the other artifacts recorded in the logs of the Peabody Museum document his travels.

The pointing hand on this spoon was not the only human form cross-ing the Atlantic in the 1850s. U.S. participation in the African slave trade had been illegal since 1807. In the 1850s, when Sparhawk was traveling, U.S. nationals were certainly not supposed to be involved in the Brazilian slave trade, though some southern slaveholders and northern merchants ignored this prohibition. Ships flying the U.S. flag illicitly carried slaves from West Africa to Brazil in the years before the American Civil War. Sparhawk's connections to both Brazil and Angola suggest that he may have had a deeper connection to this trade.[97] Even without direct involve-ment in the sale of individuals into slavery, some of the people who worked for Sparhawk in Pará, Brazil, where slavery was legal into the 1880s, were likely enslaved, as were the workers who supported his endeavors in Angola.[98] In 1864, Sparhawk and his son Bertram (born to his first wife in Brazil) applied for a joint passport, and by the following year, they were running a nearly 1,500-acre plantation in Fernando Pó in this case, one they had committed to operating with free labor.[99] The venture went hor-ribly wrong and the two Sparhawks were basically marooned until their family sent funds to rescue them. The elder Sparhawk died one month after he returned to Massachusetts in 1872.[100]

A decade after his death, his wife donated his collections to Harvard, whose accession log described the lot as "[a]n interesting collection of weap-ons, feather garments, gourd dishes, and other native work of the Amazon Indians; and of the grass-cloth garments, basketwork, carvings on wood and ivory, trumpets made of elephant tusks, and numerous other objects of native workmanship from Southern Africa."[101] The large donation linked Brazil and Africa in the Peabody Museum's records. The places recorded in the museum's ledger book followed the same path as the enslaved Africans forcibly moved to the Amazon to work the rubber and coffee plantations, which were often funded by American capital and designed to serve the needs of U.S. consumers. Did Mary Willis Sparhawk realize the larger story her donation recorded? In the years her husband and stepson were in Fernando Pó, her father Clement Willis served as an alderman in Boston and proposed the creation of a monument to those who died "put-ting down the Southern Rebellion." The Army and Navy Monument was installed on the Boston Common in 1877. Today Mary Willis Sparhawk's museum donation may suggest as much about Massachusetts's role in slav-ery as does her father's towering plinth.[102]

This carved spoon with its pointing finger may have shared a vessel with enslaved Africans, and later with the goods being sent to Massachusetts that their hands helped to create. As an unplaced thing, does it suggest a specific ceremonial function? Could a careful anthropologist link it to the identity of a respected female tribal leader? Perhaps an art historian could explain how a talented artist imbued a carved stick with as much energy as God's crooked finger on the Sistine Chapel ceiling. Or does it serve as a placeholder for a shameful, often forgotten chapter in American history? Maybe it is all of these things and a material metaphor: a piece of a human body employed for another's purpose, taken from one context to another, and after more than a century in a museum case, still pointing to a sinister history.

S. A. C.

A Mexican Tortilla: From Exotic to Ordinary

Even though it belongs to a botanical collection, this object was not taken from the ground or clipped from a stem or shrub. Nor did it grow, fungus-like, on the trunk of a rotting tree. It is a cultural artifact, a product of human hands. It is ostensibly a tortilla, but for some reason, the label-maker used the plural form of the word and enclosed it in quotes. Was this a mistake? Or did the string threaded through the hole in

77. Small, thick, round, and charred, this hundred-year-old tortilla is a botanical specimen collected in Mexico in 1897. Economic Botany Herbarium of Oakes Ames, Harvard University Herbaria.

78. Surface details on the tortilla show scorch marks from the griddle, the grind of the corn, the thickness of the "little cake," and the brittleness of the drying specimen when a hole was punched through it. Economic Botany Herbarium of Oakes Ames, Harvard University Herbaria.

the upper corner once hold more than one specimen? The handwritten label says the tortilla was "Made from Zea Mays." That's corn or maize. But nearly everything else on the label raises questions. No one at the Harvard University Herbaria, where the tortilla now lives, recognizes the handwriting or the numbering system on the label. Although the name "J. N. Rose" and the date "1897" seem to fit, Joseph Nelson Rose was a botanist with the National Herbarium in Washington, an affiliate of the U.S. Department of Agriculture. His 1899 treatise on Mexican plants includes a brief mention of tortillas, but there is no record at Harvard explaining how or when this specimen came here.[103] The reference to "O. A. Col" adds to the puzzle. Although Oakes Ames became an instructor at Harvard in 1900, the Oakes Ames Collection of Economic Botany was not established there until 1918.[104]

This is an errant tortilla in both senses of the word, a wanderer and a deviant that defies attempts to fix its provenance. A closer look at the tortilla itself raises still other questions. Until time and evaporation curled its corners, it appears to have been an almost perfect circle, no doubt a result of wet dough being rolled into a ball between the palms of two hands, then flattened and slapped onto a griddle, perhaps a too-hot griddle. That it was exposed to fire seems apparent from the black streaks—scorch marks—on its surface. Even more intriguing is the thin crack stretching from the punched-out hole where the label is attached. The crack suggests that the hole was made after the tortilla had begun to dry. A fresh tortilla is amazingly pliable. It would have been easy to poke a hole in it when fresh, more difficult after it became brittle. The wonder is that it did not break apart. Maybe its unusual thickness helped to give it stability.

In Spanish, the word tortilla means "little cake." This tortilla appears to be both smaller and thicker than the tortilla pictured in Rose's 1899 article. It is also quite different from the tortillas that found their way to the Oakes Ames Collection from an even earlier collector. In 1878, Edward Palmer, a pioneer in the emerging field of ethnobotany, sent both tortillas and implements for making them to Harvard's Peabody Museum. In the 1970s, the Peabody transferred his tortillas to the Harvard University Herbaria but kept the implements he collected and a more modern photograph that may once have been displayed with them, dividing what was once a unified collection between two modern disciplines. Palmer's tortillas, still in the big glass jar in which they were once displayed, are remarkably thin and without visible scorch marks. Although curled, they seem mostly intact, but then no one attempted to poke a hole in them. The labels on the jar, though typed, conform to the numbers in Palmer's manuscript account of his expedition.[105]

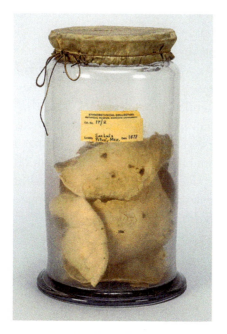

79. You can't have just one: a jar of tortillas collected by ethnobotanist Edward Palmer in San Luis, Potosí, Mexico, 1878. Harvard University Herbaria.

80. A woman preparing tortillas in Mexico, date unknown. The photograph was displayed in the twentieth century alongside artifacts collected by Edward Palmer in 1878. Peabody Museum of Archaeology and Ethnology, Harvard University.

Today, the presence of tortillas in the collections of a major university seems bizarre. In the nineteenth century, however, these humble things appeared exotic. Palmer and Rose both wrote about their travels in Mexico and offered observations about the making and use of tortillas. Comparing their descriptions alongside the specimens they left allows us to see the context in which the things they sent to Harvard were created. They also expose the range of attitudes that these two articulate white men brought to their observations of women's work in a culture that was not their own.

Palmer pioneered the field of ethnobotany, a discipline that eventually brought together plant science and ethnography. Although his major work was collecting pressed botanical specimens for the Smithsonian and other eastern U.S. museums, he was intensely interested in the way the various communities he visited used native plants. Although he organized his materials according to taxonomic classifications, his interest in the interconnections between plants and humans established a new way of collecting and documenting specimens. In 1871, he wrote a now-classic paper, *Food Products of the North American Indians*.[106]

Palmer was interested in all the tools and processes involved in harvesting *Zea mays* and in turning shelled corn into bread. He emphasized that in Mexico, Indians and "mixed race" peoples did not grind their grain dry as in the United States, but boiled it over low heat and then ground it into a paste while wet using a *metate* or grinding stone made from volcanic rock. Usually the grinder was also the baker. She arranged her pot of corn and her *metate* near a round earthen grill (*comal*) set on rocks over a small fire. Palmer was fascinated by the fluid movements of the tortilla maker as she knelt on the ground in front of her *metate* transforming wet corn into dough, gradually filling a container with the wet mass. He used words like "strength and dispatch" to describe her labor.[107]

When she was ready to form a tortilla, she took a fistful of dough from the trough, flattened it "out with the palms of her hands a little." Then "with great quickness" threw it from one hand to another, whirling and catching it, "keeping the hands close together so it can be quickly caught in case the edge needs thinning." Then, grabbing another clump of dough with her left hand, she slapped the finished disc onto the *comal* with her right. "It is astonishing how quick they are made and cooked," he wrote, adding that "[m]akers of 'tortillas' tell their whereabouts by the loud, peculiar noise resulting from the cake being thrown from the palm of one hand to another in order to render the cakes thin."[108]

Tortillas were not the only things made with the *maza* ground on the *metate*. Palmer also described the making of *pacholes*, *tamales*, and *gordos*. The only difference between a *gordo* and a tortilla, he explained was "in the extreme thinness of the latter." Unlike the tortilla, the *gordo* was sometimes cooked in the ashes like the corn "dodgers" or cakes he had known in the United States as cornmeal cake. His description raises the possibility that the tortilla displayed in *Tangible Things* may in fact have been a *gordo*. Certainly it is more visibly marked by fire.[109]

In contrast to Palmer, Rose treated tortilla-making in a perfunctory way, briefly describing the grinding and baking but paying scant attention to either tools or art. The difference may have been in the two men or in the women they observed. Surely there were both regional and personal differences in cooking methods, regardless of culture. Rose claimed to have "traveled 600 miles on horseback," observing that more than once he came to "a Mexican's hut after a long day's ride, tired and hungry, and found I had to wait until the woman of the house had made her little fire on the ground, mashed her corn on her 'metate,' patted it into little cakes, and baked them." He recalled that tortillas were usually served hot from the griddle and "passed about in a gourd or clay dish, covered with a rag or cloth," though sometimes they were warmed "by throwing them on a bed of live coals." When cold beans or cheese were folded into them, they were called *gordo*, meaning 'fat one.'"[110] Although Palmer and Rose had different definitions of a *gordo*, Rose's description of a woman "patting" rather than "throwing" the dough suggests that there was more than one way to make a tortilla and that his tortilla might have had a lot in common with Palmer's *gordo*.

Although Palmer and Rose were both interested in the ways human beings interacted with plants, their orientations were different. Palmer's instincts led toward anthropology, which is why he is remembered today as a forerunner of the field of ethnobotany. Rose's interests may have been more closely aligned with what came to be called economic botany. In that regard, he had much in common with Oakes Ames, the man who gave his name to the collection in which both Palmer's and Rose's tortillas are now found. When Ames became director of Harvard's Botanical Garden in 1909, he developed an undergraduate course that he taught for many years called "Outlines of Economic Botany." The course was not taught in Harvard Yard, but on the grounds of the Botanical Garden. To support the course, Ames added to a collection created by his predecessor,

George Lincoln Goodale. Although there is as yet no documentation for this, the tortilla may have originated in Goodale's collection.

There is better documentation for the nature of Ames's course. According to a former student, Edgar Anderson, he paid little attention to agricultural staples like wheat, rice, or corn and said nothing at all about lumber, instead turning to exotic materials like amber. He supposedly spent an entire month on arrow poisons. In response, waggish students dubbed the course "Uneconomic Botany." Even those smitten by Ames's interests did not know what to make of them. Anderson recalled, "When I finished the course I thought it the most fascinating one I had ever taken but... also the most useless." Only later did he understand that Ames "was one of the few people in this country to take a really intelligent interest in cultivated plants." Anderson later became a renowned plant geneticist.[111]

The Harvard University Herbaria has notes in Ames's tiny handwriting that he may have used in preparing lectures. He did devote a page or two to *Zea mays*, though the information he collected was somewhat random. He noted that in Holland, maize was called Turkey wheat, that in Italy, "corn food" was called polenta, and that in Mexico, it was used to make tortillas. Although most of his references date from after 1912, he read and quoted from Rose's 1899 report. He displayed an interest in the nutritional, as well as the commercial, dimensions of his topic, adding a reference from a 1916 *Scientific American* article on the problem of pellagra in corn-based foods. Given today's concern over the use of high fructose corn syrup, his reference to the development of "a substitute for maple syrup" is intriguing.[112] But there is nothing in these papers to suggest more than a passing interest in corn, and nothing that identifies the moment when somebody associated a tortilla with the "O. A. Col."

After a century in the Harvard Herbaria, the tortilla that now lives in an attic has lost its significance as a botanic specimen and its luster as an ethnographic object. In the larger culture, the once exotic tortilla has lost its italics and become just another item on a grocery list. To understand how that happened and why it matters requires knowing something about the ancient transformation of *Zea mays* into a nutritional staple, the rituals and folkways that gave it meaning, and the market forces that metamorphosed a labor-intensive breadstuff into American fast food.[113]

In 1899, a prominent Mexican senator insisted that the world could be divided into three races—the people of corn, the people of wheat, and the people of rice. The people of wheat were, in his view, the only truly progressive race. Maize, he said, was "the eternal pacifier of America's indigenous races and the foundation of their refusal to become civilized."[114] He and others campaigned to replace hand-ground *maza* with centrally milled flour and tortillas with wheat bread. They based their arguments on the images of poor peasant women bending over their *metates* hour after hour. Not until the 1940s did nutritional studies begin to push back, demonstrating that the ancient combination of maize, beans, and chilies offered adequate nutrition, and that the old practice of adding lime to the water in which the corn was boiled released important nutrients.[115]

Today, despite the availability of mass-produced tortillas, some Mexican-American women insist on using a *metate* to prepare *masa* and chilies for special occasions. Ethnic pride and history come together in their choices. As Edward Palmer understood, there is artistry in the backbreaking labor of making tortillas. Liduvina Vélez, who now lives in California, learned to make tortillas in Michoacán, Mexico, where she was born. Married at sixteen, she felt inferior to her husband's mother and sisters until she realized that she was better than they were at making tortillas. "And when I saw they made some ugly tortillas, I no longer was embarrassed.... *Uy*, my tortillas would come out so thin, puffed up so nicely!...I mean, yes, yes; I would beat them at making tortillas."[116]

Harvard's 116-year-old tortilla began a new journey in 2011 when it emerged from the attic of the Herbaria to remind Harvard students and visitors to *Tangible Things* that common objects also have histories.

L. T. U.

A Beetle Ornament: Iridescent Opulence

A string of five beetle carapaces separated by glass beads not only catches the eye because of its brilliant green iridescence, but also prompts a host of hard-to-answer questions.[117] Although this item is in the Peabody Museum of Archaeology and Ethnology, it is a small and modest thing of the kind that might turn up in a family attic or curio store. The original museum ledger entry records it among a number of things described as coming from the "Naga Hill District, Burma, India," more specifically Diliku, as a "Beetle necklace." Roland Burrage Dixon acquired it with many other artifacts during a Peabody Museum expedition in 1912–13.

Dixon had completed his doctoral dissertation at Harvard in 1900, and he remained there, becoming an assistant professor of anthropology

81. A necklace of five complete "jewel beetles" strung on cotton cord with glass beads may have announced the rank and tribal identity of its Naga wearer in the mountainous northeast corner of India at the turn of the twentieth century. The delicate nature of such adornments, however, seems to contrast with the Naga tribes' reputedly violent headhunting campaigns against each other. Fiercely independent and loyal to their culture, many Naga have never accepted outside domination, whether by the British Raj or its successor states. Peabody Museum of Archaeology and Ethnology, Harvard University.

in 1906 and curator of ethnology at the Peabody Museum in 1912. His doctoral research had been on the language of the Maidu people of California, but he conducted fieldwork in many Oceanic and Southeast Asian regions. In 1913, the year he returned from the subcontinent, Dixon published a far-reaching and controversial lead article in the *American Anthropologist*.[118] He advocated testing hypotheses in archaeology and anthropology as linked disciplines scientifically and methodically by the carefully targeted collection and analysis of specimens, rather than the indiscriminate accumulation of material. In this respect, Dixon was a methodological innovator.[119] He was promoted to full professor at Harvard in 1915. Fellow Harvard anthropologist Alfred Tozzer described him as "undoubtedly one of the most erudite ethnographers of all time."[120]

At the time of Dixon's visit, the Naga Hills District had just been incorporated within the province of Assam under the government of British India. Today it is the state of Nagaland within India. Neither of these administrative designations reflects its inhabitants' long-term resistance to state formation. Violence ended only a short time before the negotiations that led to statehood within India in 1963. The district and its neighbors conform to political scientist and anthropologist James Scott's description of large areas of upland Southeast Asia as beyond state control, in spite of repeated efforts by lowland polities to exert authority, in this instance British India succeeded by the Republic of India in the west and Burma (Myanmar since 1989) in the east.[121]

Although colonial and post-independence Indian texts, both governmental and academic, describe the inhabitants of present-day Nagaland as Naga, variously subdivided, such tribal designations are external inventions that scarcely conform to the self-descriptions of the hugely varied social groups concerned. Tribal identification depends entirely on what historian Ajay Skaria has aptly termed "colonial constructions of wildness."[122] British interest in the area was in part a consequence of its strategic significance, notably in the wake of the first Anglo-Burmese war of 1826.[123] The suitability of the area for tea cultivation also excited British interest.[124] Between 1840 and the establishment of the Naga Hills District in 1881, British colonial rule only extended gradually into the area. It was consolidated—insofar as this was possible—only in 1912, the year of Dixon's expedition.[125]

Dixon was far from the first American to visit this—for outsiders—relatively inaccessible area. By the time of his expedition, American Baptist missionaries had long been evangelizing in the Naga Hills. As early as 1836, Williams College graduate, linguist, and philologist Nathan Brown, established a mission at Sadiya (in present-day Assam), and three years later, Miles Bronson, a graduate of the Hamilton Literary and Theological Institute in New York, had overcome local suspicions that he might be a spy for the British and acquired enough vocabulary to establish a mission at Namsang (in present-day Arunachal Pradesh).[126] The charter of the East India Company had prevented such endeavors until its revision in 1813. Even after their admission, the American missionaries noted that the predominantly Anglican officers of the company, succeeded by those of the government of British India, were often not especially sympathetic toward them.[127]

The significance for Dixon's expedition of the spread of the American Baptist missions is that their continuing long-term endeavors among these diverse communities, often hostile toward outsiders, provided a precedent for an American presence. They also provided practical aid in terms of knowledge of local languages. The lingua franca of the Naga was a broken form of Assamese, which the American missionaries had set out to master first. By the early twentieth century, American missionaries were publishing dictionaries of at least some of the myriad local languages.[128] For instance, Edward Clark published his *Ao-English Dictionary* in 1911, the year before Dixon embarked on his expedition.

These upland communities were extremely varied, and in many instances, mutually antagonistic. Warfare among themselves was one of the few cultural values they shared. In these circumstances, the particular form of the beetle necklace ought to be identifiable as belonging to a specific community, but no other example with which to compare it has been found. Dixon himself was scarcely precise about it, listing it inaccurately in his own inventory as a "shell necklace."[129]

The cotton string—cotton was used among Naga communities—is threaded with five complete beetles (the head of one has been lost) of the genus *Sternocera*. Their iridescence results from a variety in surface texture that selectively reflects different light frequencies in different directions. The surfaces are remarkably durable and have scarcely deteriorated over the decades. The inhabitants of the Naga Hills gathered such beetles at the end of their natural life spans of three to four weeks and adapted them as constituents of a variety of symbolic personal accoutrements.[130] For instance, the Angami Naga set modified forewings—elytra—within ear ornaments fashioned of red dyed goat hair to be worn by warriors.[131] However, the use of entire bodies, such as we see in the Peabody artifact, appears unique in known Naga practice, for all these communities habitually used only the detached and flattened elytra. Further, the glass beads threaded between the five whole beetles on the cotton thread are most likely trade items from Bengal that had become sporadically available in the wake of British penetration up the Brahmaputra River valley from the mid-nineteenth century and onward.

By the time Dixon had acquired the beetle necklace, a fascination with the decorative possibilities of iridescent beetle elytra had long since spread across the European world. In the second half of the nineteenth century, *Sternocera* beetles, collected in parts of Southeast Asia more accessible to Europeans than the Naga Hills, had become available for use in the decorative arts. The Peabody Museum also has a circular straw lidded box covered with an elaborate design in appliquéd red and green cloth, sequins, and beetle elytra, probably from India.[132] A tea cozy made in

India for export to Britain, likely in the 1880s, incorporates beetle elytra in an embroidered foliage design.[133] In 1888, the actress Ellen Terry wore a dress covered with a thousand beetle elytra to play Lady Macbeth.[134] A year later, John Singer Sargent painted her dramatic portrait in the role while wearing the dress.[135]

By the time Dixon had acquired the Peabody beetle necklace, its principal material connoted exotic opulence, even decadence. It remains an enigmatic, apparently anomalous artifact, invested in the West with Orientalist associations. Thanks to the reports of two generations of American Baptist missionaries, the Indigenous peoples of the Naga Hills were themselves subjects of ultimate exoticism in Western eyes, not only because of their remoteness and aloofness from the fundamental values—religious, social, and political—of neighboring valley societies in both India and Burma, but because of their reputation for headhunting raids among local communities. The elaborate delicacy of their personal adornments, using cordage, animal hair, shells, and brilliantly colored feathers, as well as beetle elytra, seemed to offer an ironic counterpoint to their reputedly bloodthirsty customs.

Dixon was by no means the only anthropologist who visited the Naga Hills in the early years of the twentieth century. Even those knowledgeable outsiders most seriously involved with the Indigenous inhabitants paid sensational attention to headhunting, and after the British had forbidden the practice, to facial mutilation, which on occasion replaced it. The most influential by far in this respect were two administrative officers of the

82. A close-up of the iridescent beetles showing the head and feet on the underside of one. Peabody Museum of Archaeology and Ethnology, Harvard University.

Indian Civil Service, John Henry Hutton and James Philip Mills. Hutton was a magistrate and taxation officer in the Naga Hills between 1909 and 1935; Mills served there between 1916 and 1938. They both collected a great deal of material that they documented carefully, mostly for the Pitt Rivers Museum of Oxford University. They both recorded the ways of life of the various Naga peoples. Their practice exemplifies the way in which anthropology and colonial administration could go hand in hand, for, as anthropologist Alan Macfarlane put it, Hutton "did this, both for posterity and, as he saw it, to make it easier gradually and non-coercively to integrate this culture into the British Empire."[136] Hutton went on to become professor of social anthropology at Cambridge University, and Mills became a reader in anthropology at the School of African and Oriental Studies of the University of London. For all their assiduity, Mills, in particular, presented accounts of the Naga as determined to circumvent the British prohibition on warfare and headhunting, thereby perpetuating a prurient Western interest in seemingly ferocious yet unexplained rituals and customs. Dixon reviewed Mills's publications enthusiastically.[137]

We are left with the enigmatic beetle necklace in the Peabody Museum, just one among a host of things brought back by Roland Dixon from the Naga Hills in 1913. What could have prompted whoever made this artifact in an otherwise unknown form to have done so? Was it put together to appeal to a foreigner as a trade item, with its glass beads that had come to the Naga Hills through exchange? What might have prompted Dixon to acquire it, then describe it wrongly, and acquiesce (if he noticed) in its problematic description in the Peabody Museum registration ledger as a "shell necklace"? This unidentified and perhaps unidentifiable thing from the hills of far northeast India or far northwest Burma serves as a thing unplaced. Yet it also remains unplaced in a larger sense: that of its maker's community attempting to remain unplaced in relation to colonial administrations and national governments, whether from India, Burma, or distant Britain.

I. G.

A Board Game: Tracking Blondie

In September 1940, the Westinghouse Electric Company announced a new board game intended to "drive business" into the stores of their retailers. The children's game would promote the company's new "leisure living" advertising campaign designed to sell a wide range of electric appliances. It starred a familiar American woman who certainly needed some leisure: Blondie.[138] In 1940, *Blondie*—the still-popular daily comic strip—was only a decade old. Blondie Bumstead (née Boopadoop) is married to Dagwood, a man almost as notorious for napping and shirking housework as he is for his love of impossibly huge sandwiches. Blondie needed some help around the house, and Westinghouse saw the potential of their electric appliances to make up for her famously unhelpful—if lovable—husband.[139]

Blondie has been published in daily papers since 1930. Artist Chic Young created Blondie as a beautiful flapper-turned-secretary and a gold digger who was attracted to Dagwood's family riches (his father was a railroad magnate). Unfortunately, when the pair married in 1933, Dagwood's

83. The goal of "Blondie Goes to Leisureland"—a 1940 board game based on the popular comic strip *Blondie*—was to reach "Leisureland," an "all-electric home" made possible by Westinghouse, the maker of the "Leisure line of electric home appliances." Baker Library, Harvard Business School.

parents disinherited him and he had to get a job. Like all Americans across the country dealing with the effects of the Great Depression, they had to find a way to make ends meet. Since then, Blondie and Dagwood have been fixtures in daily papers around the world. By 1940, Blondie was also the star of a popular radio program and a series of feature films; television shows came later. Chic Young drew the strip until his death in 1973, when his son Dean Young took over. Dean Young still writes and maintains artistic control over *Blondie*. While *Blondie* was gradually modernized, the strip has maintained the same aesthetic: Blondie's sculptural curls; Dagwood's spiky hairstyle; their son (Baby Dumpling, later Alexander) and daughter (Cookie) replicate their parents' appearances; and the familiar olive-shaped nose of Daisy, their faithful dog. The elder Young trained in art school and had a clear style that marked his work as his own—a style that has been maintained by his son and artistic collaborators.

Given its recognizable style, if it were framed and hung on a wall, the Blondie board game could appear in an art museum, like any other print attributed to a known artist or group.[140] In its current acid-free housing in the historical collections of the Baker Library of Harvard Business School, "Blondie Goes to Lesisureland" requires the careful attention of archival specialists who know how to treat and care for fragile, aging paper.[141]

Appliance retailers distributed the game in a slim, beige envelope, printed with instructions, as a giveaway to customers. The game consists of a large foldout game board, numbered game pieces, a series of cards that feature specific Westinghouse appliances, and a spinner. Players follow a turning and twisting journey through a series of labor-intensive tasks ending with the goal of an "all-electric home" in Leisureland. They suffer through the tribulations of an un-electrified life: A leaky icebox does not keep Dagwood's soft drink cold; Dagwood refuses to manually fire up the furnace, leading to a chilly evening; Blondie has to wash Dagwood's shirts in an old crank-powered washer; Dagwood boils water on the old soot-producing stove to heat Baby Dumpling's bath; the same stove burns Mr. Dithers' dinner and chains Blondie to the house while she cooks. Housework is truly hard work without electricity and without Westinghouse. As a player moves through each of these trials, she may land on spaces that further punish her with mishaps: "Clothes scorched from overheated iron. Go back 4 spaces" or "Dinner for Mr. Dithers total failure. Go back 3 spaces." One wins upon arriving in Leisureland,

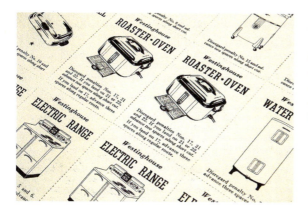

84. Game pieces for "Blondie Goes to Leisureland" featured toasters, electric ranges, water heaters, and washing machines. Baker Library, Harvard Business School.

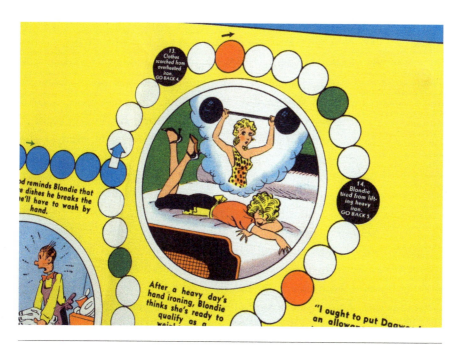

85. Exhausted after a day of ironing, Blondie dreams that she could qualify as a weight lifter. Domestic work is hard work in the un-electrified home of "Blondie Goes to Leisureland." Baker Library, Harvard Business School.

a place where Blondie can read the paper, Dagwood can snooze after a long day working for Mr. Dithers, and Baby Dumpling and Daisy can play on the floor. The domestic scene is happy, warm, and comfortable. It would have been an especially happy scene for dealers of Westinghouse appliances.

A Westinghouse advertisement from earlier in 1940 explains how selling to Blondie, one product at a time, could help retailers rake in money and transform the daily lives and labors of women. The advertisement features a middle-aged woman, a salesman, and an image of her total purchases from his store. The text proclaims, "That makes me just about all electric," to which he replies, "and you did it in just a few years." The advertisement includes an image of a ledger sheet with Mrs. Mathilde Goode's name, her occupation ("housewife") and her credit ("good") above a list of her purchases. Starting in 1933 with an iron that cost only $7.95 to finally buying a dishwasher in 1940 for $230, she spent a total of $1,125. The fictional Mrs. Goode slowly replaced each item in her house with an electric model. The headline "Every customer a $1000 potential" suggests how profitable such sales would have been. It is hard to imagine Dagwood or Blondie having good credit—he was never (in more than eighty years of asking!) able to secure a raise from his boss, Mr. Dithers, and she was a housewife (until she opened a catering company with neighbor Tootsie Woodley in 1991). Buying appliances one small purchase at a time would have made it possible for a housewife without an independent income to show her husband the value of each of the products she wished to have. In the process, she and Westinghouse could change the form of domestic work. But could these purchases really give housewives like Blondie leisure?[142]

By 1940, the vast majority of American homes had access to electricity. In the 1930s, the major electrification projects of the New Deal, the Tennessee Valley Authority, and the Rural Electrification Administration ensured that even isolated areas had power. The "all-electric house" made it easier for women to work outside the home and lessened the physical strenuousness of their housework. Despite the Great Depression, appliance ownership grew dramatically over this decade. For example, only 10 percent of American homes had a refrigerator in 1930, whereas 56 percent had purchased the large appliances by 1940. Innovations like refrigerators and washing machines may have done more to change women's work than to necessarily reduce it. The electric washing machine eliminated "wash day" from the weekly calendar and removed the heavy work of manually washing clothes, but it did not fundamentally shift responsibility for the task away from women.[143]

Blondie and Dagwood's story lines reveal that domestic work is as much about will as it is about watts. In 1933, shortly after their marriage, Young ran a strip titled "The Night Shift" in which Blondie cited "the housewife's code" that prevented her from working more than eight hours a day. Dagwood ended the strip washing dishes at the sink. Throughout the series, Blondie asks her hiding or napping husband to complete specific domestic chores. Housework is a running gag, but tough-minded Blondie makes her wishes clear, even if some readers might have wanted to hide behind the sofa with Dagwood when asked to share the load.[144]

In 1948, Blondie and Dagwood were deployed to promote a technology far more controversial than electricity: nuclear power. Westinghouse and General Electric co-sponsored a month-long exhibition in Central Park called *Man and the Atom*. A comic display entitled "Splitting the Atom" featured atomic-sized Blondie and Dagwood discovering the wonders of science at the atomic level. The strip culminated in a major coup for Dagwood, who successfully split the nucleus of uranium atom 235 and produced a deafening explosion. In the final frame, small images of "medicine," "transportation," "power," "industry," and "agriculture" surround Dagwood's challenge: "That was an awful big noise, eh Dagwood? It took a lot of power to make that noise—all wasted. Now the job is to find how that power can be used—not wasted...." Dagwood runs off the page yelling "BLONDIE!"[145] He knew that he needed his wife's know-how to harness atomic power. Perhaps Dagwood knew that his own efficient and savvy wife could solve the global problem of nuclear energy just as she had maintained their budget, electrified their home, and brought their family into Leisureland one appliance at a time. But, of course, it's just a comic strip.

Books and manuscripts, art, history, science... eight decades and counting, Blondie and Dagwood still appear in the daily paper and comfortably fit into each of these categories. In *Tangible Things*, the game "Blondie Goes

86. Ancient gaming pieces, these three-thousand-year-old sheep or goat knucklebones served as dice and divination tools in the Iron Age in western Asia. Semitic Museum.

to Leisureland" is beside the knucklebones of sheep or goats from the Semitic Museum that date to the Iron Age.[146] These bones were used like dice and could be purposed for gambling and divination. The "Blondie" game and these bones suggest the ways objects related to play—broadly defined—engage intellectual themes across disciplines. On her journey to Leisureland, Blondie found her way into core themes of twentieth-century American life recorded in museums, collections, and departments across the university. Where will Blondie go next?

S. A. C.

CHAPTER THREE

Things out of Place

One way to investigate the instability of things is to "misplace" them in full sight. This is the strategy we adopted in the third section of our experimental exhibition: an examination of things purposefully shown out of place.

Both specialists and casual visitors have certain expectations regarding what they will find in any given type of Western museum. They expect to see natural history specimens in a natural history museum and art in an art museum. However, each of these categories can be both elastic and expansive, and the boundaries that separate them are permeable. That becomes obvious if we consider the ways in which museums have opened their collections to new sorts of things. Just as fossils were added to *natural history* in the eighteenth century, sub-Saharan wooden carvings were added to *art* in the twentieth century. Although such objects had previously existed, the gatekeepers of *art* and *natural history* had not previously considered them as belonging in their domains. This does not mean that tangible things enter or exit categories in identical ways or on the same terms. Some things are added because they are novelties—as in the case of computers or viruses. Computers were new instruments to do a job that already fell under the category of *science*; before the late nineteenth century, humans had been unaware of viruses. But other things added to a given category may appear incongruous. And, if they are close enough to the boundary of that category, they may disrupt it. When boundary disruption occurs in a museum display, it can prompt viewers to reconsider the character of the interloper and the category in which it was placed.

Our experimental exhibition introduced seventeen purposely "out of place" items into displays in seven different collections. Six appeared in various galleries of the Harvard Museum of Natural History, two in the Peabody Museum, two in the Harvard Art Museums, two in the Houghton Library, two in the Collection of Historical Scientific Instruments, and one each in the Schlesinger Library and the Semitic Museum. Visitors came across these "guest objects" either by chance when visiting the collections, or by deliberately following clues in a flyer picked up in one of the *Tangible Things* venues, thereby conducting their own scavenger hunts. A clear but discreet label included the exhibition logo and a cell phone number that allowed viewers to dial in to hear a brief commentary that was also accessible through the Harvard iTunes site.[1]

In their unexpected settings, each of the guest objects raised issues regarding the characters, uses, perceptions, and understandings of things as they have been categorized in Western thought. By actually introducing foreign objects into incongruous settings, we were able to investigate consequences we might not have discerned through thought alone. In this way, we confirmed the character of our exhibition as an experiment, rather than as a finished product for visitors' consumption alone.

Our interventions in the Harvard Museum of Natural History invited visitors to rethink the division between specimens derived from nature and artifacts created by human beings. We chose as the site of our experiment the oldest and most historic galleries in the museum, those still arranged according to nineteenth-century notions of taxonomy. The Earth and Planetary Sciences Gallery in the Harvard Museum of Natural History displays row after row of minerals (arranged according to their chemical compositions) in brilliantly lit glass cases. In one of these cases, we placed a vesicle calculus, or bladder stone, from the Warren Anatomical Museum in the Medical School.[2] Egg-shaped and sliced through the middle, it seemed small and drab compared to the fantastically shaped minerals around it. One could easily see how it was formed in concentric layers. In keeping with the emphasis on chemical composition in this gallery, we noted that it contained oxalate of lime, uric acid, and phosphate of lime. This was no pearl from a Massachusetts oyster bed. It had formed within a human body and had been removed during an autopsy in Salem, Massachusetts, in 1809. This suggested that the man, like his bladder stone, was also a product of nature. It also prompted recognition of the elemental affinities between things mineral and things animal. It

87. Amid rows of colorful minerals on display in the Mineralogical Hall of the Harvard Museum of Natural History, visitors stumbled upon a large, ovoid stone that had been removed from a man's urinary bladder in 1809. The bladder stone was on loan from the Warren Anatomical Museum in the Francis A. Countway Library of Medicine.

88. Sliced in half, the egg-shaped stone shows concentric rings indicating layers built up over many years inside a man's bladder. Like rocks found in the earth, stones made by the human body (called vesicle calculi) can be rough or smooth, flaky or spiky. This bladder stone is a rough concretion of oxalate of lime, uric acid, and phosphate of lime. Warren Anatomical Museum in the Francis A. Countway Library of Medicine.

89. This pencil belonged to the writer Henry David Thoreau of Concord, Massachusetts, in the 1850s. A hundred years later, Henry Seidel Canby, a Yale literature professor and Thoreau biographer, sent the pencil with a rolled-up note in this box to Harvard's Houghton Library. The pencil was made in the factory founded by Henry's father, John Thoreau, and uncle, Charles Dunbar. Father and son both worked in the factory and were proprietors. Houghton Library.

90. Close-up of the unsharpened end of Thoreau's pencil showing the square cross-section of the writing lead—actually a graphite-clay mixture—laid into a groove in the lower half of the wood pencil and then covered by the upper piece of wood. Henry David Thoreau came up with the idea of using clay as a binder to New England graphite to solve the problem of smeary pencils. Thoreau, who signed himself as a "civil engineer," made other technological improvements to pencil manufacturing, including devising a means of injecting lead directly into the pencil core. Houghton Library.

was hard not to cringe when thinking about the unfortunate man whose body grew this rock.

In the same gallery, beside a large specimen of raw graphite, we installed a pencil from the Houghton Library that had belonged to Henry David Thoreau.[3] Although encased in wood, its core was a specimen of low-grade New England graphite milled with clay. The process developed by Thoreau gave a competitive edge to his father's pencil factory in Concord, Massachusetts, from the later 1840s and onward. Pencils like this one reliably and evenly made smear-free marks. Placed among Harvard's famous mineral collection, the pencil invited visitors to think about the everyday uses of the minerals all around them. Thoreau once wrote that if he wanted a boy to learn about the arts and sciences, he would not send him to listen to a lecture but would have him make "his own jackknife [or pencil?] from the ore which he had dug and smelted."[4]

In the Great Mammal Hall of the Museum of Natural History, we installed two more anomalous items. A patent medicine bottle from the time of the American Civil War, labeled "Macamoose, The Great Indian Tonic,"[5] took its place among the taxidermy and skeletal specimens of various species of mice.

House mice (*Mus musculus*) have long shared domestic spaces with humans. One apparently squeezed into this bottle and perished there. The bottle had been made for the U.S. Army Hospital Department between 1862 and 1865, and likely came from an army hospital store. It may have belonged to Lieutenant Charles Grosvenor Ward. After his death in battle at Drewry's Bluff, Virginia, his effects were returned to his parents in Shrewsbury, Massachusetts, in May 1864. They have remained ever after at what in 1925 became the General Artemas Ward House Museum. The

91. A patent medicine bottle labeled "Macamoose, The Great Indian Tonic," ca. 1865, contains the desiccated body of a house mouse (*Mus musculus*). The curious artifact from the General Artemas Ward House Museum was an interloper on a shelf of various species of mice in the Mammal Hall in the Harvard Museum of Natural History in 2011.

92. Who walked here before me? A stuffed coyote gazes down at a dog paw print made in a mud brick between 1500 and 1300 BCE in the city of Nuzi, Mesopotamia. The brick was placed, courtesy of the Semitic Museum, in the Mammal Hall in the Harvard Museum of Natural History.

presence of the bottle among the more clearly visible mouse specimens reminded those who saw it in the Great Mammal Hall that the lives of humans and animals are interconnected, in this case, even in death.

Our intervention in the display of taxidermy mounts of canines in the Great Mammal Hall also acknowledged the intersection of human and animal lives. We took advantage of the downward gaze of a stuffed coyote to make it appear that the object of its attention was a paw print made 3,000 years earlier by an ancestor. The paw print was in a large mud brick excavated between 1927 and 1931 from the ancient Mesopotamian city of Nuzi, and is now in the Semitic Museum. It dates from between 1500 and 1300 BCE. While it was drying, a dog walked across it, leaving an impression and offering us a glimpse of the relationship between Nuzi's Hurrian inhabitants and their canine companions.[6]

Our fifth intervention in the Museum of Natural History was in one of the most popular displays among all of Harvard's collections, the Ware Collection of Blaschka Glass Models of Plants, better known as the Glass Flowers. The Glass Flowers were commissioned by George Lincoln Goodale, professor of botany, subsequently the Fisher Professor of Natural Science, and, between 1879 and 1909, director of the Botanical Museum. Altogether more than 3,000 colored glass models represent 847 plant species. Leopold Blaschka and his son Rudolf made them between 1887 and 1936 near Dresden, Germany. They served as permanent substitutes for mutable specimens in the teaching of botany. A large selection is on long-term display in a dedicated gallery of the Museum of Natural History. Their detail and precision can deceive the eye, and generations of viewers have marveled at their astonishing verisimilitude. The combination of techniques used to make them has proved to be inimitable.

93. A long-stemmed vase shaped as a flower by Louis Comfort Tiffany, ca. 1900, on loan from the Harvard Art Museums, was set among the famous Glass Flowers on display in the Harvard Museum of Natural History. The latter is a collection of more than 3,000 scientific models artfully crafted in glass by Leopold Blaschka and his son Rudolf beginning in 1886.

In the same years that these models were commissioned, the American designer Louis Comfort Tiffany developed and patented various glass-making procedures to enable his Tiffany Studios to produce unprecedented decorative art objects. Among them was a tall-stemmed glass vase made in about 1900 in the form of a stylized flower.[7] It was given to the Fogg Art Museum in 1957, but it has only been exhibited occasionally. We introduced it as a guest object into the gallery where the Glass Flowers were displayed. In contrast to the literal, visually deceptive models crafted by the Blaschkas, the Tiffany vase is obviously an elegant human invention, evoking a single blossom of an indeterminable species on a tall stem. Yet a close look at its stem reveals a swelling, a knop that

94. Although a stylized flower, the Tiffany vase evokes botanical realism with details such as the swelling on the stem. Harvard Art Museums/ Fogg Museum.

is similar to the node on a model of grass in a case nearby. Although the vase is highly stylized, its unknown designer paid close attention to the details of plants.

Aspects of the Blaschka models themselves depend on stylization and convention: not so much the reproductions to scale of whole plants as the enlarged details and cross-sections of parts of them, which conform to the norms of scientific illustration. The comparison between the Glass Flowers and the floriform vase prompts consideration of the nature of any distinction between artistic and scientific representation. Is faithful imitation, apparently without invention, sufficient for the resulting product to be classified as art? If not, has the change in use of the Glass Flowers, from transparent teaching aid to object of wonder at the human capacity for imitative fabrication, led to their change from technical objects to artworks? Or might the presence of the Tiffany floriform vase have evoked by its instantiation of human invention a quality absent in the Glass Flowers, however marvelous the craftsmanship they exemplify may be? How are we to analyze and assess the range of human ingenuity encompassed by both? Are science and art as distinct from one another as much practice and education in each would lead us to believe?

The two guest objects we placed in the Peabody Museum raised questions about boundaries between peoples that are often replicated in the way artifacts are divided among museums. According to nineteenth-century

95. Tucked among models of canoes and kayaks in the Hall of the American Indian at the Peabody Museum of Archaeology and Ethnology was a British model of the world in the form of an eighteenth-century pocket globe, on loan from the Harvard University Archives. Pocket globes were memory aids for schoolchildren and others wanting a portable map of the heavens and Earth. Tracks of famous explorers were marked as lines on the globe so that users could see their routes. The explorers shown and the cartography of the terrestrial and celestial spheres were typically influenced by national politics.

96. The terrestrial globe, a mere three inches in diameter, sits in its spherical case covered with sharkskin. The case is lined with a map of the celestial sphere. Made by James Ferguson, London, ca. 1757, this pocket globe shows the route of Commodore George Anson, who circumnavigated the world between 1740 and 1744. Harvard University Archives.

ways of thinking, Europeans had art and history; non-Europeans had culture. Those divisions are still reflected in the collection policies of many museums. The Hall of the American Indian includes a vitrine devoted to models of various kinds, including miniature canoes and kayaks.We added a Western artifact to this display, a miniature terrestrial globe and its sharkskin case lined with a map of the heavens.[8] The Scottish astronomer, instrument maker, and portrait miniaturist James Ferguson created this pocket globe in about 1757, incorporating the most up-to-date geographical information then available to Europeans. It

97. The dress, belt, and beads, worn by a girl dressing up as an Indian at a New Hampshire summer camp in the 1940s, were displayed in a gallery of the Peabody Museum of Archaeology and Ethnology alongside some authentic clothing of Indigenous peoples and anthropological models of their villages. The costume represents an early twentieth-century American tradition in which children dressed up as Native Americans and romanticized them as living simply in nature. When juxtaposed with authentic and interpretive things in the gallery, the costume brought to the fore tensions between the ways that Natives and outsiders saw themselves and each other.

98. A beaded necklace that was part of a Native American costume sewn by Sarah Jenney Gilbert Kerlin in the late 1940s for her granddaughter to use at campfires at Singing Eagle Lodge on Squam Lake, New Hampshire. Arthur and Elizabeth Schlesinger Library on the History of Women in America.

entered the University Archives in 1914 with other materials once owned by Ebenezer Storer, a Harvard graduate (A.B., 1747, A.M., 1750) and Boston wholesale merchant who was treasurer of Harvard College from 1777 to 1807. These miniature versions of skillfully designed things, both indigenous and European, encapsulate knowledge of aspects of the world and ways of navigating it.[9] They also display the widely shared human practice of creating small versions of large things.

The fourth floor of the Peabody Museum also contains miniatures, early twentieth-century scale models of indigenous North American dwelling sites. These models, created by Euro-Americans, include local topography and small figures of inhabitants going about their daily tasks. Such models have been roundly criticized in recent decades for, among other perceived failings, their representation of an idealized, timeless "anthropological present," implying an unchanging set of circumstances and routines that deny Native people places in history. It is also striking that the models exclude overt representations of any signs of contact between Natives and newcomers. Today the models are exhibited so that students can question them on just these and other terms, rather than view them as accurate accounts of the various peoples they represent.

Alongside these models, in an existing horizontal display case, we introduced another example of a Western fantasy of American indigeneity: a fabric dress with belt and beads made in stylized imitation of a Plains Indian woman's hide dress.[10] Sarah Jenney Gilbert Kerlin made this dress and its accoutrements in the late 1940s for her granddaughter, Catharine Wilder Guiles (Radcliffe Class of 1959), who gave these items to the Schlesinger Library in 2006. Such clothing was the formal wear for girls assembling for Saturday evening campfire meetings each week at the Singing Eagle Lodge on Squam Lake, New Hampshire. Like the Camp Fire Girls, the Boy Scouts, and other groups, the Squam Lake Camp incorporated Indian motifs to give campers a sense of being in a primitive place in tune with nature. "Playing Indian" was integral to the program. Like the anthropological scale models, the camp dress conveyed Indians as non-Indians wished to see them. Our introduction of Catharine Wilder Guiles's camp dress into an institution dedicated to the collection and study of authentic ethnological material was risky. For us, the challenge of how to arrange this exhibit prompted further consideration of the Western manipulation of the very idea of authenticity. It highlighted the sometimes fictive and often antagonistic relations that have often existed—and continue to exist—between Indigenous and incoming Americans.[11]

99. Set alongside seventeenth-century European and American silverware at the Sackler Museum was a pierced silver band that once adorned the tall hat of a Peskotomuhkati (Passamaquoddy) woman, living in Maine or New Brunswick, Canada, ca. 1875. The hatband was on loan from the Peabody Museum of Archaeology and Ethnology, Harvard University.

100. This pierced silver band with scalloped trim was made by a white silversmith in Maine or eastern Canada as an item to trade with the Peskotomuhkati in the nineteenth century. Peabody Museum of Archaeology and Ethnology, Harvard University.

101. An extraordinary goblet, made ca. 1600 from a coconut and carved with Bible scenes, was installed, courtesy of the Busch-Reisinger Museum, among a display of rare printed Bibles in Houghton Library as part of *Tangible Things*, Harvard University, spring 2011.

We invited another comparison between North American cultures by taking a Peabody Museum artifact and relocating it to the Arthur M. Sackler Museum of the Harvard Art Museums. The object was a nineteenth-century silver hatband for a tall felt hat like those formerly worn by Peskotomuhkati (Passamaquoddy) women in northeast Maine and New Brunswick.[12] These hats were derived from European men's top hats. They were adorned with silver bands embellished with elaborately incised decoration and cutwork. One such hat with a silver band is shown in a portrait of a Penobscot woman known as Sarah Molasses by the Maine artist Jeremiah P. Hardy dating from about 1835. The original hangs in the Bangor (Maine) Public Library, and a copy by Hardy's daughter Anna Eliza Hardy is in the Peabody Museum.[13] White silversmiths in Maine and eastern Canada made such silver hatbands as Indian trade items. Even so, the Peabody Museum example looked anomalous in a case of European and American silver at the Sackler Museum. It was clearly the

102. Scenes from the story of
Samson are carved into the
coconut, which was mounted
in gilt silver and topped
with a lid by Hans Peter
Müller, Breslau, ca. 1600.
Harvard Art Museums/
Busch-Reisinger Museum.

odd thing out beside items such as an elaborate sideboard dish with a scene
of Hercules drawing his bow on Nessus abducting Deianira, made by the
silversmith Jacob Bodendeich in London between 1676 and 1677,[14] and
an ornate two-handled cup and cover by Boston silversmith John Coney,
given to Harvard College in 1701 by the lieutenant governor of the province of Massachusetts Bay, William Stoughton, who had presided at the
Salem witch trials in 1692–93.[15] The hatband served as a reminder that
wealthy, socially privileged consumers did not have a monopoly on crafts
in precious metal, and that silver can evoke a far wider social and cultural
range of people than is normally the case in art museum displays.

Houghton Library hosted two guest objects. We incorporated one into
a temporary exhibition, *The Bible in Type: From Gutenberg to Rogers: An
Exhibition Commemorating the Four-Hundredth Anniversary of the King
James Bible* (January through June 2011). This exhibition focused on
printed bibles. We inserted a lidded cup, fashioned from a coconut and
set in ornate silver gilt mounts by the Breslau artist Hans Peter Müller
(active ca. 1600) that depicted an elaborately contrived representation of
scenes from the story of Samson in the biblical book of Judges.[16]

103. A framed dress fragment, said to have belonged to Priscilla Mullins, a Pilgrim on the *Mayflower* and, by 1623, the wife of John Alden, the *Mayflower*'s cooper. According to Alden family lore, first published in 1814, Miles Standish, the Plymouth colony's commander, was a rival for Priscilla's hand. The love triangle was immortalized in an 1858 poem by Henry Wadsworth Longfellow, a descendent of Alden. The fragment, which belongs to the Radcliffe Picture Collection, was displayed in a case devoted to the library of John Harvard at Houghton Library.

104. Frayed and moth-eaten, the blue fragment of Priscilla Mullins's dress has striped areas woven in the wool. Arthur and Elizabeth Schlesinger Library on the History of Women in America.

If the coconut cup among the bibles prompted reflection on modes of representation, our display of a fragment of a dress said to have belonged to Priscilla Mullins, the heroine of a poem by Henry Wadsworth Longfellow, invited reflection on another kind of mythology.[17] According to a family tradition, John Alden, a young immigrant to the newly founded Plymouth Colony in 1623, carried a proposal of marriage to Priscilla from the colony's gruff military commander, Miles Standish. Priscilla supposedly responded, "Why don't you speak for yourself, John?" Henry Wadsworth Longfellow popularized the story in his poem "The Courtship of Miles Standish" (1858). The story was so well known by the time descendants of Priscilla donated the swatch of fabric to the college that no one needed to ask its significance. Priscilla became a model for a woman's right to choose her own mate. As a reminder that Radcliffe had its own myths, we set it beside a shrine-like display of a book thought to have belonged to John Harvard, the minister for whom Harvard College was named after he donated his library and half of his estate to the fledging school.[18] Whether authentically connected to Priscilla Mullins or not, we used the fragment of cloth to complement the male Harvard's celebration of its colonial origins. In doing so, we also invited visitors to consider the mythical elements in Harvard's own sense of its past.

We also evoked questions of gender by our choice of venue for the display of the so-called President's Chair, an elaborately turned British three-square great chair from the second half of the sixteenth century that had been acquired by Edward Holyoke when he was president of Harvard College between 1737 and 1769 to lend dignity to the office.[19] A portrait by John Singleton Copley, painted in about 1760, depicts Holyoke sitting in his acquisition.[20] Successive presidents thereafter have used the chair on ceremonial occasions, most prominently at their installations and at Harvard's annual commencements. As Harvard remained an exclusively male bastion (servants apart) for much of its existence, the President's Chair assumed an identity as symbolic of expressly male authority. This changed only in 2007 with the installation of Drew Gilpin Faust as Harvard's twenty-eighth president, the first woman to occupy the position. Faust had been dean of the Radcliffe Institute for Advanced Study, the successor to Radcliffe College, since 2001, so to emphasize the change that had taken place—at least symbolically—we displayed the President's Chair in the Arthur and Elizabeth Schlesinger Library on the History of Women in America at the Radcliffe Institute.

105. Made in England or Wales between 1550 and 1600, the turned great chair was
bought by Edward Holyoke, president of Harvard College from 1737 to1769. Holyoke
added the spherical oak pommels, which he made himself. With a triangular board seat
secured to a central rear post topped by a knobby square back, the three-legged chair
was an uncomfortable and tippy seat for Harvard's president during commencements. To
compensate, the odd whale tail was added to the rear leg as a stabilizer, and the cushion
was added to the seat. Harvard Art Museums/Fogg Museum.

106–107. Loose rings hang from the knobby turnings
on the back of the President's Chair, rattling when a
person leans against them. The needlepoint cushion
has offered a small measure of comfort since 1979.
Harvard Art Museums/Fogg Museum.

Two interventions were subtly slipped into the Collection of Historical
Scientific Instruments in the Science Center. A section of the IBM
Automatic Sequence Controlled Calculator (ASCC), called the Harvard
Mark I after its arrival at Harvard in 1944, is so large that it is installed
in a well-trafficked corridor of the Science Center rather than in the
Putnam Gallery of the collection itself. This was the first programmable
calculator capable of performing long computations and is often held up
as the first true computer. Illustrated text panels explaining the opera-
tion of the Mark I run at waist level beside it. One of the early photographs reproduced shows team member Robert L. Hawkins attending

108. What might a homely American corncob pipe from 1919 have to do with the sleek, art deco, state-of-the-art Harvard Mark I computer of 1944, the world's first programmable calculator? The pipe, on loan from the Harvard University Herbaria, was tucked into the Mark I machinery on display in the Science Center corridor courtesy of the Collection of Historical Scientific Instruments.

109. Missouri Meerschaum corncob pipe, 1919. Harvard University Herbaria.

110. Robert L. Hawkins, a Harvard technician, smokes a corncob pipe while working on the multiply-divide unit of the IBM Automatic Sequence Controlled Calculator (known as the Harvard Mark I computer) during its installation in the Cruft Laboratory at Harvard University, February 1, 1944. Collection of Historical Scientific Instruments.

to the machine while smoking a corncob pipe. On a part of the instrument nearby, protected by a transparent acrylic cover, we were able to install an actual corncob pipe from the Economic Botany Herbarium of the Harvard University Herbaria,[21] playfully challenging viewers to work out the reason for its otherwise unexplained presence.

We intended the temporary presence of each guest object to be disruptive, but not to ridicule its host exhibition. We did not introduce them to discredit the assumptions underlying the existing displays, but rather to prompt exploration of further avenues of thought. The otherwise concealed or fugitive aspects of tangible things are not necessarily superior to standard classifications and treatments, many of which have led to extremely effective thoughts and actions. Some existing arrangements are indeed open to criticism, however, especially for their indifference to the pernicious effects of ethnic, gender, class, and economic resource disparities. As historians, our task is to try to reveal, understand, and explain contingency. We aimed to demonstrate that, in any given set of circumstances, there is never simply one viable or fruitful way of thinking or behaving.

That insight became even more important as we selected four guest objects for more extended analysis after the exhibit closed. In the galleries, each of these objects performed the work we had intended, provoking visitors and our own students to rethink received categories. As we did additional research, however, we became even more convinced of the power of the method we had used. By quickly, almost randomly, reassigning a small set of objects to new settings, we unexpectedly opened up areas of inquiry in our own fields that we had not considered earlier. A tin bluebird displayed in the Museum of Natural History led Laurel Ulrich to consider aspects of female activism that she had not previously understood. The skull of a helmeted hornbill bird from the Museum of Comparative Zoology gave Ivan Gaskell an opportunity to probe the boundary between nature and art in new ways.[22] The placement of an artist's palette used by John Singer Sargent in a history-of-science exhibition that Sara Schechner had curated led her to ponder the psychology of color.[23] Finally, Sarah Carter encountered new ways of thinking about historical memory when we placed a late eighteenth or early nineteenth-century walking plow from the General Artemas Ward House Museum into Harvard's Semitic Museum, alongside a cut-away life-size reconstruction, incorporating original artifacts, of a private house of a kind found in Israel and Judah between about 1200 and 586 BCE.[24]

Each of these more extended case studies demonstrates a central theme of our project, that tangible things are multivalent, mutable in substance and association, and capable of mediating relations among humans and between humans and their complex environments. Our own choices, manipulations, and contrivances were designed to make this goal more readily apparent than would be possible in collections selected, arranged, and exhibited in accordance with habitual nineteenth-century categories.

An Artist's Palette: The Psychology of Vision

What do we make of a large wooden palette thickly covered with oil paint and set among contemporaneous scientific instruments for the study of color vision, illusion, and emotion?

111. John Singer Sargent's artist's palette, borrowed from the Harvard Art Museums, was placed in an exhibit case alongside late nineteenth-century scientific instruments used by experimental psychologists and philosophers to explore color vision and optical illusions. Clockwise beginning to the left of the palette are Titchener's color pyramid, an ophthalmotrope (illustrating forces of the eye muscles), models of the eye in brass, glass, wood, and papier-mâché, a zoetrope (in the form of a slotted, dark green cylinder in which the paper movie strip is placed and spun), William James's black-and-white striped waterfall illusion (seen on edge at the right side of the case), Holmes's stereoscope, a zoetrope movie strip, Holmgren's test for color blindness, a model of the human brain, and a hypnoscope. The exhibit case was in the Putnam Gallery of the Collection of Historical Scientific Instruments.

112. An oil paint-encrusted wooden palette used by John Singer Sargent in the late nineteenth or early twentieth century. Harvard Art Museums/Fogg Museum.

The palette in question belonged to the American artist John Singer Sargent. It is a magnificent and manly thing, nearly two feet long and over a foot wide, with curves that accommodated the artist's grip and made room for his torso. The oil paint on its surface rises up in rugged mountain chains. It is a topographical map formed by the artist's will, and it remains a mystery how Sargent's brush could move from this dark mess to canvases of nuance, color, and emotion.

The palette belongs to the Department of American Paintings, Sculpture, and Decorative Arts of the Harvard Art Museums/Fogg Museum. It was a 1933 gift from the artist's sisters in his memory.[25] Art museums preserve palettes, brushes, and artists' pigments as relics of great masters, allowing us to meditate on how the artists could manipulate these humble tools of their craft to soar to great heights of artistry that are anything but common. Artists are often depicted with their palettes, the symbolic things that proclaim their subjects' vocation. But palettes as tangible things can be admired as more than vehicles through which a painter is somehow magically transformed from a mere craftsman into an artist. Of all artists' tools, the palette offers the most tantalizing glimpse into the artist's working method of laying down color.[26] And nothing could be more important. As the English art critic John Ruskin wrote, "The whole value of what you are about depends, in a coloured sketch, on the colour *merely*. If the colour is wrong, everything is wrong: just

113. The rugged terrain formed by dried oil paint on Sargent's palette shows the energy with which the artist pushed the paint around. Harvard Art Museums/Fogg Museum.

as, if you are singing, and sing false notes, it does not matter how true the words are."[27] Sargent, however, observed that "[c]olour is an inborn gift," but he thought the eye could be trained to appreciate light and dark values.

William James, a contemporary of Ruskin and Sargent, was trained in art, biology, and medicine but found his calling as a philosopher and psychologist at Harvard University. Sargent was on friendly terms with the James family. Not only did he paint portraits of William's brother, author Henry James,[28] and daughter-in-law, Alice Runnells James,[29] but he was much beholden to Henry for a boost to his career in America.[30] Aside from this, we would not expect much of an overlap in the interests or activities of John Singer Sargent and William James, much less the tools of their trades.

In the 1880s, James established a psychological laboratory in Harvard's Department of Philosophy and, in 1892, invited Hugo Munsterberg to direct it.[31] James and Munsterberg were pioneers in what became known as the New Psychology, which banished the old philosophical method of introspection. Instead, it relied on highly controlled experiments with equipment borrowed from the domains of physics and physiology to explore the relationship between mental events and physical experiences. Research topics included the psychology of the senses, the timing of mental acts, and studies of judgment, memory, and attention.[32]

The advantages to philosophy were many. As Herbert Nichols, a Harvard psychology instructor, explained in 1893, "The minds of these workers are not wandering in dialectics and vagrant hypotheses....Hypotheses they have, and must have. Often they hold conflicting opinions. But the referee is always present—Nature herself."[33] Harvard was so proud of the new psychological laboratory that it showed off its scientific equipment at the World's Columbian Exposition in Chicago in 1893.

Ruskin intuitively sensed that colors and notes were of fundamental importance in the arts, but philosophers, psychologists, physicists, and physiologists questioned their basic nature. Were colors and tones fundamental, irreducible elements of nature? How did combinations of colors or tones act upon physiological receptors in the eye or ear? How did the brain receive and interpret the sensations? And most fundamentally, do sensations give us direct access to real objects or events in nature, or only to signals from which we infer the properties of external objects or events?

Philosophers like James were particularly interested in vision. Psychological experiments explored perceptions of color, motion, space, and their relationship to emotions and sense of time. Perceptions, however, were often at variance with the phenomenal world. For instance, a subject looking at a two-dimensional photograph through a stereoscope "saw" the scene in three dimensions. Experiments with zoetropes and other predecessors of modern animation showed that the mind inferred motion from an interrupted series of slightly different images. This effect was due to persistence of vision—that is, the ability of the eye to retain an impression of an object for a fraction of a second after its disappearance. Other devices, such as the black-and-white striped "waterfall illusion," caused spectators to experience motion aftereffects—the illusion of fixed objects moving in the opposite direction of adjacent objects whose real motion one had just been watching. The waterfall illusion was named after the experience of hikers who, after having stared at descending water, averted their gaze to the cliff alongside the waterfall and perceived the rocks to be moving upward. These exercises raised philosophical questions about ontology (the study of being) and epistemology (how we know about the world). Philosophers and scientists asked what truths can we discover in nature if senses like sight do not give us direct access to real objects, but only untrustworthy signals about them.

The story of the roots of experimental psychology in Harvard's philosophy department is told today in the Science Center as part of a permanent exhibition of the Collection of Historical Scientific Instruments.[34] In January 2011, as part of the *Tangible Things* experiment, Sargent's palette

114. Instruments for exploring color, vision, illusion, and emotion: an artist's palette loaded with paint, plaster and papier-mâché models of the human eye, a tin of worsted wool yarn, spinning mirrors for hypnosis, a plaster brain on a pillow, and a zoetrope movie strip, "Raining Pitchforks." The palette was on loan from the Harvard Art Museums. The scientific instruments were on permanent display at the Collection of Historical Scientific Instruments in 2011.

was removed from its usual home in the Fogg Museum and placed in the Science Center display case that held nineteenth-century apparatus for the psychological study of vision. Before *Tangible Things*, the palette had been exhibited only in an art museum context in a show examining Sargent's methods: *Sargent in the Studio: Drawings, Sketchbooks, and Oil Sketches.*[35] The new juxtaposition of the palette with scientific instruments encouraged visitors to reevaluate it as an artist's instrument and the psychological apparatus as tools for understanding people's experiences of art.

In the display case with Sargent's palette were interactive models of the eye artfully made of papier-mâché, wood, plaster, and brass, illustrating the optical, mechanical, and anatomical parts of this organ.[36] Nearby was a zoetrope with two movie strips.[37] Each strip was double-sided, one sporting happy images (such as "Magic Ocean" with a swimming whale) and the reverse showing disturbing images (such as "Raining Pitchforks" attacking a man walking under an umbrella). Outside the psychological laboratory, the zoetrope was a parlor toy, but in the lab, it was used for studies of illusions, animations, and emotional responses to imagery. Another toy-turned-scientific-instrument was the refracting stereoscope designed in 1859 by Oliver Wendell Holmes, professor of anatomy and physiology at Harvard Medical School.[38] In the lab, it was a tool for understanding binocular vision and depth of field.

Also in the exhibit case was the waterfall illusion constructed by William James, allegedly from a professor's black-and-white striped bathing suit.[39] This apparatus looked like a bold piece of modern art, as did Edward Titchener's color pyramid, a three-dimensional model of visual sensations defined by color, brightness, and saturation.[40]

Nearby was Munsell's "color globe."[41] Using a photometer to measure color, Boston artist and educator Albert Munsell had developed a numerical system of describing and mapping the attributes of color—hue, value, and chroma—along three axes with visually uniform steps. (If you sliced through Munsell's globelike color solid, you would find the familiar color-matching cards we see today in the paint sections of hardware stores.) Munsell was keen to use his painterly skills and scientific theory to teach color to students, and had created his "color globe" for this purpose. Patches of the sphere were painted with different colors. Rotation of the globe produced visual bands of white, gray, and black, depending on the intensity of the colors mixed.

Another instrument on display both mixed and separated colors. This was the heliostat, a window-ledge device that tracked the Sun in order to direct a beam of light into the laboratory, where it was separated by prisms or gratings into particular colors, which could then be selected and recombined by mirrors.[42]

And lastly, near Sargent's palette, there was Holmgren's test for color blindness, which was nothing more than a tin box of colored worsted wool yarns.[43] Favored in the railroad and shipping industries, this scientific instrument could be mistaken for a knitter's scrap basket.

At first glance, some of these scientific instruments do not look scientific at all. Why not an artist's palette loaded with paint? William James, Hugo Munsterberg, and the other psychologists sought truths about humanity and the physical world by using instruments to explore and manipulate color vision, illusions, and human emotions. Were these not also the goals of John Singer Sargent?

S. J. S.

A Tin Bluebird: Calling for the Vote

People walk by birds every day. Hidden in trees and shrubs, they awaken us with their chirping or startle us with an expected flash of color, but most of the time, they live around us unnoticed. People have to be taught to see birds.[44] That can be true even in museums. We added this die-cut tin bird advertising votes for women to an existing exhibit in the Harvard Museum of Natural History, hoping that it might startle visitors into thinking differently about the stuffed birds inside the glass case. Many people probably walked right by. But those who spotted the tin bluebird in the back of the case were understandably surprised. What was a blatantly political artifact doing in an exhibit devoted to the presence of color in the natural world? Was this a joke in need of explanation?

The original exhibit had five beautifully preserved bird specimens, all blue, their feathers ranging from aqua to deep indigo. There was little

115. Perched among blue-feathered birds in an exhibition at the Harvard Museum of Natural History, a die-cut tin bluebird sign surprised visitors with its voting-rights message. Made in Massachusetts in 1915, the tin bird was on loan from the Women's Rights Collection of the Arthur and Elizabeth Schlesinger Library on the History of Women in America.

explanatory text, only the evocative English names of the birds printed on small white cards with italicized Latin names below. A tiny red-legged honeycreeper (*Cyanerpes cyaneas*) perched near a hefty black-throated magpie-jay (*Calocitta colliei*). Around them were a swallow tanager (*Tirsila viriolis*), a buff-breasted paradise kingfisher (*Tanysiptera sylvia*), and the inevitable eastern bluebird (*Sialia sialis)*, the obvious model for our tin specimen. A nearby kiosk explained that feather color was not applied like pigment, but rather created by unseen nanostructures that enhanced and reflected light. By pressing an oversized button, visitors could see the colorless web of a bird feather as it appeared through an electron microscope.

In such an exhibit, the tin bird was a provocation. Anyone could see that it was unlike the others, made of metal and paint rather than feathers. It was not a bird, but a representation of a bird. We hoped that the students in our course and other museum visitors would recognize that the regular

116. A slogan on the yellow belly and tail feathers of this cheery die-cut tin bluebird sign urged Massachusetts male voters to support a "VOTES FOR WOMEN" state constitutional amendment at the polls on November 2, 1915. Arthur and Elizabeth Schlesinger Library on the History of Women in America.

117. A typical field-guide image of a bluebird in the early twentieth century, from Chester A. Reed's *Bird Guide: Land Birds East of the Rockies from Parrots to Bluebirds* (1909). Ernst Mayer Library, Museum of Comparative Zoology.

118. A large preserved rare bird roosts on the hat of Katharine Lane Weems, photographed as a young woman, ca. 1918. Arthur and Elizabeth Schlesinger Library on the History of Women in America.

specimens in the case were also fabrications. Their eyes were glass. Their inner organs were gone. These were not actual birds, but the outer wrappings of creatures long dead. True, the taxidermist's art gave them the appearance of live birds by stuffing their desiccated carcasses so they replicated the original size and shape. The feathers and beaks were real, but the display was a human invention nonetheless. In nature, the five birds perched on the museum's white twigs could never have flocked together. Some came from New England, one from as far away as New Guinea.

Although the tin bird seems less "real" than the museum specimens, it is more closely related to the natural world than one might think. It is not a fantasy bird but a recognizable image, despite its size, of the Eastern Bluebird (*Sialia sialis*). It is not accidental that its stylized profile is oriented in exactly the same way as those of Eastern Bluebirds in typical field guides from the period.[45] In the era in which the tin bluebird was created, bird watching became a popular pastime, and field guides emerged as a new genre in nature writing. As killing birds for sport or commerce gave way to conservation, scientists too began to focus on observation rather than collecting.[46] When they created their tin sign, the Massachusetts suffragists built on the popularity of bird-watching. They also built on a long tradition, though they may not have known it, of political engagement over birds.

It all started with a transition in female fashion. In the 1880s, an earlier emphasis on clothing that emphasized the lower part of a woman's body, first with broad skirts, then with bustles, gave way to an interest in shoulders and heads. Wide-brimmed hats displayed flowers, fruits, lavish plumes, and eventually birds' wings, beaks, and bodies. The Schlesinger Library has a photograph taken around 1918 of Katharine Lane, the teen-aged daughter of a prominent Beacon Hill family. An entire bird, preserved in much the same way as the specimens in the exhibit case, looks like it has just taken a nose dive and landed beak down on the hat's brim. What now looks like a freak accident was then a fashion statement.[47]

On two trips through an uptown shopping area of New York in 1886, the ornithologist and bird preservationist Frank Chapman counted forty different species on women's hats. Among them were three bluebirds, two red-headed woodpeckers, nine Baltimore orioles, five blue jays, a swallow-tailed flycatcher, and a laughing gull.[48] Chapman was not laughing. Although bird collecting was for him both a private passion and an essential part of his work as curator at New York's American Museum of Natural History, he was newly awakened to the potential for destruction in popular uses of birds.[49] Although Chapman's writings helped awaken the public, it was women—writers, reformers, and housewives—who spearheaded a new environmental movement. In the 1880s and 1890s, they responded to the news that the millinery trade had decimated coastal rookeries from Maine to the Florida Keys.[50]

The New Hampshire nature writer Celia Thaxter despaired over the indifference of the hat-wearing women she knew. Most could not imagine a world without unlimited natural resources. The thinking at the time was that the animal world was made for human use, and to most people then, it seemed bottomless. To take up the cause of birds, some argued, was as silly as trying to "save the little fishes in the sea." Thaxter had no use for such thinking. In one of her essays, she described a woman laughing at her speech on preservation, and then walking away with "a charnel-house of beaks and claws and bones and feathers and glass eyes upon her fatuous head."[51] In 1896, two wealthy Boston women, Harriet Hemenway and Minna Hall, began a campaign against the use of feathers and plumes in women's hats. They gathered pledges from friends listed on the Social Register and then helped to found the nation's first enduring Audubon Society. Similar groups formed in neighboring states and then, with support from the woman's club movement, the Audubon Society became a national association.[52]

The growth of bird-watching helped shift attitudes from a focus on the economic potential of the natural world to an ethic of preservation.[53] At

Smith College, Florence Merriam was astonished to see her fellow students wearing her favorite birds on their hats. Outraged, she began publishing newspaper stories with titles like "French Milliners and Bird Murder." She and her friend Fanny Hardy engaged John Burroughs as a campus speaker, organized a campaign against wearing feathers, and led students on bird walks to help them "see how the birds look, what they have to say, how they spend their time, what sort of houses they build, and what are their family secrets." In 1889, Merriam published *Birds Through an Opera Glass*, sometimes considered the first field guide to North American birds.[54]

Early field guides merged science and sentiment, often presenting birds as if they were people next door. Writers like Merriam noted when birds were rude to their neighbors or when a father bird helped out with baby tending, laudably giving his "wife" a rest. These early nature writers also worried about the immigration status of troublesome birds like English sparrows.[55] In *Birdcraft* (1895), another of the popular early field guides, Mabel Osgood Wright used domestic imagery to describe the song of the bluebird: "Heard at a distance it has a purling quality. Uttered close at hand, as when the birds go to and fro about their nests, it sounds as if their domestic arrangements were being discussed with the subdued, melancholy voice so often assumed by unwilling housewives. Then the male will fly off on a marketing expedition, murmuring to himself, 'Dear, dear, think of it, think of it!'"[56] In an age when bird songs could be thought to reflect human speech, it was not too far-fetched to imagine a progressive citizen bluebird warbling, "Votes for Women! Votes for Women!"

Although female organizers nodded to convention by enlisting men as presidents of the new ornithological societies, they also found ways of asserting their own claims. By 1899, all but one of the secretaries of the nineteen state societies were women, and they were often responsible for submitting information to the national Audubon Society magazine, *Bird-Lore*, which Mabel Osgood Wright began in 1899. Women's stories not only campaigned against frivolous fashions, but also emphasized the dangers to game birds from male hunting and the need to teach boys not to rob birds' nests of their eggs. Initially, women focused on activities familiar to women. In Rhode Island, one society organized a display of 150 hats attractively made without the use of wild plumage. They called their new creations "Audubonnets." But growing threats forced them to engage with politics, though as with many progressive campaigns in this period, they couched their activism in allusions to home, family, and children—their own and those of the birds.[57]

Bird watching pioneered what we today might call "citizen science." It brought together the new profession of ornithology with a growing interest in public service on the part of men, as well as women. Through the Audubon Society, birdwatchers of both sexes helped to replace the traditional holiday bird hunt with the "Christmas count," an ongoing Audubon tradition today.[58] The theme of good citizenship permeated the literature. Mabel Osgood Wright even co authored a book for children called *Citizen Bird*, in which a naturalist father engages his children in object lessons derived from the study of avian behavior. "As a Citizen the Bluebird is in every way a model," they wrote, highlighting his work in eradicating grasshoppers, crickets, and caterpillars that might pose a danger to plants.[59] Florence Merriam offered a more lyrical notion of the bluebird, building on the contrast between the blue of its wings and back and the reddish-brown or "cinnamon" color of its breast. These, she wrote, were "poet's signs" that the bird belonged to both the earth and the sky. She attributed its "wavering way of lifting its wings when perching" as evidence of life poised between the practical work of the earth and the "wild ethereal spirit" of the sky.[60] In her view, the common bluebird was an ideal progressive reformer. It was about to become a champion of women's suffrage.

At the turn of the twentieth century, the suffrage movement in Massachusetts, once dubbed "the capital of stuffy feminism," was in the doldrums. Its leaders had always behaved more decorously than their flamboyant New York counterparts, but with the death in 1895 of Lucy Stone, the movement itself seemed to be dying. In 1889, there had been ninety suffrage leagues in the state. By 1895, only twenty-six remained. When Maud Wood Park enrolled in Radcliffe that year, she could hardly find a suffragist on campus. Over the next decade, she and others brought new life to the cause by enlisting college women and working-class activists and by implementing new tactics and forms of organization. The new suffragists held outdoor meetings on street corners and in popular vacation spots, canvassed in railroad stations and at factory gates, and even talked a circus manager into draping his elephant with a "Votes for Women" banner. Their most popular speaker was Margaret Foley, an Irish Catholic in Dorchester who had been active in the hat-trimmers union. At one event, she ascended in a hot-air balloon while throwing leaflets to the crowd below.[61]

In 1914 and 1915, the Massachusetts state legislature agreed to send a woman suffrage amendment to voters. The suffragists did everything they had done before and more. Among their new tactics was an experiment in outdoor advertising. In the months before the referendum, they distributed 100,000 brightly painted "Votes for Women" bluebirds around the state, tacking them on buildings, posts, and fences, and even suspending them from window shades in private houses.[62] Perhaps the suffrage bluebird was inspired by the success of *The Blue Bird*, a play by the Belgian dramatist Maurice Maeterlinck that was performed at the Schubert Theatre in Boston in October 1913.[63] If so, the play merely reinforced an already well-established use of bluebirds as emblems of resilience, hope, happiness, and good citizenship.

On October 15, 1915, pro-suffrage women staged a massive parade in Boston with 15,000 marchers and thirty bands. On November 2, the male citizens of the state went to the polls, and in the largest turnout ever for an amendment quashed the women's vote by a margin of 132,000. Women leaders blamed the liquor interest. On the day of the election, saloons passed out pink slips saying, "Good for two drinks if woman suffrage is defeated."[64] But divisions among women also contributed to the defeat. Although the suffragists were well organized, they faced a well-funded Massachusetts Association Opposed to the Further Extension of Suffrage to Women. The "Antis," as they were called, included a disproportionate number of upper-class women, as well as some social reformers who believed women were more effective working outside the political system. Disdaining to parade in public, they draped their homes in red bunting and distributed paper roses to male voters, assuring them that there was no need for the new amendment, which was for them "a rash and dreadful act."[65]

Undeterred by defeat, the suffragists continued their campaign. Had they known it, they might have taken heart from a poem by a then-forgotten Massachusetts poet. Emily Dickinson was fond of bluebirds because she considered them creatures of "independent hues" who arrived in her orchard in early spring while trees were still leafless and skies gray and who persisted long past the time when other birds went south. During the Civil War, she enclosed one of her bluebird poems in a letter to her friend Thomas Wentworth Higginson, who later became editor of *The Woman's Journal*, a pro-suffrage publication.

> After all Birds have been investigated and laid aside—
> Nature imparts the little Blue-Bird—assured
> Her conscientious Voice will soar unmoved
> Above ostensible Vicissitude.
> First to the March—competing with the Wind—

Her panting note exalts us—like a friend—
Last to adhere when Summer cleaves away—
Elegy of Integrity.[66]

Dickinson was not writing about the flamboyant male bird with his brilliant blue feathers, but about the less visible female. Eventually, the wom-
en's voices prevailed. After Congress finally passed the women's suffrage
amendment to the federal Constitution in 1919, Massachusetts became
the eighth state to ratify it.

L. T. U.

A Hand Plow: Plowshares and Swords

The small walking plow, or moldboard plow, displayed in the Semitic
Museum at Harvard is at once a familiar and a strange object.[67] As a
historical item from the General Artemas Ward House Museum, an
eighteenth-century house museum owned by Harvard, it suggests a colonial revival aesthetic, one that consciously remembered the forgotten and
mythologized past of the Revolutionary General Artemas Ward through
his family's things. It further documents the daily lives experienced by
laborers on a New England farm. In the Semitic Museum, across the gallery from an Iron-Age plow point (1200–586 BCE) displayed in an exhibit
devoted to *The Houses of Ancient Israel: Domestic, Royal, Divine*, the delicate
plow suggests the long global history of agricultural technology, from
colonial New England to ancient Israel. Placed in a deliberately anachro-
nistic setting, it also invites reflection on its symbolic meaning. Farming—
when contrasted with warfare—has rhetorical value. In many cultures, a
plow represents peace and prosperity. Looked at historically, however,
farming may also suggest violence, dominance, and colonization. Who
owned the land this plow might have furrowed? Who decided how it
would be used?[68] Plows like this one were in use in New England in the
eighteenth and early nineteenth centuries. It is hard to date this common
form precisely. Local blacksmiths typically made plows as needed. The
curved moldboard would have turned the wet New England soil to prepare for planting and would have once been fully shod with strips of iron.
In contrast, the Iron-Age plow point in the gallery—known as a scratch
plow—simply had to score the surface of the dry land in ancient Israel.
By the 1820s, shod plows were replaced with cast iron patent plows that

119. To the right of the Semitic Museum's reconstruction of a typical Iron-Age house from ancient Israel, complete with farming implements, *Tangible Things* installed a late eighteenth- or early nineteenth-century New England plow belonging to the General Artemas Ward House Museum.

120. The walking plow, likely made in Massachusetts in the late eighteenth or early nineteenth century, has a curved moldboard to turn over the soil. It was used by the family of General Artemas Ward.

121. A photograph of the Ward House attic taken in the 1890s shows the plow—its handles visible left of center—in company with a spinning wheel, snowshoes, a cradle, an old trunk, a chair, a bed warmer, a spade, and a balance. General Artemas Ward House Museum.

offered less resistance as they turned the earth. Thomas Walter Ward, the son of the illustrious general, purchased cast iron plows in the 1820s to prepare the fields of his farm for planting.[69]

The small plow sits at just over two feet tall with the beam stretching to over five feet. Although its diminutive size makes it tempting to see it as a child's toy, it could have accommodated an adult man, holding it upright by the handles and walking behind it in the furrow that it carved in the fields. Its size may also be why it survived for two centuries—perhaps it was not as useful as the larger, heavier plows that fill the Ward family barn. Easily carried to the family attic, it may have survived because it served another purpose.

By the time the Artemas Ward House was left to Harvard in 1925 to become a "public, patriotic museum," as the donor expressed it, it had already functioned as a local house museum for decades. Elizabeth Ward and her nieces Clara Denny Ward and Florence Ward maintained the homestead as a shrine to their ancestor Major General Artemas Ward, the first commander-in-chief of the Massachusetts forces during the American Revolution. This plow spent countless years in the crowded attic of the Artemas Ward House. Its curved handles are visible in a ca. 1890s photograph of the attic. Along with a spinning wheel, a snowshoe, an old chair, and a dusty trunk, the plow suggested the depth of the family's material legacy. As artifacts of the colonial revival, these objects were part of a broader movement to remember and recreate stories and plausible fictions about America's past. The Ward women who preserved the homestead were like the individuals who mourned the loss of the Hancock House on Boston Common, interpreted George Washington's Mount Vernon, or jumped in front of wrecking balls to save historic architecture. For them, American history was personal, national, and material. This small plow became a tool for shaping this history and their memories.[70]

The small plow is also a rhetorical tool. It has stood for productivity and the possibilities of a fecund landscape, as opposed to the destruction of war and violence. The biblical verse "They will beat their swords into plowshares and their spears into pruning hooks" (Isaiah 2:4) suggests the depth of this connection. War no longer seems possible when its violent implements are transformed into a technology of peace and stability.

This metaphor appealed to the leaders of the American Revolution. The Society of the Cincinnati was founded in 1783 by Continental Army officers who hoped to join together to secure money and benefits owed to them by the government. The founders selected a historical figure with a clear association to the land: the great Roman general Cincinnatus. As the Roman historian Livy explains, during a national crisis, a group of senators sought Lucius Quinctius Cincinnatus (520–430 BCE) in his fields. Livy recreates the scene: "whether leaning on a stake in a ditch which he was digging, or in the employment of ploughing, engaged at least on some rural work, as is certain, after mutual salutations had passed, being requested by the ambassadors to put on his gown, and listen to the commands of the senate."[71] He agreed to serve as dictator to save Rome. When his duty was done, he relinquished his power peacefully and returned to his fields.

This tale appealed to the former Continental Army officers: Civic duty forced them to serve, while their homes and farms demanded their attention once the war ended. George Washington was sometimes compared to Cincinnatus because he chose to return to Mount Vernon after two terms in office. The obverse of the medal of the Society of the Cincinnati depicts Cincinnatus as he is about to serve his country—on his left a sword, on his right a plow. Perhaps these noble associations were part of the meanings that this plow had for the family of General Artemas Ward?

Prior to the adoption of a singular national currency, plows even appeared on printed banknotes along with ships to indicate the forces that drove the economy of early New England.[72] In this context, a plow suggested an investment and a bright future through individual labor made possible by a stable and peaceful society. What aspects of the plow and its world do these metaphors hide?

Because this tool was used to furrow the land, it highlights the physical realities of farm life in central Massachusetts. Plowing the land is a key step in preparing soil for the cultivation of crops. A plow would break and turn over the earth to allow a farmer to sow seeds. In New England, farming dramatically changed the landscape, as illustrated by the Harvard Forest dioramas. By the mid-nineteenth century, 60–80 percent of New England's forests were cleared to make way for farms. The changing landscape of New England (as well as the day laborers who plowed and transformed it by their work) is central to the story of the plow.[73]

More important, the Wards were not the first people to inhabit the land occupied by their farm. The Nipmuc people have lived in central Massachusetts for thousands of years. In 1762, General (then Colonel) Ward was even appointed guardian of the local Hassanamisco Band of the Nipmucs. Members of the Hassanamisco Nipmuc likely made several items in the Ward house, including the general's snowshoes and a grain riddle, a farm tool for separating grain from chaff.[74] Ownership of land has been the key political issue for Native peoples like the Nipmuc since European settlers first arrived. The Hassanamisco Indian Museum presents the situation succinctly: "The 3½ acre Hassanamisco Reservation is the last portion of a 1728 land grant made to the Nipmuc tribe by the Massachusetts Bay Colony whose eager colonists were clamoring to settle on the tribe's original grant of 7500 acres." The complex history of the tribe's land ownership has been central to the federal government's decision not to recognize the group as a nation, though the tribe has long been recognized by the Commonwealth of Massachusetts. Plows like this one transformed Nipmuc land into settled farms. In this context, is the plow still a symbol of peace and prosperity? Is it still the opposite of the sword?[75]

S. A. C.

A Carved Bird Skull: Nature or Culture?

Visitors to an art museum would not expect to see a specimen from a natural history museum. There is usually no place in the Harvard Art Museums for any of the approximately twenty-one million things in the Museum of Comparative Zoology. Artworks and natural history specimens do not mix. Westerners regard them as fundamentally different in kind. Not only are the latter things in nature, ostensibly originating and existing independently of human volition and action, but Westerners regard what they designate as artworks as the most thoughtfully contrived and effectively invested of human creations. To draw attention to at least some of the ambiguities inherent in the fundamental Western distinction between things in nature and things in culture, we chose a thing from the collection of the Museum of Comparative Zoology that itself exemplifies the natural world but that has clearly been subjected to human intervention. That thing is the skull of a bird called the helmeted hornbill.[76] It retains its natural appearance as a bird skull, with some colorful feathers attached, but its unusually prominent upper bill has been elaborately carved.

All natural history specimens are in some sense human artifacts in that each has been selected, prepared, and exists as it does solely in consequence of human intervention. A taxidermy mount may be derived from

122. An alcove off a painting gallery at the Arthur M. Sackler Museum displayed a large eighteenth-century album of bird sketches and a nineteenth-century skull of a helmeted hornbill as part of *Tangible Things* in 2011. The album is the work of Jean-Baptiste Oudry and his assistants who rendered ninety-six bird studies in black ink and watercolor. It belongs to the Fogg Museum, which, like the Sackler, is part of the Harvard Art Museums. The helmeted hornbill (*Rhinoplax vigil*) is an ornithology specimen of the Museum of Comparative Zoology.

123. Art and nature are combined on the carved skull of this helmeted hornbill. The *Rhinoplax vigil* specimen was collected in Sumatra, Borneo, or the Malay Peninsula and then traded to China, where an artist intricately carved the upper beak and forehead of the thick skull. Museum of Comparative Zoology.

a once-living creature, treated to preserve its external appearance, so that it seems to be a living thing momentarily arrested. But in spite of using parts of the actual body of the creature it represents, it is no less contrived than a waxwork. Insofar as it is derived directly from a creature, a mount is natural; insofar as it is the result of human contrivance, it is an artifact. Similarly, though not identically, the helmeted hornbill skull from the Museum of Comparative Zoology is a thing in nature and a natural history specimen insofar as it retains its identity as a preserved bird body part, and an artifact—indeed an artwork—insofar as it embodies human creativity manifested through carving.

The helmeted hornbill (*Rhinoplax vigil*) is native to the rainforests of Southeast Asia, from southern Myanmar and southern Thailand through the Malay Peninsula to the islands of Sumatra and Borneo. For more than 150 years, Western scholars appear to have known only the head and bill of a bird that remained mysterious. In 1599, the Bolognese naturalist Ulisse Aldrovandi described and illustrated a specimen then in the collection of the grand duke of Tuscany in Florence in the first volume of his great work on ornithology.[77] He thought that it had come from India via Damascus and Venice with the name Semenda. In 1758, the naturalist and librarian to the Royal College of Physicians, George Edwards, published an illustrated description, again known to him only from a skull, in the first supplementary volume to his *A Natural History of Uncommon Birds* (1758). Evidently, he was not acquainted with Aldrovandi's account:

C is the Beak of a Bird unknown to us: it was lent to me by the obliging Mr. Furzer, of New-Inn, London, who told me it was brought from the island of Sumatra, in the East Indies, where it is called the

124. The eye is painted wood. It is glued to the bird skull along with white feathers painted red and greenish yellow. Museum of Comparative Zoology.

Friendly Wood-bird, as its Indian name imports; and that it defends men from danger when they sleep in the woods. . . . I take this Bill to be very rare, as I have not seen a second of it; and I believe this to be the first figure of it that was ever published.[78]

In 1780, the Comte de Buffon included the helmeted hornbill in his monumental study of natural history as the ninth species of the Calao, or rhinoceros birds. He cites Edwards's description and notes: "We have nothing of this bird but the bill."[79] A year later, professor of natural history and mineralogy at the University of Halle and celebrated as the naturalist on James Cook's second voyage of circumnavigation between 1772 and 1775, also based his description in his *Indische Zoologie* on that of Edwards.[80]

The use of the term *casque* (helmet) to describe the upper part of the bill is due to Buffon. The birds, which can be up to five feet in length, use their solid and weighty casques to break up rotting wood and dislodge bark in search of edible insects. Long-distance trade between Southeast Asian maritime regions and China was established by the thirteenth century, Borneo being the major source of helmeted hornbill casques for the Chinese trade.[81] Though softer than ivory, the keratin casque is solid. Chinese connoisseurs came to value this unusual material even more highly than ivory or jade.[82] Most likely emulating indigenous Borneo artists, Chinese artists skilled in the carving of this exotic imported material produced miniature figurative relief sculptures. The casque of the Harvard skull is carved with a celebrated scene from China's partly mythological and partly historical past: King Wen's discovery of the retired statesman Jiang Ziya while fishing. Born Ji Chang, King Wen of Zhou ruled between 1099 and 1050 BCE. With Jiang's advice, King Wen helped to overthrow the Shang dynasty and is honored

125. The carving depicts a well-known Chinese story: King Wen of the Zhou dynasty discovers the long-retired statesman Jiang Ziya fishing without a hook. Jiang Ziya had earlier served King Zhou, the last ruler of the Shang dynasty, but after coming to hate the tyrant, he retreated into seclusion, hoping that he might someday help to overthrow him. He waited a long time with the philosophy that the fish would come to him of its own volition when it was ready. Curious about this improbable method of fishing, King Wen begins a conversation with the old man and realizes that he is the advisor he has long sought. Jiang Ziya becomes his minister and later helps his son, King Wu, conquer the Shang dynasty. Museum of Comparative Zoology.

as the founder of the Zhou dynasty.[83] Often—as in the present case—the artist embellished the upper mandible with decorative motifs. Another use in China was to cut casques into sheets that could be colored with the secretion of the bird's preen gland, giving them a red sheen, that were then carved to form high-status ornamental belt buckles.[84] The nineteenth century was the peak in this trade and art form. Thereafter, the dwindling population of helmeted hornbills owing to relentless hunting led to a decline.

As a thing out of place, we installed our particular helmeted hornbill skull from the Ornithology Department of the Museum of Comparative Zoology beside an album of watercolor drawings of birds in the Arthur M. Sackler Museum of the Harvard Art Museums. The parchment-covered album consists of eighty-three leaves of off-white antique laid paper onto which some of the ninety-six drawings have been

126. Are you looking at me?
A watercolor drawing of a bird in
Jean-Baptiste Oudry's avian album.
Harvard Art Museums/
Fogg Museum.

127. A bird with attitude marches
across the page of an avian album
of watercolor drawings by French
artist Jean-Baptiste Oudry, from the
first half of the eighteenth century.
Harvard Art Museums/
Fogg Museum.

pasted, while others have been drawn directly on the leaves. They are by the French eighteenth-century artist Jean-Baptiste Oudry and his associates.[85] Oudry was employed by King Louis XV of France to paint animals and birds associated with the royal hunt, and by the duke of Mecklenburg-Schwerin to paint rare birds and animals in his menagerie.

Rather than relying on the direct observation of actual birds, Oudry and his associates derived most of the drawings in the album from images by earlier artists and from decorations on imported Chinese porcelains. Unlike the illustrations in natural history publications, such as those of Edwards, Buffon, and Forster, these representations were not attempts at a methodical, comprehensive identification and categorization of bird species. Rather, they served as models for further artworks, notably for prints used by other artists as patterns for decorations on ceramics, textiles, and furniture. All these endeavors, however—those of the Chinese sculptors no less than the European naturalists and artists—served to domesticate the exotic. Just as helmeted hornbill skulls were rarities from distant foreign lands for the Chinese, so were the Chinese ceramics from which

Oudry and his associates derived their drawings of birds. The exoticism of distance and difference outweighs a distinction between art and nature.

We further embedded the helmeted hornbill skull from the Museum of Comparative Zoology within the display of European and American art in the Arthur M. Sackler Museum by placing the case containing the skull and the album in a niche flanked by two other objects from the Harvard Art Museums chosen to reinforce the context of mid-eighteenth-century French artistic practice. On the right, we hung an etching after a portrait of Jean-Baptiste Oudry by Nicolas de Largillière. Elaborated with additional framing elements, it was executed by Oudry's wife, Marie-Marguerite Froissé.[86] On the left, we placed a trompe l'oeil still-life painting of woodcock and quail carcasses hanging against a plain wall by Oudry and Froissé's son, Jacques-Charles Oudry, who had been taught by his father.[87] Specializing in painting animals, the hunt, and its trophies, the younger Oudry spent much of his career at the Habsburg court in Brussels in the Austrian Netherlands.

The juxtaposition enhanced the apparent exoticism of the Southeast Asian helmeted hornbill skull, embellished by a Chinese sculptor for a Chinese market—no European recipient was intended or expected—by appearing culturally out of place. Further, its undisguised animal appearance—its transformation had not superseded or concealed its natural origin as the head of a bird—contrasted with the total transformation of all other natural materials used by artists to create their paintings, prints, and drawings in the immediate, as well as the general, proximity. The helmeted hornbill skull allowed viewers to consider the ambiguity of distinctions: between the domestic and the exotic, whether between the European world and Asia or within different parts of Asia itself; between a thing in nature collected and classified in a zoology museum, and things clearly human-made as artworks within an art museum. Are these distinctions quite as clear-cut as the characters of the institutions that usually house them would suggest?

I. G.

CHAPTER FOUR

Things in Stories—Stories in Things

As an exhibition, *Tangible Things* emphasized categories. As an undergraduate course, it focused on stories. The overall goal was to explore the long and complex history of Harvard's relationship with the worlds beyond its gates, although we regard Harvard as just one institution among many amenable to this kind of investigation. Initially, we looked for two kinds of stories—stories that included objects and stories about objects.

Stories about objects often begin with a basic set of questions: What is it? Who made it? How did it get here? What is it worth? These questions produce narratives about provenance and value, the kinds of stories that dealers and collectors require and that viewers of the popular PBS television show *Antiques Roadshow* have come to expect. Historians, on the other hand, usually reach for a bigger set of questions. For them, the focus is seldom on the objects themselves but on larger themes that objects might evoke or illustrate. As a consequence, in historical narratives, objects usually play at best a supporting role. The usual strategy is simply to acknowledge the existence of each object—as the first, the oldest, the most important, or the most telling example of whatever it is the narrator is trying to tell. Both of these approaches have value. Our task was to bring them together. When seemingly narrow queries about where things came from and how they got there are placed next to seemingly bigger questions, interesting things begin to happen. Sometimes the central characters in a story change. Sometimes entirely new stories begin to emerge.

Harvard's history, like much conventional history, has often been about "great men," the presidents, professors, and graduates who have made Harvard what one local newspaper columnist sardonically refers to as TWGU, "The World's Greatest University." This kind of history is, of course, a variant of the classic nineteenth-century narrative about the progress of Western civilization, or the familiar American story about expanding opportunities. Lots of things in our exhibition could fit into a narrative about famous people and oldest things: a surviving volume from John Harvard's library, bequeathed in 1683,[1] beside which, in the lobby of Houghton Library, we installed a fragment of a dress said to have belonged to Priscilla Mullins, a member of Massachusetts's Plymouth Colony;[2] the blue sash worn by George Washington in 1776 when he took command of the Revolutionary Army;[3] and, moving forward into the nineteenth century, Louis Agassiz's microscope[4] and Henry David Thoreau's pencil.[5] There are many firsts at Harvard and a lot of things to brag about.

But a closer look at almost any object in the exhibition forces revision of the triumphal story. For one thing, Harvard was not always first. The nation's first serious museum was not in Cambridge but in Philadelphia, where the painter Charles Willson Peale began exhibiting art works and "Wonders of Nature" as early as 1786. Washington apparently gave his blue sash to Peale after the painter had used it in a set of portraits. It was on display at Peale's museum until the museum closed in 1846, after which much of the collection was sold to P. T. Barnum who apparently passed the sash along with other relics to his partner Moses Kimball, creator of the entrepreneurial Boston Museum. In 1899, Kimball's heirs attempted to deposit Washington's sash at Harvard's Peabody Museum, but the Peabody rejected it, passing it along to Boston's Old South Association, which eventually gave it back even though there was little enthusiasm at Harvard for such a piece of Americana. It remained in storage until an enterprising intern ran across it about the time we were searching for objects for *Tangible Things*. Happenstance, as well as fore-sight, built Harvard's collections. A Yankee reluctance to throw things away may have preserved some of today's most treasured items.

Harvard's strangely assembled but demonstrably rich collections have many stories to tell. According to college lore, John Downame's *The Christian Warrior*, published in London in 1634, is the only rem-nant of John Harvard's original bequest of books to survive the 1764 fire that destroyed the library in Harvard Hall. It survived because it was checked out (and overdue). It is now kept in a special case in the lobby of Houghton Library, treated more as a relic than as a document. But what if we tried to situate the book and the 1764 fire in a bigger story? The elaborately illustrated title page of the book uses baroque imagery to illustrate a Christian theme—a war with the devil and his minions. Within a year of John Harvard's death, this cosmic war had become a literal war as Massachusetts Bay Colony joined Connecticut Colony, Saybrook Colony, and Plymouth Colony forces in an attempt to exterminate the Pequots.

Over the next century, Harvard men fought the forces of "savagery" on the one hand and "popery" on the other with arms, and sometimes with books. Tiny pieces of type excavated in Harvard Yard document the presence of a crude press set up at the so-called Indian College. The English Society for the Propagation of the Gospel in New England funded the creation of the brick Indian College around 1655 with the goal of educating Native Americans who would supposedly then carry the gospel into their home communities. Cash-strapped Harvard welcomed the donation. Between 1655 and 1672, the Indian College press turned out psalm books, almanacs, and an Algonquian translation of the Bible, supporting early hopes of converting pacified Indians. But a devastating war in 1675–76 between settlers and Indians ended that dream. Caleb Cheeshahteaumuck, class of 1665, was the first Wampanoag to graduate from Harvard College. Tiffany Smalley, class of 2011, was the second. Other artifacts in Harvard's collections, including a bow seized during one of many conflicts between colonists and local Indians, help to explain that astonishing gap.[6] The imagery of war on Downame's title page was prophetic.

The "cabinet of curiosities" lost in the library fire of 1764 included the skull of an Indian warrior and also a piece of tanned "Negro skin." Harvard's history, like the broader history of the United States, is laced with stories of racial conflict, violence, and despair. The tangible things documenting these stories range widely, from a woodcut made by Peter Fleet, the enslaved assistant to an eighteenth-century Boston printer[7]; an engraved teapot that the eighteenth-century English dictionary maker Samuel Johnson bequeathed to his African servant[8]; swatches of so-called "Negro cloth" from an antebellum textile manufacturer[9]; and a set of daguerreotypes that Louis Agassiz commissioned of South Carolina slaves in the hope of substantiating his theory of polygenesis, the idea that Africans and whites had separate ancestors.[10] When taken seriously, such objects push beyond the self-congratulation that is so much a staple of any institutional history. They also locate Harvard in larger histories of racism and race-based violence and conflict.

Some objects at first glance seem to have little to do with either Harvard's or the nation's larger history. At the General Artemas Ward House Museum in Shrewsbury, for example, locks of hair, bits of fabric, and shards of broken crockery memorialize dead relatives. But among a collection of tools in an old box, one of our seminar students found a piece of bone with curious carving that looked like it might have been the handle of some sort of implement. After assiduous research, he identified it as the handle of a quirt, a riding whip brought from Nebraska by a westward-leaning son who had apparently secured it from the Ponca Indians living near his homestead.[11] A different set of stories from the Great Plains survives in a set of busts derived from life masks taken from Plains Indian warriors imprisoned in Florida between 1875 and 1878.[12] Some of the prisoners, including a man named Nock-ko-ist, anglicized as Bear's Heart, ended up at the Hampton Institute, an institution dedicated to the education of American Indians, as well as freed slaves. A ceramic plate decorated by Nock-ko-ist was among the objects displayed in the "muddle."[13]

The pressed seaweed in the *natural history* section of the exhibit fits comfortably into its category.[14] It is not just a scientific specimen, however.

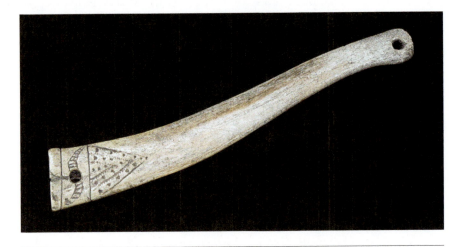

128. The incised bone handle of a quirt (riding whip), made in Nebraska by Omaha or Ponca people, ca. 1870–90, was found among a box of tools in Shrewsbury, Massachusetts. Although at first it appeared unrelated to anything or anyone associated with the General Artemas Ward House, the quirt handle is in fact a tangible link between the local family and a relative who had ventured west to establish a homestead on the prairie. General Artemas Ward House Museum.

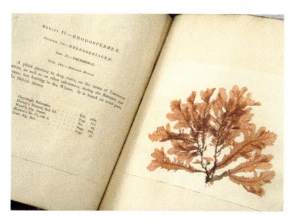

129. A book of dried seaweeds combines artfully pressed plants with their technical descriptions. John Cocks, *Algarum Fasciculi; or A Collection of British Sea-weeds, Carefully Dried and Preserved, and correctly named after Dr. Harvey's "Phycologia Britannica"* (Dublin, 1855). Farlow Herbarium of Cryptogamic Botany, Harvard University Herbaria.

It is a cultural expression. Harvard's abundant collections of pressed plants show how a passion for botany brought together laypersons and scientists, women and men, in an enterprise that engaged both scientific curiosity and sentiment. To take just one example, the Emily Dickinson Herbarium in Houghton Library,[15] documents more than the poet's engagement with nature. Through a mutual interest in botany, she and her friend and future editor, Thomas Wentworth Higginson, expressed their mutual concerns with the fecundity and transience of material life.[16] The collection and classification of botanical specimens also united science and art in the work of Blanche Ames Ames, who used her skills as an artist to illustrate her husband's vast collection of orchids. A close look at Ames's work brings together still other narrative topics—from a shovel factory to the aesthetic orchidaciousness of Oscar Wilde.

The lectures in our undergraduate course provided a chronological narrative of Harvard history, moving from John Harvard's library through the astronomical explorations of the eighteenth century into the romance of transcendentalism and the rise of Louis Agassiz and his peers, and then from the World's Columbian Exposition of 1893 to the codification of new disciplines like anthropology into the twentieth-century expansion of museums and archives. But cutting across that linear narrative was the exhibition itself with its built-in tension between stability and change. Working with the seemingly smaller stories found in material things, students discovered related ideas about race, gender, and sexuality, puzzling interfaces between science, art, and everyday life, and both disturbing and inspiring narratives about the buildings, monuments, and legends that surround them. Choosing their own entry points into the exhibition, they also discovered the challenges and joys of creating history.

On a smaller scale, the exhibit offered these same opportunities to our visitors. The labels and brief audio prompts that we provided via cell phones suggested only a few of the stories that lay hidden in our seemingly miscellaneous agglomeration. The body language of our visitors told us that our experiment with open-ended display was working. After a few minutes in the gallery, most visitors found themselves bending over to peer more closely at objects that caught their attention. It was not just that the typeface on our labels might have been too small. People really did want to get close to the things that engaged them. This curious collection of objects provoked questions that in turn invited people to tell their own stories—about things they had seen, experiences they had had, or narratives they hoped might be true.

Tangible things are inseparable from the stories people create about them as they find them, make them, use them, and then use them again in different ways. One of the complex uses of objects is their identification and collection, often followed by a further refinement of their initial categorizations. This is a prime way in which Westerners have made knowledge claims about things in the world. Historians can use all this data—the succession of stories and the things themselves—to understand how people use tangible things in endlessly varying and frequently changing ways to articulate their relations with one another, individually and communally, and with the worlds they inhabit. The past accounts for most of human existence, and in telling and retelling ever-changing stories about the past, translating it to the present, historians have the opportunity—too infrequently taken—to make use of tangible things, those often bewildering and confusing material traces of the past. We hope that readers of this book might be inspired to tell their own stories about the past and its relations with the present by making use of tangible things they have at hand.

Objects as Portals

All human-made material things have the potential to convey information—and in some cases, they even convey viewers to another world or state of being. Three items in *Tangible Things* exist as portals to constellations of powerful human sentiment that seem to dwarf the six nineteenth-century categories often employed to sort and contain material things. Missives from deceased relatives and friends, warnings about evil spirits, and the possibility of everlasting love all take material forms. Stories unlock these intangible emotions and ideas.

Sometimes objects directly communicate the incorporeal. Spirit writing or automatic writing was a method employed in the nineteenth and early twentieth centuries to allow the living to communicate with the dead through mediums. Spiritualists, as believers were called, advocated that a mere veil separated life and death. Trained practitioners allowed the living to talk to their departed loved ones. A small schoolroom slate offers just such messages from the spirit world:

Blessed sister

I preached what I believed was truth, but I found myself far away from it at times. The heaven I taught people to go to was too narrow and selfish to hold even the people of Elmira. I have had my eyes opened, and by the grace of Christ I no longer preach Episcopalian fol-de-rol.

Rev. (crossed out) S.D. [B . . . illegible]

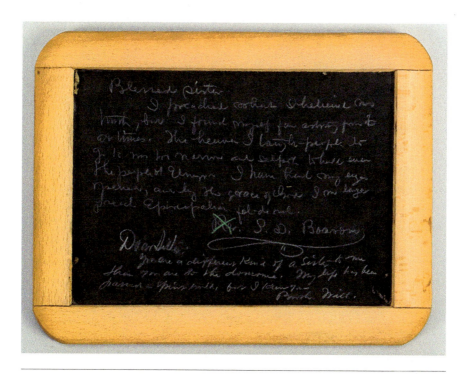

130. Messages to the living from the dead were conveyed through "automatic writing" in chalk on a portable slate sometime between 1882 and 1919, and were treasured by the Herrick family. Arthur and Elizabeth Schlesinger Library on the History of Women in America.

131. A close view of the slate with "spirit writing," showing a revision of the text of one spirit by another. Arthur and Elizabeth Schlesinger Library on the History of Women in America.

Dear Sister:
You are a different kind of a sister to me than you are to the d....My
    life has been passed [in?] spirit world, but I know you.
Brother Will[17]

Here, two spirits are sending messages to a living friend. One is a disgruntled minister, who seems to have found the failings of his faith after death; the other, "Brother Will," announces himself to his sister. Neither can be identified with certainty, though these objects were passed down in the Herrick family and are preserved as part of the family papers in the Schlesinger Library. Sometime between 1882 and 1919, spirits visited the home of Louisa Herrick, a wife, mother, and minister living in upstate New York, who had turned to spiritualism to support her family. The slates may not be definitively identified, but what is certain is that they document what was supposed to be an ephemeral encounter, linking life and death with a trace of chalk on a board. This message was supposed to be wiped clean for future communications, yet it was preserved. Perhaps this trace provided the living with comforting proof that their loved ones were not gone.[18]

These everyday chalkboards were transformed through a specific set of religious practices into portals. An individual's encounter with these common objects and their deliberate misuse (for spirit writing rather than schoolroom ciphering) imbued these objects with the power to transport viewers to another world. Reading the slate that contains father Oman Herrick's note to his daughter, "Did you see me come in the door? It seems so strange to me that I may come here and write, stand beside you and you not be conscious of it," one wonders, is he still here? Would touching the slate be like touching his hand?

In 1853, American sculptor Harriet Hosmer made a cast of the clasped hands of the poets Elizabeth Barrett Browning and her husband Robert Browning.[19] Nathaniel Hawthorne described this evocative cast in his 1859 romance *The Marble Faun* as "symbolizing the individuality and heroic union of two high, poetic lives."[20] The hands each clearly belong to a unique individual, with Elizabeth Barrett Browning's hand finished with a delicate dress edge and a narrow ruffled cuff, resting within her husband's hand, his wrist encircled with pressed shirtsleeve. The two hands appear to have equal parts in creating the sculpture. Though

132. This plaster cast of the clasped hands of poets Robert and Elizabeth Barrett Browning commemorated a friendship between the American sculptor Harriet Hosmer, who made the original cast in Rome in 1853, and the nineteenth century's most famous literary couple. Arthur and Elizabeth Schlesinger Library on the History of Women in America.

133. A loving touch and partnership are evident in the wrapping of Robert Browning's fingers around those of his wife Elizabeth. Arthur and Elizabeth Schlesinger Library on the History of Women in America.

Elizabeth's hand is inside that of her husband's, it is not dwarfed by it. Instead there is a sense of partnership. More of her hand is visible than his. Instead of a handshake, the left and right hands are clasped, one right and one left, as if created side by side. As Elizabeth declared in her poem "A Man's Requirements," "Love me with thine hand stretched out / Freely—open-minded," Robert's hand is open to receive hers.

Perhaps Hawthorne saw their union as heroic because the sickly Elizabeth defied her family and was disinherited to marry the younger and relatively unknown artist, or perhaps because they sought to live in a world defined by poetry, art, and aesthetics. The clasped hands conveyed that message to Hawthorne and seem to convey the depth of their relationship to modern viewers.

To Hosmer, the hands were an eternal representation of the intimate moment in which they were cast. She noted in a speech she gave in Chicago in 1896 that she cast the hands herself: Elizabeth only consented to the procedure "provided that you [Hosmer] cast them yourself. I will not sit for a formatore."[21] Hosmer explained that she resisted recasting the hands in brass or anything more permanent than plaster, the pink flesh-colored plaster of the hands in the Schlesinger Library. The pinkish cast feels immediate, intimate, and frail. The hands are very precise, with the bones and veins apparent, suggesting the specificity and individualism that Hawthorne noted. Plaster seems more accessible and touchable than the bronze version at the Metropolitan Museum of Art. In the same speech, Hosmer also exclaimed, "It will be interesting to see the handwriting of these hands." These hands are a link to the poetry and letters the Brownings wrote—their heroically romantic works—as well as to their love.

134. A divination basket on a gourd base, containing fifty-four items, belonged to
a diviner among the Chokwe people in the Benguela Highlands, Angola, at the
beginning of the twentieth century. Peabody Museum of Archaeology and Ethnology,
Harvard University.

The sickly Elizabeth predeceased her husband by almost three decades.
She was buried in the Protestant cemetery in Florence. Clasped hands
have been a symbol for relationships, as in Masonic links, as well as marriage, for millennia. In the nineteenth century, clasped hands could appear
on sailor's bodies as tattoos or on tombstones as symbols of unity even after
death. Perhaps such a symbol links to the final line of Elizabeth's still
most famous poem, "How do I love thee, If God choose / I shall but love
thee better after death." The Brownings' clasped hands suggest a love that
lasted beyond earthly concerns.

Rev. Merlin W. Ennis, a member of the American Board of Foreign
Commissioners, was not necessarily thinking of the ethereal in this way
when he donated a divination basket to Harvard in 1939.[22] Because Ennis
was a Congregational Christian missionary working in Angola, this divination basket probably had no spiritual meaning for him. By deposit-
ing it in a museum when he returned to his home in Massachusetts, he
confirmed its status as simply a cultural curiosity. It was a document of
a "passing" culture.[23] Yet, for the Chokwe people who likely relied upon

this *lipele*, the Luvale term for a divination basket, it was a tool for revealing the unseen aspects of daily life and the future. It was a vehicle through which one could understand the everyday and its profound challenges. It was also a means of communicating. It was both a material object like a stool or a house and simultaneously sentient, "capable of thinking, hearing, judging, and responding."[24] In this way, it became a gateway to other, often hidden, aspects of life.

The basket is woven from plant fiber, probably *jikenge* roots, on a gourd base and is filled with fifty-four divination objects, *jipelo*, employed by a diviner. The *jipelo* include a range of animal bones, carved wooden and shaped clay figurines, a wooden spool, a bottle stopper, various plants and seeds, jewelry, and even a miniature basket. Typically, such baskets would be woven by postmenopausal women and then "stolen" by diviners through a ritual process. Diviners, with community help, would then fill a new *lipele* with *jipelo* from an old, worn out basket. Through a specific initiation ritual, the basket and its accoutrements acquire the ability to convey information about the underlying causes of human suffering and daily events.

Through a process of chanting and shaking the *lipele*, a diviner reveals patterns in *jipelo* inside the basket, explaining why illness, death, or other misfortunes affect his clients. In the hands of a skilled practitioner, such a *lipele* allows one to access an unseen world. Patterns of objects could be read, just like spirit writing on a chalkboard. By removing this object from its context, Rev. Ennis ended its spiritual life cycle. Its *jipelo* could

135. When juxtaposed with other items in the Chokwe divination basket through the act of shaking, these human figurines helped the diviner interpret the misfortunes of his clients. Peabody Museum of Archaeology and Ethnology, Harvard University.

136. A spotted blue cloth tied around an unknown thing and bound to a bundle of small sticks is one of many mysterious items in the Chokwe divination basket. Peabody Museum of Archaeology and Ethnology, Harvard University.

no longer serve ritual purposes. This thing, which anthropologists view as both a "way of doing" and a "way of knowing," loses its ability to give diviners access to hidden information. It ceases to serve as a portal to another side of the world.[25]

Lost loved ones, romantic love, and personal suffering rarely appear in museum settings, though these themes are central to the lives of visitors. These intimate feelings are seldom discussed in public, but some material things have the potential to invoke these abstract concepts. Perhaps these feelings seem most at home in an anthropological setting, like the Peabody Museum of Archaeology and Ethnology, where objects like the Angolan divination basket may be contextualized, sanitized, tamed, and explained. In the Peabody Museum, however, the basket loses its ritual power—it is no longer associated with a diviner, and it is far away from any potential petitioner. It has lost its ability to discern the causes of sickness or death, to see the forces that shape daily life. The spirit writing slate is also related to religious practice, but it is drawn from a historical collection. While the exact source of its creation is hazy, this chalkboard supposedly documents a specific communication from the spirit world to ours, one in which spirits actually address and sign their missives—from a father to his dear daughter, from a brother to a sister, from a reformed Anglican minister to a medium. These messages retain the specificity of their historical context and still seem to pierce through the veil between life and death.

Both the divination basket and the spirit writing slate may be best understood in the context of the religious practices of the people who created them, whether members of the Chokwe culture group in Angola in the mid-twentieth century or a family of spiritualists and ministers from upstate New York in the late nineteenth and early twentieth centuries. They both required a translator, whether a diviner or a medium, to link users to an unseen reality. In a similar way, the cast hands of Elizabeth and Robert Browning became a vehicle for eternal love only through the work of artist Harriet Hosmer. In the end, the thing on display is simply the portal, the means to touch and access the material knowledge shaped by Hosmer's hands, the shaky writing traced by the Herrick family medium, or the dozens of *jipelo* arranged and shaken in a diviner's *lipele*. It is not just the things that matter. Rather, it is the people they allow us to remember, touch, and meet. Tangible things open doors to human feelings, emotions, and states of being that would otherwise disappear with their owners. As Hosmer noted above her sketch of the Brownings' clasped hands, "Parted in death we say, / Yet hand in hand they hold their eternal way."[26] And hand in hand, they will remain in an archival box in the Schlesinger Library.

S. A. C.

A Nostalgic Painting: The Message

Edward Lamson Henry's little painting *The Message* tells a small story that, when interpreted in the context of its time, tells a much larger story about the relationship between race and gender in the United States in the late nineteenth century.[27]

Henry completed the painting in 1893, too late for inclusion in the World's Columbian Exposition held in Chicago that year, though it would have been right at home among his other works displayed there. His massive canvas *The First Railroad Train on the Mohawk and Hudson Road* appeared in the Transportation Building alongside an antique engine. It memorialized an event that took place in 1831, ten years before he was born. Henry traded in nostalgia. Born in South Carolina, he served for a time on a Union transport ship during the Civil War. After the war, he studied painting in Europe and established a studio in Greenwich Village, but he was ambivalent about progress. Like other white Americans, he was also conflicted about the consequences of a new racial order that seemed to be emerging. In his works, African Americans usually appeared as relics of a lost world of simplicity and racial harmony.[28]

In *The Message*, a young white woman perched on the seat of a rustic wagon reaches toward a small black boy standing on the road beside her. She is the dominant figure in the scene, poised on a pedestal-like seat with her bright blue bonnet shimmering in the sun. But he holds the message alluded to in the title. Is it a love letter? A summons to the bedside of a dying friend? An invitation to a party? Whatever its meaning, the contents are safe because the little go-between probably cannot read. He is ragged. His elbows poke out of a torn shirt; suspenders hold up his too-big trousers. In the background, looking over a railed fence, a woman who might be his mother stands beside another child. Is she the silent monitor of the story or an unknown player? We cannot know.

In an age when new barriers of race were coalescing in both the North and the South, Henry's painting represented more than nostalgia. As tensions over race and sex came together in an epidemic of lynching, a

137. In 1893, Edward Lamson Henry painted *The Message,* a nostalgic scene of a white woman in a wagon stopping alongside a black boy standing on the dusty road and holding a letter. Henry used his large collection of Americana in his Catskills home as source material for anecdotal paintings of rural places in earlier times that, by the late nineteenth century, seemed a remote ideal. Harvard Art Museums/Fogg Museum.

young journalist named Ida Wells Barnett joined the venerable abolitionist Frederick Douglass to protest the refusal of the committee for the World's Columbian Exposition to include displays by the nation's blacks. In a powerful essay, Douglass confronted the nation over its inability to fulfill the promises of emancipation. "We have long had in this country, a system of iniquity which possessed the power of blinding the moral perception, stifling the voice of conscience, blunting all human sensibilities and perverting the plainest teaching of the religion we have here professed.... That system was American slavery. Though it is now gone, its asserted spirit remains."[29] In this context, the railed fence that extends across the width of the picture seems to be a racial boundary. Its meaning is ambiguous. The boy is on the same side of the fence as the white woman, though he is clearly subordinate. Is she his teacher? His benefactor? A symbol of a better world?

Central to the racial politics of the fair was the elevation of white women, as symbols and as individuals. The symbolism was most apparent in the statuary surrounding the Grand Basin. The dominant figure was a sixty-five-foot-high statue of *The Republic*, a female figure by Daniel Chester French. Unlike the *Statue of Liberty*, which had recently been erected in New York Harbor, the fair's *Republic* was less a mother of exiles than an imperial mascot. In one hand, she held a liberty cap suspended on a long pike, in the other, an eagle-topped globe. Resplendent in gold leaf, she wore a crown of electric lights on her head. Though elevated, she was a static figure, fixed to her pedestal, seemingly unconnected to the real world and lacking feminist energy.[30]

She had living imitations at the exposition. Although Bertha Honoré Palmer, the chairwoman of the exposition's "Lady Managers," insisted that American women were ready to step down from their pedestals, her own portrait showed her in a glistening white gown with a diamond tiara on her head and a sparkling scepter in one hand.[31] Even more intriguing was the participation of May Sheldon French, a Midwestern woman who, after marrying into wealth, became by her own estimation the first white

138. *The Republic* was a formidable sixty-five-foot-tall statue of a woman holding a liberty cap on a pike and an orb surmounted by an eagle. Sculpted by Daniel Chester French, she stood guard at the World's Columbian Exposition in Chicago. This image is taken from *Harper's Weekly*, 1893. Widener Library, Harvard Library.

woman to explore the African interior. Brandishing a pistol and clad in a regal gown spun from silver extracted from her own mines, she awed sultans and tribal monarchs, carrying a banner suspended from her walking stick with the Latin phrase *noli me tangere*, "touch me not." In Chicago, she regaled audiences at both the Congress of Women and the Congress of Anthropology.[32] She presented herself as an exemplar of a new kind of colonialism, one achieved not by military might, but by "the establishment of industrial manual training stations and medical and nurses' posts, and the presence of practical, honest, sober, decent, industrious white men and women, whose daily life will carry the highest precepts of enlightenment."[33]

Sheldon won an award for the exhibit of her "Palanquin Camp Outfit," equipment that allowed her to serve tea in proper style while on safari. The certificate, used for all the awards at the exposition, not only exemplified her concept of feminized imperialism but the iconography of the fair itself. In the upper left corner of the page, a resplendent Goddess of Liberty extends her benevolent hand toward three naked children, each representing a different part of the as-yet "uncivilized" world.[34] The certificates elaborated a vision of the world present from the earliest age of European exploration of North America and Africa. A white goddess represented both authority and benevolence as half-clothed natives bent to her will. Significantly, the same relationship of dependence is evident even in the earliest antislavery painting in the United States, Samuel Jennings's 1793 *Liberty Displaying the Arts and Sciences*, which features a white goddess (in the guise of a schoolteacher) presiding over an assembly of grateful slaves.[35]

In contrast to the glittering displays of art and commerce in the official buildings of the fair, the Midway offered visitors an imagined journey around the world through a conglomeration of sideshows and ethnographic displays arranged in a continuum from the most to the least civilized nations.[36] *Harper's Illustrated Weekly* published images of nighttime crowds touring the Midway under the glow of electrical lights that emanated from street lamps and looped around the huge ferris wheel that dominated the scene. According to news reports, visitors to the Midway could encounter virtually all the peoples of the world, from the cliff dwellers of New Mexico to the Arctic "Eskimaux." They could ride an Egyptian camel, have tea in an Indian pavilion, or peer at the so-called "Black Amazons" of Dahomey crouching half-naked around their cooking pots. The ideas exemplified in these displays are made explicit in a rude caricature published in *Harper's* of an African American family

139. "Life of Aunt Jemima" was a promotional pamphlet published by the producers of self-rising pancake flour, R. T. Davis Mill and Manufacturing Company of Missouri, ca. 1895. It called pancake-flipping Jemima "the most famous Colored Woman in the world." Arthur and Elizabeth Schlesinger Library on the History of Women in America.

supposedly greeting their former master in the Kentucky Pavilion. When asked what he was doing there, the man replied that he was like an old shoe "dat's been blacked" and had come to get "some polish."[37]

All this has taken us a long way from Henry's little painting. The rough seat of a horse-drawn wagon is a pedestal only in its relation to the ragged figure on the road. Henry surely had no intention of painting an allegory of racial politics or late nineteenth-century Western imperialism. Yet his portrayals of simple people in rural settings conformed to both contemporary notions about the nineteenth century as an age of progress and to a yearning in the heart of an urbanizing and increasingly fractured America for the supposed stability of a seemingly simpler past. For an increasing number of Americans, that nostalgia included a mythical Southern past in which African Americans and their masters lived in peace and harmony. That sort of nostalgia was on display on the Midway in an exhibit sponsored by a Midwestern milling company that featured a former slave named Nancy Green as Aunt Jemima. Clad in a long skirt with a bandanna wrapped around her head, she flipped pancakes for visitors, drawing upon sentimental attachments to old-time Southern cooking to sell Aunt Jemima's now-legendary pancake mix.[38]

The figure of Aunt Jemima was inspired in part by minstrel and vaudeville representations of antebellum slaves, but also by a host of "mammy stories" that centered on the figure of a nurturing servant devoted to the care and feeding of her white owners and their children. Like the Uncle Remus stories of Joel Chandler Harris, they mixed authentic memories of actual persons with sentimentalized notions about racial harmony. Like Henry's painting, these stories reassured white Americans that if interfering northerners and uppity blacks would stay out of the way, respectful relations between African Americans and their former owners might be restored. In this imagined world, a white woman in a blue bonnet required a black woman in a kerchief, and each depended on the other. The dim figure in the background of Henry's painting wears the same sort of headwear as Aunt Jemima, though instead of confronting the viewer with an open-lipped smile, she rests one hand contemplatively on her chin as if she is pondering the significance of the message being exchanged between the boy and the woman in the wagon.

That gesture suggests an alternative reading of *The Message*. Perhaps the note was not passed from the woman to the boy but from the boy to the woman, and before that verbally or in writing from the woman behind the fence. The power of a painting like this is that it can convey different meanings to different viewers. Of course, the perceived meanings depend on how the reader imagines the relationships. Did the woman behind the fence have anything to say to the woman in the wagon? One point of connection might be food, as the caricature of Aunt Jemima makes clear. A quite different object in Harvard's collections takes that connection a step further.

What Mrs. Fisher Knows About Old Southern Cooking is a collection of recipes published in San Francisco in 1881. The author did not have the advantage of an education, but she was an expert cook. Born somewhere in the South, she migrated to California after the Civil War. She was no Aunt Jemima. Proud to be called *Mrs.* Fisher, she had won prizes for her pickles and preserves at several California fairs. She may have also worked as a caterer. Impressed by her skill, a San Francisco women's group wrote down her recipes as she described them and then funded the publication of her book. The Southern cooking she described was lavish in its use of butter, eggs, cream, and tropical fruits like pineapples and coconuts. This was cooking as the gentry remembered it, with jellies, custards, and fancy cakes. There were apparently no collard greens in Mrs. Fisher's book. Unlike later ethnic recipe books, it contains only two examples of rural Southern food, one of them misidentified. Her recipe for hoe cakes, a simple mixture of boiling water, cornmeal, and salt, dropped by spoonfuls onto a hot griddle is clear enough.. That the compilers labeled the second recipe "Circuit Hash," demonstrates their reliance on oral transcription.

140. The embossed cover of the first published African American cookbook, *What Mrs. Fisher Knows About Old Southern Cooking* (San Francisco, 1881). Born a slave, Abby Fisher moved to California after the Civil War and established her own business, winning prizes for pickles and preserves and securing the patronage of elite San Franciscans. Arthur and Elizabeth Schlesinger Library on the History of Women in America.

Since the primary ingredients in this dish were sweet corn and beans, they obviously misunderstood the word "succotash."[39]

Despite her dependence on her patrons, Mrs. Fisher commanded respect often denied African Americans in the years after the Civil War. She included only two, seemingly off-hand comments on the kind of life she may have lived before emancipation. Both have to do with the care of her own children. In a recipe for blackberry syrup, used to cure dysentery, she said, "This recipe is an old South plantation remedy among colored people." And in a recipe for infant "pap," she offered a rare autobiographical note: "I have given birth to eleven children and raised them all, and nursed them with this diet. It is a Southern plantation preparation." To raise eleven children to adulthood was something of a miracle for any mother, regardless of her color.[40]

Mrs. Fisher's book carries its own proud message even as it nodded to the nation's fascination with the supposedly harmonious life of pre–Civil War plantations.

L. T. U.

Transits of Venus

In May 1761, John Winthrop packed up "two young gentlemen…, an excellent clock, Hadley's octant…; a refracting telescope,…and a nice reflecting telescope, adjusted by cross levels" and embarked from Boston for Newfoundland to observe the transit of Venus.[41] His departure was hasty. Only days before had the president and fellows of Harvard College approved Professor Winthrop's request to take the college apparatus behind enemy lines to serve the cause of science. Winthrop knew he had no time to waste if he were to reach Newfoundland and properly calibrate his equipment before the imminent transit.[42]

The transit was a rare astronomical alignment in which the planet Venus crossed the face of the Sun as seen from Earth. Transits of Venus occur in an unusual sequence. They happen in pairs that are eight years apart, but the separation from one pair to the next alternates from 105.5 years to 121.5 years. Winthrop's extraordinary pains to travel to St. John's in Newfoundland (1761) and later to Lake Superior (1769) were part of the largest international scientific collaboration ever attempted up to that time. With courage, royal warrants, letters of safe passage, and the best equipment to be had, astronomers set out for St. Helena, Sumatra,

141. Thomas Hancock, uncle of the famous
signer of the Declaration of Independence,
John Hancock, gave Harvard College this
reflecting telescope by Benjamin Martin
of London in 1761. Professor John
Winthrop took it on his transit-of-Venus
expedition to Newfoundland. On
long-term loan to the Collection of
Historical Scientific Instruments from
the Science Museum, London.

142. An instrument for measuring angles
precisely between the Sun, Moon, and stars,
this gilt brass octant was made by Benjamin
Martin of London. It was a 1764 gift to
Harvard College from the town clerk of
Boston, Ezekiel Goldthwait, to replace an
octant he had earlier given to John Winthrop
for use during the transit of Venus. The first
octant had been lost in a fire. Collection of
Historical Scientific Instruments.

Pondicherry, Siberia, and other places remote from Europe to observe
each transit simultaneously from stations scattered all over the globe. The
physical hardships were real, as was the presumption that science should
rise above political conflict. The shared goal was to determine the distance from the Earth to the Sun by triangulation, and hence, the dimensions of the solar system—one of the great unsolved problems of the day.[43]

Much of Winthrop's own story—his provincial professorship, expedition
planning, and scientific results—was shaped by the scientific instruments
at his service. Many of these survive in Harvard's Collection of Historical
Scientific Instruments, where they bear witness to the social and political
entanglements of their acquisition and use by this Harvard astronomer.

When called to act, John Winthrop had the opportunity to be the only
observer of the transit of Venus in North America and the most western
observer internationally on June 6, 1761. As Harvard's Hollis Professor

of Mathematics and Natural Philosophy, he was also the most able and best equipped American astronomer (although not as well equipped as colleagues in Europe). But as late as April, it was not obvious that he would get support for an expedition. He was situated in what Europeans considered an "infant Seminary" and had no personal resources.[44] So he turned to his former student, James Bowdoin, who was now a wealthy merchant, influential political leader, and friend of science. As a member of the Council of the General Court of Massachusetts Bay, he relayed a letter from Winthrop to the royal governor, Francis Bernard, and endorsed it in the council chamber.[45] On April 18, the governor took the request to the House of Representatives and persuaded its members that Massachusetts should not be outdone by European monarchs who were sending warships with mathematicians all over the globe. The assembly agreed to "serve the Cause of Science and do Credit to the Province"[46] by having its sloop carry Winthrop to Newfoundland, and upon his return, reward him with £30, nearly half a year's salary.[47]

With the backing of the governor, the Council, and the House of Representatives of the General Court of Massachusetts Bay, it would have been hard for the president and fellows of Harvard College to say no to the plan when it came up for a vote on May 5, 1761. But Winthrop wanted to take Harvard's finest and newest instruments, which would be at some risk. Winthrop would be sailing into a war zone, for the French and British were still fighting over territories along the northeastern seaboard in the French and Indian War. Fortunately, Governor Bernard had given Winthrop letters of safe passage, addressed to both English and French commanders, to secure the expedition from disappointment by the enemy.[48] On top of this, Harvard required Winthrop to insure the instruments so that it would not suffer if they were lost during the voyage. Winthrop agreed to this condition. Satisfied that care would be taken, Harvard voted to allow its professor and apparatus to be employed in this affair.[49]

On May 5—a spring day during which it snowed!—John Winthrop got the good word. On May 9, he embarked from Boston with two students onboard the sloop chartered by the General Assembly. His destination was Cape Bona Vista, but learning that it was still iced in, he landed in St. John's, Newfoundland, on May 22 with only days to set up his equipment before the transit of Venus on June 6.[50]

Finding St. John's to be bounded on the east with high mountains, Winthrop and his students, Samuel Williams and Isaac Rand, set up their observatory on a hill some distance from the town where the rising Sun could be seen. Winthrop had brought a pendulum clock made by

Thomas Tompion of London around 1675.[51] The ancient clock was no match for modern astronomical regulators that could be had in London, but it was the best available to Winthrop in Boston.

At St. John's, the clock was secured to a tree trunk set into the ground under a tent. (The screw holes are still visible in the case's back.) It was regulated by means of equal altitudes of the Sun observed by a reflecting telescope and gnomon "with an assiduity which the infinite swarms of insects, that were in possession of the hill, were not able to abate, tho' they persecuted us severely and without intermission, both by day and by night, with their venomous stings," Winthrop reported.[52] This telescope was made by Benjamin Martin of London in about 1760, and had been presented to Harvard in April 1761 by Thomas Hancock, the uncle of John Hancock, the political leader.[53] The Martin telescope and Tompion clock were also the principal instruments used during the actual transit, a day described as "serene and calm." Other instruments included a small refractor mounted on a level, a gift of Christopher Kilby, chief agent for Nova Scotia, and a Hadley's quadrant, given by Ezekiel Goldthwait, Boston's town clerk and the Suffolk County register of deeds.[54] These were used mostly to show off the spectacle to various local dignitaries who gathered on the hill and were probably brought along as a courtesy to the donors.

Winthrop's expedition to Newfoundland lasted eleven weeks, and his return with equipment intact on July 25 was celebrated in the local papers. He published *Relation of a Voyage* in Boston and another version in the *Philosophical Transactions* of the Royal Society. The expedition was also immortalized in a famous portrait of Winthrop painted by John Singleton Copley.[55] Items in the portrait include Winthrop's diagram of Venus on the Sun in 1761 and Venus's Hill, the St. John's site where he made his observations. The telescope on the table, however, is one he used in 1769.

The political landscape was much altered by 1769 when Winthrop considered organizing a second expedition to observe the transit of Venus. In 1761, the enemy had been the French, and he had the full support of the colonial British government. In 1769, Winthrop and influential friends of Harvard's scientific undertakings—among them James Bowdoin, John Hancock, and Benjamin Franklin—were subversives in the eyes of the crown appointees in Massachusetts.

Beginning in 1764, the English Parliament, looking to offset the debt brought on by the French and Indian War and hoping to defray the costs of running the colonies, placed restrictions on colonial trade and increased taxes with the Sugar, Currency, Stamp, and Quartering Acts.

143. John Singleton Copley's portrait of John Winthrop, painted between 1771 and 1773, shows the astronomer holding his technical drawing of Venus crossing the Sun. Behind him is the St. John's, Newfoundland, site where he made his observations in 1761. The brass telescope on the table is a favorite by James Short of London, ca. 1758, which he acquired after the transit with the aid of Benjamin Franklin. Harvard Art Museums/ Fogg Museum.

144. Paul Revere's engraving of British warships landing their troops in Boston in October 1768. American Antiquarian Society.

The Americans fought back, asserting that the new taxes were unconstitutional, and Boston merchants organized boycotts of British luxury goods. In July 1765, the Sons of Liberty, an underground organization, began a campaign of intimidation and violence that ultimately forced British stamp agents to resign. The repeal of the Stamp Act in 1766 temporarily let off some steam, but the signing of the Declaratory Act and Townshend Revenue Acts (1767) imposed new taxes and established a Board of Customs Commissioners in Boston to act as enforcer.

In 1768, Samuel Adams—the clerk of the Massachusetts House of Representatives and Winthrop's former student, now better known as the patriot brewer—challenged the Townsend Acts' legality and fomented rebellion in a circular letter sent to the legislative bodies of the other English colonies. Refusal to revoke the letter led to the dissolution of the General Court of Massachusetts and the arrival of British warships in Boston harbor. Meanwhile, Boston's chief customs collector, Joseph Harrison, decided to make an example of John Hancock, who was caught smuggling wine onboard his ship, the *Liberty*. Harrison had the ship seized and towed away from the wharf. An angry mob responded by beating up Harrison and other customs officers, smashing the windows in their homes, and torching Harrison's boat. Terrified customs officers and their families fled to a fortified harbor island and called for British regiments to keep order.

There were other challenges too. On a snowy night in January 1764, Harvard Hall was consumed in flames, and with it the college library and scientific apparatus. Among the items lost were the instruments Winthrop had used to observe the transit of Venus (with the exception of the Martin telescope and the Tompion clock, which were stored at Winthrop's house).[56] Recovery came with gifts of money, apparatus, and expertise. In particular, Benjamin Franklin offered his services while in London as an agent for the Pennsylvania assembly.[57] In consultation with Winthrop, he handpicked apparatus from London's finest instrument-makers and had these shipped to Harvard. Remarkably, the precious cargo was permitted to enter the port of Boston despite the boycott of English goods, and the bills of lading show that duties were paid.[58] Here is another instance of science rising above politics.

In the midst of these tensions, Franklin forwarded to Winthrop a pamphlet published in 1768 by Nevil Maskelyne, the Astronomer Royal, containing instructions for the next transit of Venus.[59] Encouraged, Winthrop tried to organize an expedition to Lake Superior, the closest place to New England where the full transit could be witnessed. The problem was that the assembly that had funded Winthrop's expedition in 1761 did not exist when he received Franklin's letter of July 1768. It had been dissolved on orders from London for its support of the rebellious acts of Samuel Adams.

So once again, Winthrop wrote to James Bowdoin, a member of the Council of the General Court of Massachusetts Bay, to solicit his help in getting the project funded.[60] He knew that Bowdoin would support the mission on its scientific merits, but he offered him reasons (such as improved surveys and cartography) to approach the royal governor, Francis Bernard, or General Thomas Gage, the commander-in-chief of all the British forces in North America.[61] Since it was Gage who had just sent warships and troops to Boston to control the violence, Winthrop's request was rather cheeky! In politics, Winthrop sided with Samuel Adams and the Sons of Liberty in the 1760s, and he would be a leading patriot in the 1770s. Bowdoin's position was seen as so subversive that when reelected to the Council in 1769, the governor refused to let him take his seat.[62]

While waiting for the reply, Winthrop began to put together the instruments for the expedition.[63] His own health was too frail for the journey and he was ambivalent about one of his students leading the trip in his stead. Therefore, he was stingy in what he would lend from the college, offering only the old, second-rate apparatus. On the other hand, he wanted to give the student a good chance of success and so was audacious in attempting to borrow first-rate items from loyalists and customs officers like Joseph Harrison, who had been among those beat up and burned out of their homes by Boston's mob. Let the fine apparatus of these gentlemen go on the trek, Winthrop apparently thought, but let us not risk Harvard's brand new treasures in the canoes or on the pack animals.

In spite of political differences, General Gage responded politely and offered much advice, letters to post commanders, and wilderness guides—but no money. The governor applauded the research trip but claimed himself unauthorized to finance it.[64] In the end, Winthrop consoled himself with observations of the transit in Cambridge, using all the new apparatus secured by Franklin since the fire. Made by Short, Dollond, Ellicott, Sisson, and Bird, these instruments were as fine as any to be had overseas and comparable to those that outfitted the European transit expeditions.[65] Financed by colonists and expressing their scientific aspirations, these instruments had made it through the rough political waters that were surging between London and Boston.[66]

The instruments that survive today are more than brass and glass, wood and lead. Imported at great expense from a metropolis to a province, they helped to determine the dimensions of the solar system in 1761 and 1769 in the midst of armed conflict and the affirmation that politics should give way to the cause of science.

S. J. S.

Changing Stories about American Indians

One of the fundamental founding stories of the American nation vindicates the displacement of the original inhabitants by newcomers who began arriving to settle as recently as the seventeenth century. Some Americans still accept the notion of Manifest Destiny by which, in the words of the journalist John O'Sullivan who coined the term in 1845, they have "overspread the continent allotted by Providence for the free development of our yearly multiplying millions."[67] Yet many people have questioned or challenged this story, provoking controversy.[68] Some newcomers who were sympathetic to Native Americans long assuaged their guilt with the notion that Indians were fated to disappear, either through attrition or absorption within colonial society. This is the story of the "vanishing Indian." Native Americans and some others expend great efforts to refute it. Demonstrating that Indians are not disappearing means telling other stories. How does this happen?

Two sources of new stories are Indian gambling casinos and museums. The success of the Foxwoods Resort Casino of the Mashantucket Pequot Tribal Nation in Connecticut, which opened in 1992, is a prominent example of Indian casinos engendering economic and political influence.[69] Among the most conspicuous projects financed by the casino is the Mashantucket Pequot Museum and Research Center, reportedly the largest tribal museum in the United States. Museums are a conspicuous way of asserting indigenous cultural continuity, for unlike many anthropological museums within the socially dominant sector of American society, Native American museums give considerable weight to contemporary conditions. This is true of the National Museum of the American Indian (NMAI), which opened in Washington, DC, in 2004. A predominantly Native staff worked with Indigenous community curators to create the long-term exhibits, transgressing museological conventions but telling stories of Indian life, past and present, from an Indian point of view unfamiliar to many in American society.[70] Such changes have in turn helped to promote a paradigm shift in stories told by those who dominate American society about the Indigenous peoples' past and present. Harvard has played a role in promoting this shift through two institutions in particular: the Peabody Museum and the Harvard University Native American Program (HUNAP).

HUNAP emerged in 1990 from a program begun in 1970 at the Graduate School of Education to train American Indian educational leaders. It expanded to become a university-wide endeavor, and in 1998, the central administration designated HUNAP an interfaculty initiative of Harvard University to focus on scholarship and teaching throughout the university (with a focus on Indigenous nation-building), Native outreach, and student recruitment and support.

Since 2005, the Peabody Museum has collaborated with HUNAP and the department of anthropology to lead an undergraduate teaching excavation. The site is the Harvard Indian College in Harvard Yard, built in

1655 for the Christian education of Indians. The undertaking ended in 1670, and the building was demolished in 1693.[71] The excavation opening and closing ceremonies took place with local Native participation, reminding all present of the Indigenous moral claim to precedence of identification with the site. Since 2008, the results have been displayed in an exhibition at the Peabody Museum organized with student participation: *Digging Veritas: Archaeology and History of the Indian College and Student Life at Colonial Harvard.*[72] The Harvard Yard Archaeology Project is a conspicuous part of the renegotiation by Harvard of its relationship with Indigenous Americans. It is part of a newly emerging story in which things in Harvard collections—principally in the Peabody Museum—play a vital role.

Although the excavation did not uncover any specifically Native American items, in 2007, student archaeologists found several pieces of metal printing type used in the production of John Eliot's 1663 translation of the Bible into the Massachusetts variant of the Eastern Algonquian language.[73] The Eliot Bible is of particular importance in Native life as a vital source of information about eastern Massachusetts language forms that are currently being used in the Wôpanâak Language Reclamation Project. Wôpanâak is the language of the Wampanoag peoples of southeastern New England that until recently was dormant. The revival of the spoken, as well as written, language since 1993, as a result of the work of Wampanoag tribal member Jesse Little Doe Baird, represents a further change in the story of Native Americans, exemplifying a determination not to acquiesce in the submergence of Indigenous cultural identity in that of the dominant society.[74]

Harvard has shown itself to be especially keen to foster good relations with the various Massachusetts Wampanoag bands. Before 2011, Caleb Cheeshahteaumuck, A.B., 1665, had been the last Wampanoag to graduate from Harvard College. He died of tuberculosis within a year. His Native classmate Joel Iacoombs perished that same year in a shipwreck before he could receive his degree. In a symbolic act, once again seeking to change the story of colonizer–Indigenous relations, Harvard conferred a degree on Iacoombs posthumously in a ceremony in May 2011.

No tangible things are associated directly with Iacoombs, but a small woven textile bag transferred to the Peabody Museum by the American Antiquarian Society in 1890 has traditionally been called Caleb Cheeshahteaumuck's bag on the basis of a nineteenth-century label.[75] However, the bag conforms to a type of tubular woven raffia bag from

Côte d'Ivoire and Liberia described by two Peabody Museum scholars in 1992.[76] Might trade between West Africa and New England have brought it to the East Coast of America before Cheeshahteaumuck's death in 1665? The student who researched the bag in the 2002 seminar, Claire Eager, concluded that "the likelihood that the bag ever came into contact with Caleb in life is slim," but points out that "his story remains integral to its history because of his influence on its rediscovery and research" since HUNAP has used Cheeshahteaumuck as a symbol in its nation-building outreach and teaching.[77] Here is an African thing that has become part of an American Indian story, occupying an ambiguous role in the collections of the Peabody Museum, for it was illustrated on the museum's website in 2009 as a "Bag belonging to Caleb Cheeshahteaumuck, Aquinnah Wampanoag, Harvard's first Native American graduate, Class of 1665."[78] As Eager pointed out, "a 'false' story would be just as important to the whole history of the bag as the true ones.... Caleb belongs to the bag now, even if it never belonged to him."[79]

Even as Indians themselves are presenting their own stories, non-Indian scholars are increasingly welcoming and exhibiting Indian points of view. An example at the Peabody Museum was the long-term exhibit (2009–12) *Wiyohpiyata: Lakota Images of the Contested West.* Peabody curator Castle McLaughlin and Lakota artist Butch Thunder Hawk highlighted a ledger book in Houghton Library filled with drawings by Plains Indians that was found at the site of George Armstrong Custer's defeat in 1876. Their exhibition presented Lakota perspectives on colonial westward expansion. The Chicago newspaper reporter James W. Howard (whose pen name was Phocion) acquired the ledger book soon after the battle. He ascribed the drawings to a single artist whom he fancifully named Half Moon. However, recent examination by McLaughlin and Thunder Hawk suggested that at least five artists were responsible.[80]

Howard's invention of Half Moon, like the identification of the West African bag with Caleb Cheeshahteaumuck, exemplifies the deep-rooted Euro-American ideological propensity to associate tangible things, no less than decisions and accomplishments, with individuals rather than with collectivities. Yet few nineteenth-century or earlier Indian artifacts can confidently be associated with identifiable individuals. One Indian item in the Peabody Museum, also exemplifying the Plains Indian drawing tradition, that *can* confidently be associated with an identifiable person is a pottery plate painted by a Cheyenne warrior named Nock-ko-ist, or Bear's Heart.[81]

145. A pottery plate painted by a Cheyenne warrior named Nock-ko-ist (Bear's Heart) for the Euro-American market, ca. 1878–82. Peabody Museum of Archaeology and Ethnology, Harvard University.

Nock-ko-ist was one of seventy-two Plains Indians captured and transported to Fort Marion in St. Augustine, Florida, after the Red River War in Indian Territory in 1874 and 1875. They were imprisoned between 1875 and 1878, but fell under the idealistic regimen of U.S. Army Captain Richard Henry Pratt. Pratt famously sought to "kill the Indian and save the man" by westernizing his prisoners' appearance, teaching them English, converting them to Christianity, and teaching them a trade.[82] His strategy attracted the attention and support of contemporary idealists, including the author of *Uncle Tom's Cabin* (1852), Harriet Beecher Stowe, who published a two-part article on Fort Marion in 1877.[83] Nock-ko-ist, though, hung onto the skills he had brought with him into captivity, filling a book with twenty-four drawings recounting his experiences following his capture. He used the conventions derived from Plains Indians' pictorial records long practiced on rocks, robes, tipi covers, and tipi linings, as adapted by many Indian artists in colonists' ledger books. Pratt presented Nock-ko-ist's drawing book to William Tecumseh Sherman, commanding general of the U.S. Army and an amateur painter.[84] Nock-ko-ist drew on the same repertory of images for his plate as he had used in his ledger drawings: Similar representations of two mounted figures on the plate, each chasing a buffalo, can be found in a drawing in the book.[85]

In 1878, seventeen of the Fort Marion prisoners were sent to the Hampton Normal and Agricultural Institute in Virginia, originally founded to educate formerly enslaved African Americans. At Hampton, Nock-ko-ist adapted his drawing style to the decoration of painted ceramics for a Euro-American market.[86] This included the incorporation of Nock-ko-ist's anglicized name painted around the rim of the plate as a signifier of Indian authenticity and compliance. A New England philanthropist, the founder of various vocational schools and a financial supporter of the Hampton Institute, Mary Porter Tileson Hemenway, may well have acquired the plate, for her heirs gave it to the Peabody Museum in 1930. Nock-ko-ist took the name James Bear's Heart and left Hampton in 1881 for the Cheyenne and Arapaho reservation in Indian Territory, where he worked as a carpenter. He died of tuberculosis in January 1882.[87] Pratt and his supporters may have been well intentioned, but as white voices give way to those of Indians, a story of laudable humane treatment has been superseded by one of cultural genocide.

As a hybrid object that represents attempts at rapprochement with American Indians on the colonizers' terms, the Peabody Museum has no qualms about exhibiting the plate decorated by Nock-ko-ist. Yet he also appears in another item in the Peabody's collections: one of sixty-four plaster busts modeled by the sculptor Clark Mills in 1877 after life masks of the Plains Indians held at Fort Marion.[88] Although they are vividly lifelike, derived from impressions in plaster of the faces of individuals and then painted with a brown wash to resemble flesh, these busts were not conceived as portraits by their instigator, the Smithsonian Institution, which was collecting likenesses of ethnic types worldwide for anthropological study. Therefore, although the names of the sitters were recorded, the busts of the Fort Marion Indians were labeled solely with their tribal affiliations. The Peabody Museum received a duplicate set of busts from the Smithsonian.

Because they were directly derived from their subjects, these busts carry a charge of immediacy that makes them difficult to curate in current circumstances. Many anthropologists now try to respect Indigenous peoples and their values, regarding them in terms of the emergent story about Indians as representatives of social groups that have been wronged over generations. The institutional imperative to comply with the Native American Graves Protection and Repatriation Act of 1990 (NAGPRA) has in some cases strengthened this story. Under NAGPRA, federally recognized Native entities can request repatriation from institutions in receipt of federal funds of human remains and artifacts in various categories, such as grave goods and items used in religious observance. The Peabody had instituted repatriation prior to the passage of the act and embraced it as an opportunity to strengthen long-term ties with Indigenous communities.[89] Although the Fort Marion busts do not fall under NAGPRA, heightened curatorial sensibilities have affected their treatment. Descendants have ceremonially visited their ancestors' busts; in deference to their sensibilities, the busts are not considered appropriate for exhibition. Now, reserved primarily for Indian use, they serve Indian stories.

The uses of these various Indian things in Harvard collections—Caleb Cheeshahteaumuck's bag, Nock-ko-ist's plate and bust, and many others—reflect changes in the stories told of them. Even if unreflecting white supremacism and a belief in Manifest Destiny still taint hegemonic received opinion, the stories told of—and by—Indians in institutions of learning have changed. Viewing at least aspects of the past and present while "facing east from Indian country," in historian Daniel Richter's phrase, through the prism of tangible things is no longer as difficult as it once was for Native and newcomer alike.[90]

I. G.

Unexpected Discoveries: The Joy of Object Photography

During the past decade I have photographed thousands of museum objects at several different collections, both in the United States and the UK. To an outsider, this type of work might appear monotonous or uninspiring—the photography simply a method of automated capture in which the photographer documents the appearance of an object and then disappears from view. In addition, museum objects are almost never easy to work with. They are often fragile, reflective, or difficult to light in one way or another. They may possess any number of physical or historical qualities that complicate handling and photographing. A boring, complicated job then. So why, after capturing all those images, am I still excited to photograph objects?

My answer has two distinct parts. The first lies in the often incredible stories (some obvious, many hidden) embodied and inspired by every object that makes its way onto my backdrop. The second is the joy found in the challenge of capturing and revealing the visual elements (often details) that help enrich every object's narrative.

While working in history-of-science museums, I have spent a great deal of time documenting the material culture of scientific discoveries, photographing everything from fifteenth-century astrolabes to World War II–era vacuum tubes. While some objects are obviously magnificent and historically important, there are many others that may appear relatively commonplace or trivial. The recurring surprise is that almost every single one of these things, including the uninspiring ones, have stories to tell; each thing sparks thoughts of the designer, the maker, the user—the story of the object's life.

In addition, history-of-science collections, perhaps due to the interdisciplinary nature of the field, often house unexpected and delightful surprises. At the Museum of the History of Science in Oxford I was asked to shoot a few of its lovely collection of Japanese netsuke. When I was working at the Collection of Historical Scientific Instruments at Harvard several years later, I chanced upon a glass bottle filled with an unidentified liquid. The bottle had an older label consisting of a solitary question mark in blue ink, a tag that said so much with so little. (I suppose the fact that it was written in ballpoint pen at least helped to roughly date the time in which the tag was written.) Though it appeared to pass along very little information, I was careful to shoot the label. At least the eventual cataloger of this object would get to share in the whimsical encouragement of an earlier person's befuddlement.

Tangible Things attempted to address the challenges inherent in categorizing museum objects. The show therefore contained many unusual and surprising items that elicited the same inquisitive reaction that I had often experienced when working with the unexpected. The more involved I became with the exhibit, the more excited I felt to photograph many of the objects as part of the de-installation process.

When shooting objects such as these, I follow one basic rule of photographic composition: *fill the frame.* This means that for every shot, I strive to fill the viewfinder of the camera (either by standing more closely to the object or by using a long focal-length lens) in order maximize the amount of information landing on the CCD sensor (in the old days this would have been film). In other words, the greater the percentage of pixels exposed to image data, the finer and more delicate the details that can be resolved. It is often these very details that provide rich new stores of information about the subject.

This particular series of images demonstrates this quest to both document and uncover new information. It also shows the way in which this search for detail can create an overall sense of movement toward and even *into* the object being photographed—in this case a summer gown once worn by David Greene Haskins at Harvard in 1834–35.

Photographs 146 and 147 are typical of those found in both exhibition catalogs and museum databases: front and back views of the object on a neutral background. Such images are useful in that they provide a sense of the object as a whole. In this case, the subject is evenly lit,

146–147. Front and back of a gown worn by a Harvard College student during the summer of his sophomore year, 1834–35. Harvard University Archives.

without special lighting effects or glare, which allows the viewer to get a sense of the overall nature of the object: an item of clothing made out of delicate fabric.

As the camera draws more closely, images 148 and 149 each capture an element of the gown that references the broader elements of its construction. Here one can get a sense of the layered nature of the cape across the shoulders and the hand-stitched shirring that gives the garment its shape.

As we move in more closely still, the sequence 150–153 reveals much about what was important to both the maker and the wearer and continues to be important to the preservation of this gown. At this range of magnification, the camera often captures details that can otherwise elude the observer's eye. For instance, though I had looked directly at these elements through the viewfinder of my camera, it was not until I viewed them at a larger scale on my computer screen that I became aware of the great extent of the repair shown in 150 and the area of discoloration around the sleeve hook in 151 (which may merit attention from a conservator).

148–149. Cape with tasseled fringe and shirring at back of summer gown. Harvard University Archives.

150–153. Close-up images (*left to right from top*) showing repair, sleeve hook, cuff button, and detail of fabric weave. Harvard University Archives.

These detailed photographs were taken with a specialized lens designed for macrophotography. Traditionally, the macro- prefix stipulates that the image projected onto the film plane will be larger than the size of the subject. Though this definition is used more loosely in the digital era, it means that images taken with such a lens (when used correctly) can

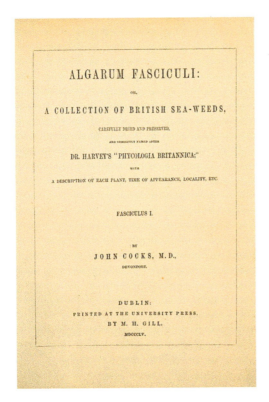

154. Title page of John Cocks, *Algarum Fasciculi; or A Collection of British Sea-weeds, Carefully Dried and Preserved, and correctly named after Dr. Harvey's "Phycologia Britannica"* (Dublin, 1855). Farlow Herbarium of Cryptogamic Botany, Harvard University Herbaria.

capture a great amount a detail. It is a common tool in forensic work and is incredibly useful in capturing a level of detail that the human eye may not normally be capable of resolving. Through these images we can focus on the uneven shape of the button that reveals its handmade origin, the slight irregularities in the gingham check, and the uneven thickness of the individual strands of the homespun thread. These are details that help us uncover this gown's story.

Another object that responds well to close visual scrutiny is John Cocks's *Algarum Fasciculi: or, a Collection of British Sea-Weeds, carefully dried and preserved, and correctly named after Dr. Harvey's "Phycologia Britannica"* (1855). Among its many wonderful surprises are lovely marbled endpapers, actual pressed specimens instead of illustrations, and the many ghost impressions left by the specimens on their identifying pages.

As I photographed some of the most representative seaweed samples in the book, I became increasingly aware of the amount of painstaking effort that must have gone into the construction of every single copy of this comprehensive work. In addition, I was struck by the fact that

155–157. A page opening showing a pressed specimen of *Chondrus crispus* (Irish moss) followed by a close-up of the specimen. This particular species of seaweed is an industrial source of carrageenan. Farlow Herbarium of Cryptogamic Botany, Harvard University Herbaria.

many of the specimens appeared to be in remarkable shape for their age. Though I am neither a librarian nor a curator, I wondered and hoped that my images might be able to help these specialists uncover more of the history of this particular volume. Furthermore, I was awed by the unexpected beauty of the specimens. My close-up images were meant to capture their three-dimensional nature, but I found that they began to approach a certain level of abstractness that began to hint at art more

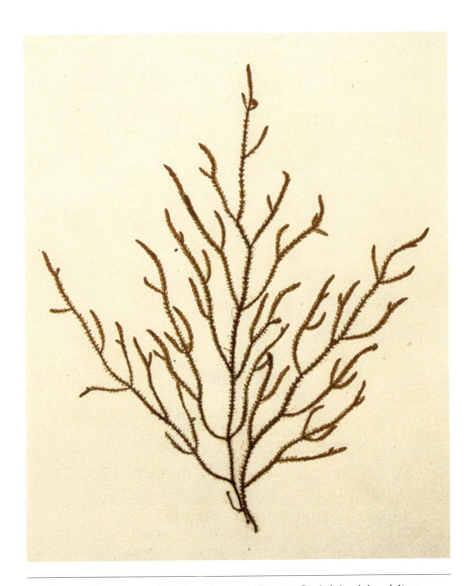

158. A pressed specimen of *Cladostephus verticillatus* in Cocks's book has delicate intact hair-like structures. Farlow Herbarium of Cryptogamic Botany, Harvard University Herbaria.

159–160. A specimen of *Delesseria sinuosa*, a seaweed that grows on the stems of the common large algae known as Oarweed. Farlow Herbarium of Cryptogamic Botany, Harvard University Herbaria.

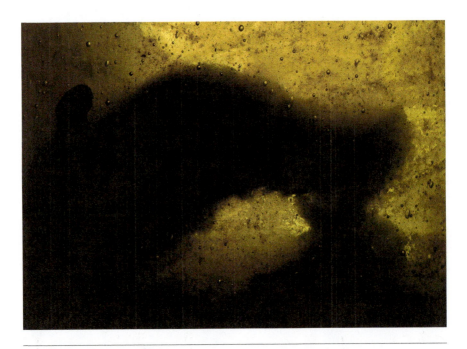

161. The shadow of the desiccated body of a house mouse (*Mus musculus*) as seen through the glass of a patent medicine bottle, ca. 1865, labeled *Macamoose, The Great Indian Tonic*. By its very nature glass often creates problems for photographers because of its reflectivity. This patent medicine bottle was fairly standard in this respect, though the many imperfections in the glass helped minimize the most glaring reflections.

The challenge here was to document the mummified mouse stuck in the bottom of the bottle. I wanted to be able to explain why this bottle was so incongruously displayed with the *Mus* family specimens at Harvard's Museum of Natural History.

After a failed attempt to photograph the mouse directly down the neck of the bottle, I decided to silhouette it, which was quite successful. I particularly enjoy the way in which the bubbles and waviness of the glass seem to suggest that it is swimming about in the liquid tonic, and not just lying in an empty bottle. General Artemas Ward House Museum.

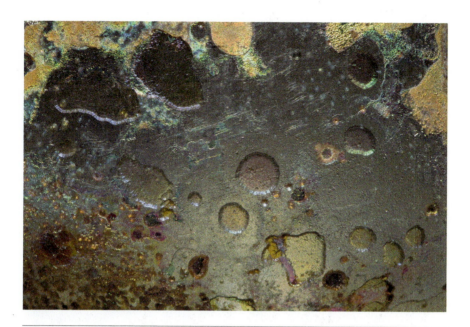

162. Iridescent and pockmarked surface of a four-handled glass jar, Roman, fourth to fifth century. I always exercise extra caution when handling and photographing glass. It is almost impossible to know how many shocks a glass object may have survived during its life (bumps that may have weakened it but not in obvious way), so it's always important for the handler to take extra care.

This vase was quite obviously delicate. The surface shows an incredible iridescence; a quality that I found out from talking to a friend at the Harvard Semitic Museum is caused by a chemical deterioration of the surface of the glass. This process makes the surface very friable, which made me more than usually nervous about touching it. With this in mind, I kept handling and lighting to a minimum, setting up the shot so that the vase was lit from the top, which makes it glow in a way that is particularly lovely. I was also pleased by the way in which this macro image captures the delicate multi-hued tones of the surface and its myriad pits and scratches. Semitic Museum.

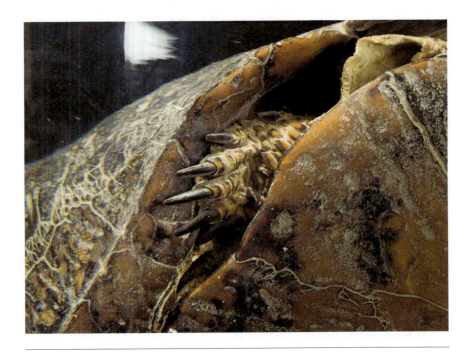

163. Clawed foot partially retracted into the shell of Blanding's turtle specimen (*Emydoidea blandingi*) caught and preserved by Henry David Thoreau in 1847. When I look at this turtle in its jar, I find myself irresistibly drawn to the thought of Thoreau catching it. In my mind, the writer and naturalist has been asked by Louis Agassiz to collect specimens from and around Walden Pond in Concord. While he may be uneasy about the inevitable end of the captured creatures, he would have been pleased to be asked by Agassiz himself, and this perhaps soothes him. It's an early mid-summer morning. Having looked on-and-off for several weeks, Thoreau has finally spotted a Blanding's turtle (this very turtle!) sunning itself on a half-submerged log in the pond. He quietly wends his way toward the turtle (muddying his boots in the process), takes a breath, and then lunges from behind. Success – the beautiful turtle is his! He quickly wraps it in a damp canvas sack and begins the trip back to his cabin.

The vividness of this tableau in my head (however far from the truth), made me look for a way to evoke a sense of this creature's former aliveness. Of all the images that I shot of this object, I think this one is perhaps the best in this regard. Though dead for over 150 years, the turtle has seemed to have just slipped into the water, evading Thoreau's grasp one last time. Museum of Comparative Zoology

164. Looking deep into a large piece of Burmese amber, the fossilized resin of the pine tree (*Pinaceae*), Myanmar. This piece of burmite is a glorious thing—like preserved fire. The incredible orange-red of the crystallized resin, the satin-like feel of the polished surface, and its size (it's the largest piece of amber I've ever handed) make it feel almost talismanic. Although almost any stone picked up on any ramble could easily be much older than this amber, the tiny flecks of the million year-old insects and insect parts (seen here as small dark flecks) highlight the magic of this object: It is a time capsule.

When I first looked at the specimen, I was concerned that I wouldn't be able to capture all of the aspects of its radiance. However, like the image of the mouse caught in the Macamoose tonic bottle, I found that backlighting really helped. By silhouetting the insect remains caught inside and refracting light through the object, the burmite glowed beautifully, making it and the ancient insects within seem to come alive within their time capsule. Archives of the Economic Botany Herbarium of Oakes Ames, Harvard University Herbaria.

165. Walrus ivory carving of a dog-sled team made by an Netsilik Inuit artist in Kugaaruk, Nunavut, Canada, in the twentieth century. This carving of a dog sled team is one of my favorite *Tangible Things* objects. There is a lovely sense of motion in this sculpture; the rockered shape of the base and the straining aspect of the dogs convey the great amount of effort needed to haul a cargo of seals, which the Netsilik traditionally used for food, lighting, and heat.

From some angles, such as directly ahead or above, the dynamic nature of the carving is not expressed. It was important to me to photograph it from angles that helped it to come alive as much as possible. I believe that this image of the sled exiting the frame is the most successful in this regard. Peabody Museum of Archaeology and Ethnology, Harvard University.

than science. This can be read as a commentary on the practice of science in the mid–nineteenth century, where the worlds of art and science were perhaps less opposed than they are in our Postmodern world—another potential story to be told.

These two series demonstrate that careful photography can be a very useful tool for anyone who works with objects—from curator to conservator. This form of image capture, though perhaps rivaled by drawing in its ability to force the viewer to deeply engage with a subject, is unequalled in its capacity to quickly compress a wealth of three-dimensional information into an easily disseminated two-dimensional reference. In addition, the camera extends the resolution of the human eye, making the normally invisible visible, and so enabling us to learn more. What is this thing? What was it used for? What kind of life has it had? How did it get *here?* These questions can all be addressed (and sometimes even answered) by careful, considerate, close-up photographic work.

In an exhibition such as *Tangible Things*—which brings together many different types of things—there is no standard setup for photographing the objects. Some items are quite large (the statues of Norma and Normann, the Galapagos tortoise carapace), while others are quite small (a tiny Babylonian cylinder seal, the knuckle bone dice). Some reflect light (the Myer Myers' silver cann), and others are so matte as to almost disappear into a neutral background (*Loulie's Hand*). Some objects visually "pop" the moment they are placed on the table (an always welcome occurrence), while others take ages to set up and light. Despite these differences, the goal is to always try to capture as much information about the objects as possible, so that the photographs can help tell the objects' own stories.

Harvard Collections that Contributed to Tangible Things

Harvard University is an institution of Byzantine complexity. The administrative structure of its nearly fifty collections is difficult to grasp. Although there is a centralized structure for its libraries, with a common catalog and links to many digital images, this cannot be said of its other collections. The six museums associated with the Faculty of Arts and Sciences have since 2012 been organized into a consortium, the Harvard Museums of Science and Culture, but access to collections still resides in the individual museums. Beyond the Faculty of Arts and Sciences, some collections operate within the various professional schools, yet others are independent entities within the university answering directly to the Office of the Provost. One consequence is that there is, at best, limited coordination among collections, and many function without regard to others.

There follows a very brief descriptive statement about each of the collections that contributed to *Tangible Things* to aid readers in their orientation and navigation. In order to be as true to their self-defined purposes as possible, parts of these statements are taken directly from individual collection websites and mission statements.

Arnold Arboretum of Harvard University
www.arboretum.harvard.edu

Established in 1872 in partnership with the city of Boston and planned in collaboration with renowned landscape architect Frederick Law Olmsted, the Arnold Arboretum occupies 281 acres in Boston's Jamaica Plain and is part of the Emerald Necklace, a series of linked parks around Boston. It is a living collection of trees, shrubs, and woody vines, and the grounds are open to the public. Researchers have access not only to the living collections but also the arboretum's comprehensive curatorial documentation and the herbaria, extensive library, and archival holdings. The Arnold Arboretum is known for research on the nature of plant diversity from the perspectives of genomic, developmental, organismic, evolutionary, and ecosystem biology. The Arnold Arboretum is an independent unit within the university under the aegis of the Office of the Provost.

Baker Library of the Harvard Business School
www.library.hbs.edu

Designated a special library in 1911 and named after benefactor George F. Baker, the Baker Library collections cover most aspects of management including accounting and control, agribusiness, banking, business and economic history, commerce, economic philosophy, finance, information technology, international business, management education, manufacturing, marketing, political economy, and transportation. The Historical Collections encompass 700 years of original materials documenting the evolution of business practices. Among them are many physical artifacts in addition to rare books, manuscripts, advertising ephemera, broadsides, prints, pamphlets, photographs, and corporate archives.

Botanical Museum and Harvard University Herbaria
www.huh.harvard.edu

The Botanical Museum was founded in 1858 by Asa Gray, Fisher Professor of Natural History, and originally known as the Museum of Vegetable Products. By 1890, its public exhibits were seen as a complement to Louis Agassiz's Museum of Comparative Zoology. The Harvard University Herbaria is an entity that includes six herbaria (collections of dried plant specimens): the Gray Herbarium, the Herbarium of the Arnold Arboretum, the Economic Herbarium of Oakes Ames, the Oakes Ames Orchid Herbarium, the Farlow Herbarium of Cryptogamic Botany, and the New England Botanical Club Herbarium; three specimen collections: the Bailey-Wetmore Wood Collection, the Paleobotanical Collections, and the Botanical Museum Collection; and associated research libraries and archives. Only with the construction of a new building in 1954 were these various institutions at Harvard brought together, although they were administered separately for approximately twenty more years. The best-known collection within the Botanical Museum Collection is the Ware Collection of Glass Models of Plants, colloquially known as the Glass Flowers. These are on public display in the Harvard Museum of Natural History, since 2012 a constituent of the Harvard Museums of Science and Culture within the Faculty of Arts and Sciences.

Collection of Historical Scientific Instruments
chsi.harvard.edu

This collection had its origins in a rescue mission by the founding curator, David P. Wheatland, who encountered discarded scientific instruments in the attics and stairwells of Harvard's science buildings and took them into his office for safekeeping beginning around 1928. By 1949, with his office overflowing with "foundlings," Wheatland secured new space with the help of the provost of Harvard College, and the Collection of Historical Scientific Instruments was born.

Its mission is to preserve, document, and care for scientific apparatus portraying the history of science teaching and research at Harvard from the colonial period to the present. Even so, many objects in the collection predate Harvard, going as far back as the Middle Ages, and were the gifts of Wheatland and other generous donors. The Collection of Historical Scientific Instruments was originally associated with the Harvard library system. It was placed under the stewardship of the Department of the History of Science in 1987, and in 2012, joined the Harvard Museums of Science and Culture within the Faculty of Arts and Sciences.

Harvard Art Museums
www.harvardartmuseums.org

The Harvard Art Museums are three museums under a single administration. The Fogg Museum opened in 1895 and now holds Western paintings, sculpture, decorative arts, photographs, prints, and drawings dating from the Middle Ages to the present. The Busch-Reisinger Museum opened in 1903 as the Germanic Museum, dedicated to the art of the German-speaking lands of central and northern Europe. The Arthur M. Sackler Museum opened in 1985 to care for the Asian, ancient, and Islamic and later Indian art previously in the Fogg Museum. The Harvard Art Museums were originally associated with the Department of Fine Arts (now the Department of History of Art and Architecture) in the Faculty of Arts and Sciences. Since 1990, the Harvard Art Museums have been an independent unit within the university, and since 2002, have been supervised by the Office of the Provost.

Harvard Museum of Natural History
www.hmnh.harvard.edu

This museum was founded in 1998 as the public face of three research museums—the Museum of Comparative Zoology, the Harvard University Herbaria, and the Mineralogical and Geological Museum at Harvard University—whose exhibition galleries had long coexisted in the same building. Its mission is to present the collections of the parent museums to the public and be a showcase for Harvard research. It was the model for the structure of the Harvard Museums of Science and Culture and has been a constituent entity of it since 2012.

Harvard Museums of Science and Culture
hmsc.harvard.edu

Established in 2012, this museum consortium is the public face of six research museums affiliated with the Faculty of Arts and Sciences. These include the three entities that have governed the Harvard Museum of Natural History: namely, the Museum of Comparative Zoology, the Harvard University Herbaria, and the Mineralogical and Geological Museum; and three museums whose public programs had been run independently: the Peabody Museum of Archaeology and Ethnology, the Semitic Museum, and the Collection of Historical Scientific Instruments. Although the individual museums retain control of their collections and all research activities, they work together through the consortium on public programming and some collaborative exhibits.

Harvard University Archives
library.harvard.edu/university-archives

The Harvard University Archives collect, organize, preserve, and provide access to a record of life at Harvard in the form of original sources.

These are documentary, digital, and other objects from the seventeenth century onward. This activity is tied integrally to records management services for the university. The Harvard University Archives form part of the Harvard Library.

Houghton Library
hcl.harvard.edu/libraries/houghton/

Houghton Library opened in 1942 to care for rare books and manuscripts in the Harvard College Library. The core of the collections consists of the contents of the former Treasure Room in Widener Library, the Harvard Theatre Collection, rarities and special materials transferred from the Widener stacks, and inaugural gifts of books and manuscripts by important Harvard benefactors, including Arthur Houghton, a businessman and arts patron, and Philip Hofer, founding curator of the library's Department of Printing and Graphic Arts.

Mineralogical and Geological Museum at Harvard University
www.geomus.fas.harvard.edu

The Mineralogical Museum at Harvard dates back to 1775, when minerals were exhibited in Harvard Hall in Harvard Yard. Benjamin Waterhouse, a chemist and cofounder of the Harvard Medical School, established a teaching collection in 1784. During the nineteenth century, the collections were under the care of the Department of Chemistry in Boylston Hall. The Geological Museum was established independently in 1876 and became associated with the Department of Geology and Geography. In 1891, the Mineralogical Museum was given a home within the University Museum building on Oxford Street, Cambridge, where it was joined in 1901 by the Geological Museum. The two museums were merged formally in 1977 and have four main collections: minerals, rocks and ores, meteorites, and gems. The conjoined museum is currently associated with the Department of Earth and Planetary Sciences. The public exhibition galleries of the collections remain in the old University Museum building, which is now known as the Harvard Museum of Natural History, since 2012 a constituent of the Harvard Museums of Science and Culture within the Faculty of Arts and Sciences.

Museum of Comparative Zoology
www.mcz.harvard.edu

Founded in 1859 by Louis Agassiz, professor of zoology and geology, the Museum of Comparative Zoology focuses on the comparative relationships of animal life, the structures of living things, their natural classifications, and their relationship with their environments. Its collection includes extant and fossil invertebrate and vertebrate specimens. The museum is associated with the Department of Organismic and Evolutionary Biology, and its public galleries form part of the Harvard Museum of Natural History, since 2012 a constituent of the Harvard Museums of Science and Culture within the Faculty of Arts and Sciences.

Peabody Museum of Archaeology and Ethnology
peabody.harvard.edu

Founded in 1866 to focus on the peoples and cultures of the Americas, the Peabody Museum cares for collections of archaeological and anthropological material from cultural traditions around the globe, with the general exception of Mediterranean, North African, and West Asian classical antiquity. It is dedicated to the documentation, preservation, and study of human origins, prehistory, historic cultures, and contemporary societies. It investigates the emergence and interconnectedness of human populations and cultural and ethnic traditions, including their biological and environmental contexts. It conducts archaeological excavations, notably in Central America. The museum is associated with the Departments of Anthropology and Human Evolutionary Biology, and since 2012 has been a constituent of the Harvard Museums of Science and Culture within the Faculty of Arts and Sciences.

Arthur and Elizabeth Schlesinger Library on the History of Women in America and the Radcliffe Archives of the Radcliffe Institute for Advanced Study
www.radcliffe.harvard.edu/schlesinger-library

Named in 1965, although founded in 1908, the Schlesinger Library was originally the library of Radcliffe College, the institution for women's education associated with Harvard since 1879. When Radcliffe and Harvard officially merged in 1999, the college was repurposed as the Radcliffe Institute for Advanced Study within Harvard University. The library collections focus on women's rights and feminism, health and sexuality, work and family life, education and the professions, culinary history, and etiquette. The library administers the Radcliffe Archives of Radcliffe College and the Radcliffe Picture Collection.

Semitic Museum
www.semiticmuseum.fas.harvard.edu

Since its founding in 1889, the Semitic Museum has assembled and cared for collections from the ancient Mediterranean, North Africa, and West Asia and has engaged in archaeological excavations from Tunisia in the west to Iraq in the east. The museum is associated with the Department of Near Eastern Languages and Civilizations. It is a constituent of the Harvard Museums of Science and Culture, formed in 2012, within the Faculty of Arts and Sciences.

Storer Memorial Collection of Medical Medals of the Boston Medical Library in the Francis A. Countway Library of Medicine
www.countway.harvard.edu/chom

Horatio Robinson Storer, a gynecologist, collected coins and medals relating to medicine. These included portrait medals of individuals and medals related to hospitals, medical colleges, societies, nursing, pharmacy, and diseases. In 1900, Storer gave the bulk of his collection in memory of his father to the Boston Medical Library (established in 1875). Today, the Storer Memorial Collection of Medical Medals is housed with the Boston Medical Library in the Francis A. Countway Library of Medicine, which opened in 1965 at Harvard Medical School. The Countway Library also contains the Harvard Medical Library (founded in 1816) and the Warren Anatomical Museum (established in 1847). The Center for the History of Medicine oversees the rare holdings of the Boston Medical Library and Harvard Medical Library: the incunabula, historical books, manuscripts, archives, physicians' personal libraries, paintings, prints, photographs, and medals.

General Artemas Ward House Museum
www.wardhouse.harvard.edu

Artemas Ward was the first commander of the colonial forces in Massachusetts; he was superseded by George Washington as commander of the Continental Army in 1775, though he was promoted to major general and retained seniority second only to Washington. He served in the Massachusetts judiciary and legislature (as president of the Executive Council, 1777–79), in the Continental Congress (1780–82), and in the Second and Third U.S. Congresses (1791–95). A direct descendent and namesake donated the Ward family house in Shrewsbury, Massachusetts, to Harvard in 1925 as a "public patriotic museum." The house and barn contain the material possessions of five generations of the Ward family and serve as a microcosm of many aspects of eighteenth- and nineteenth-century Massachusetts and its relations with the wider world. The museum is administered within the Office of the Provost.

Warren Anatomical Museum in the Francis A. Countway Library of Medicine
www.countway.harvard.edu/menuNavigation/chom/warren.html

The Warren Anatomical Museum has its roots in the teaching and research collection of John Collins Warren, professor of anatomy and surgery at Harvard Medical School (1809–47). In 1847, Warren gave his collection to the school, thereby establishing the museum. In 1861, the Warren Anatomical Museum was opened to the public, and in 1906, it moved to the new Harvard Medical School campus in the Longwood Medical and Academic Area of Boston. In 1999, the Warren Anatomical Museum was relocated to the Francis A. Countway Library of Medicine. The Center for the History of Medicine took over curatorial responsibility for the museum and created exhibition space within the library. The collection includes anatomical and pathological preparations, anatomical models, photographs, prints, paintings, drawings, medical instruments and machines, and medical memorabilia.

Notes

CHAPTER 1

1. George Brown Goode, *The Principles of Museum Administration* (New York: Coultas & Volans, 1895), p. 22.
2. Familienähnlichkeit: Ludwig Wittgenstein, *Philosophical Investigations: The German Text, with a Revised English Translation*, trans. G. E. M. Anscomb, 3rd ed. (Oxford, UK: Blackwell, 2001), esp. §§65–71.
3. Ludwig Wittgenstein, *Preliminary Studies for the "Philosophical Investigations" Generally known as the Blue and Brown Books*, ed. Rush Rhees, 2nd ed. (New York: Harper and Row, 1960), p. 27. First published in 1958, these are notes from lectures that Wittgenstein delivered at Cambridge University in 1933–34.
4. Blanding's Turtle (*Emydoidea blandingi*), Herpetology Collection, Museum of Comparative Zoology, Z111.
5. Prepared skin of a pink fairy armadillo (*Chlamyphorus truncatus*), collected by Louis Agassiz in Mendoza, Argentina, 1872, Mammalogy Collection, Museum of Comparative Zoology, 3207.
6. Orchid (*Epidendrum lorifolium*) with watercolor drawing by Blanche Ames Ames, 1923, Orchid Herbarium of Oakes Ames, Harvard University Herbaria, 00070528.
7. Vesuvianite, Mineralogical Museum, 136534.
8. Simon Schama, *Dead Certainties (Unwarranted Speculations)* (New York: Knopf, 1991), Part 2, "Death of a Harvard Man," pp. 73–318.
9. Textile fragments from Spiro Mounds, Muscogee people, Spiro, OK, USA, before ca. 1450, Peabody Museum of Archaeology and Ethnology, Gift of Charles C. Willoughby, 39-21-10/13077. These were the subject of Shannon Morrow's seminar paper in fall 2010.
10. Pestle with a carved bird's head, Concord, MA, USA, stone, Peabody Museum of Archaeology and Ethnology 69-34-10/2382.
11. Two cuneiform tablets with envelopes from Nuzi, Mesopotamia, ca. 1500 BCE, clay, Semitic Museum, 1899.2.355 and 1899.2.70.
12. The personal seal of ᵈSin-Ishme-anni, an administrator, and its impression, Mesopotamia, Old Babylonian, Semitic Museum, 1899.2.514; clay tile stamped "LEXFR," Jerusalem, 1st century CE, Semitic Museum, 1902.53.90.
13. Fragmentary oracle bones, Henan Province, China, Peabody Museum of Archaeology and Ethnology, Gift of Langdon Warner, 15-44-60/D836.40.
14. Fragment of a papyrus manuscript of Plato's *Republic*, Oxyrhynchus, Egypt, ca. 250–300, Houghton Library (transferred from Harvard Semitic Museum, the Gift of the Egypt Exploration Fund, 1904), MS Gr SM3739. See the bibliography on this fragment compiled

by Daniel Mach and Justin Stover, *Digital Papyri at Houghton Library*: http://hcl.harvard.edu/libraries/houghton/collections/papyrus/bibliographies/SM_3739.html (accessed June 15, 2012).

15. Letter employing cross-hatching to "my dear sister Bessie," Nov. 4, 1855, Huntting-Rudd Family Papers, Arthur and Elizabeth Schlesinger Library on the History of Women in America, MC 284.

16. The Huntting-Rudd Family Papers were given to the Schlesinger Library by various donors between 1977 and 1979. See the online finding aid: http://oasis.lib.harvard.edu/oasis/deliver/findingAidDisplay?_collection=oasis&inoid=5236&histno=0 (accessed June 15, 2012).

17. Abby Fisher, *What Mrs. Fisher Knows About Old Southern Cooking: Soups, Pickles, Preserves, etc.* (San Francisco: Women's Co-operative Printing Office, 1881), Arthur and Elizabeth Schlesinger Library on the History of Women in America, 641.613 F533w. An earlier cookbook by an African American, Malinda Russell, *A Domestic Cook Book: Containing a Careful Selection of Useful Receipts for the Kitchen* (Paw Paw, MI: T. O. Ward for the author, 1866), is known in only one copy in the Janice Bluestine Longone Culinary Archive, William L. Clements Library, University of Michigan, Ann Arbor, C 1866 RU.

18. Silkscreen poster, *Women Are Not Chicks*, Chicago Women's Graphics Collective, 1972, Arthur and Elizabeth Schlesinger Library on the History of Women in America, GR-15 2002-M130.

19. Edward Lamson Henry (1841–1919), *The Message*, 1893, 23.5 x 30.5 cm (9 1/4 x 12 in.), Harvard Art Museums/Fogg Museum, Gift of Theodore E. Stebbins, Jr., 2003.279.

20. Head of a female figure of the Spedos variety, marble, Cyclades, Greece, 2500–2400 BCE, Harvard Art Museums/Arthur M. Sackler Museum, The Lois Orswell Collection, 1998.242.

21. Aphrodite torso, marble, Greater Greece, ca. 250–100 BCE, Harvard Art Museums/Arthur M. Sackler Museum, The Lois Orswell Collection, 1998.239.

22. *Loulie's Hand*, marble, Hiram Powers, Florence, Italy, original made 1839, replicas made through 1877, Harvard Art Museums/Fogg Museum, Gift of Professor James Hardy Ropes, 1928.115.

23. Cann, silver, Myer Myers, New York, NY, 1750–60, Harvard Art Museums/Fogg Museum, Bequest of David Berg, 1999.306.1. This was the subject of Jennifer Stolper's seminar paper in spring 2003.

24. Conical tea bowl with *Yōhen*-type glaze, stoneware, Kimura Moriyasu, Kyoto, 1999, Harvard Art Museums/Arthur M. Sackler Museum, Gift of Moriyasu Kimura, 2000.23. (In Japanese usage, family name precedes given name: Kimura Moriyasu.)

25. Cenotaph cover, silk lampas on satin foundation, Ottoman Empire, seventeenth century, Harvard Art Museums/Arthur M. Sackler Museum, The Stuart Cary Welch Collection, Gift of Edith I. Welch in memory of Stuart Cary Welch, 2009.202.48.

26. Mask, Teotihuacán, gray limestone with traces of polychromy, Mexico, third–seventh centuries, Harvard Art Museums/Fogg Museum, Bequest of Grenville L. Winthrop, 1943.1055. This was the subject of Katherine O'Leary's seminar paper in fall 2010.

27. *Blolo Bla* figure (spirit spouse), iroko wood, Baule peoples, Côte d'Ivoire, nineteenth–twentieth centuries, Harvard Art Museums/Fogg Museum, The Lois Orswell Collection, 1998.311.

28. Marjorie B. Cohn, *Lois Orswell, David Smith, and Modern Art*, with the Lois Orswell/David Smith Correspondence, ed. Sarah B. Kianovsky (Cambridge, MA: Harvard University Art Museums; New Haven and London: Yale University Press, 2002).

29. *Cabbage Leaf*, gelatin silver print, Edward Weston, San Francisco, CA, 1931, printed later, Harvard Art Museums/Fogg Museum, Gift of Sam Pratt, P2003.250.

30. Bottles of chemicals marked "Medical College of Alabama," Rousseau Frères, Paris, ca. 1862, Collection of Historical Scientific Instruments, 4516, 4529, 4609, 4618, 4654, 4661, 4671.

31. "Mondrian," Edwin H. Land, Cambridge, ca. 1975–1985, Collection of Historical Scientific Instruments, 2004-1-0255.

32. Plaster casts from the Boston Phrenological Society: Dr. Johann Gaspar Spurzheim (1776–1832), Anne-Josèphe Théroigne de Méricourt (1762–1817), and René Descartes (1596–1650), USA, before 1835, Warren Anatomical Museum in the Francis A. Countway Library of Medicine, WAM 03562.001, 03364, 03499.

33. Sundial with *qibla* indicator, Turkish, ca. 1675–1725, Collection of Historical Scientific Instruments, 7046.

34. Project Moonwatch telescope belonging to Fred Whipple, Micronta, Japan, ca. 1957, Collection of Historical Scientific Instruments, 2006-1-0119.

35. Armillary sphere, USSR, ca. 1960, Collection of Historical Scientific Instruments, 2006-1-0109.

36. Bedspread (black, tan, and red) for Harvard Graduate Center, plaid woven cotton, Anni Albers, Cambridge, MA, 1949, Harvard Art Museums/Busch-Reisinger Museum, Gift of Anni Albers, BR67.20. This was the subject of Barbara Elfman's seminar paper in fall 2010.

37. Crimson field-hockey dress, Radcliffe College, ca. 1925, Elizabeth Wright Plimpton Papers, Arthur and Elizabeth Schlesinger Library on the History of Women in America, SC 98.

38. Blue sash of watered-grosgrain ribbon worn by George Washington, France(?), ca. 1775–83, Peabody Museum of Archaeology and Ethnology, Gift of the Heirs of David Kimball, 979-13-10/58761.

39. Framed military epaulet, France(?), ca. 1780, General Artemas Ward House Museum, HU 1695. This was the subject of Catherine Jampel's seminar paper in fall 2005.

40. Parasitic tapeworm (*Taenia* sp.), Boston, 1893, Department of Invertebrate Zoology, Museum of Comparative Zoology, 37376.

41. Rudolf Schlechter, *Beiträge zur Orchideenkunde von Zentralamerica I: Orchidaceae Powellianae Panamenses (Repertorium specierum novarum regni vegetabilis*, ed. Friedrich Fedde, *Beihefte* 17), (Dahlem, DE: Verlag des Repertoriums, 1922), p. 35, quoting notes by Charles W. Powell.

42. See David Freedberg, *The Eye of the Lynx: Galileo, his Friends, and the Beginnings of Modern Natural History* (Chicago and London: University of Chicago Press, 2002) on the "paper museum" of Cassiano dal Pozzo, and the projects of Federico Cesi and the Accademia de Lincei, founded in 1603, with many further references.

43. Lorraine Daston and Peter Galison, *Objectivity* (New York: Zone Books, 2010), pp. 84–98.

44. For instance, *English Botany*, thirty-six volumes on the plants of Britain published between 1790 and 1813, carried the name of James Sowerby, the illustrator, on the title page. That of James Edward Smith, founder and president of the Linnean Society of London, who wrote the formal descriptions, did not appear until Volume 4. To Smith's annoyance, this massive work was generally known as "Sowerby's *Botany*"; James Sowerby and James Smith, *English Botany; or Coloured Figures of British Plants, with their Essential Characters, Synonyms, and Places of Growth*, 267 parts in thirty-six vols. (London: The Author, 1790–1813). See Daston and Galison, p. 95.

45. For example, Harriet Thistelton-Dyer contributed numerous botanical illustrations to *Curtis's Botanical Magazine* at the behest of her father, Joseph Dalton Hooker, director of the Royal Botanical Gardens, Kew, and his colleague, her husband, William Thistelton-Dyer, beginning with *Jasminum didymum*, in 1878; Joseph Dalton Hooker, *Curtis's Botanical Magazine, Comprising the Plants of the Royal Gardens of Kew, and of Other Botanical Establishments in Great Britain, with Suitable Descriptions*, 3rd Series, 34 (London: Reeve & Co., 1878), Plate 6349.

46. Oakes Ames, *Orchidaceae: Illustrations and Studies of the Family Orchidaceae, Issuing from the Ames Botanical Laboratory, North Easton, Massachusetts*, seven fascicles (Boston: Merrymount Press, 1905–22).

47. Ames's younger close colleague at Harvard, Charles Schweinfurth, described them as "a partnership such as is seldom seen in the scientific world," an indication of respect even allowing for the conventions of encomium; Charles Schweinfurth, "Mrs. Oakes Ames as a botanical illustrator," *Philippine Orchid Review* 6, 1, 1955, p. 5.

48. Ames, *Orchidaceae*, Fascicle five (Boston: Merrymount Press, 1915), Dedication (unpaginated).

49. See Anne Biller Clark, *My Dear Mrs. Ames: A Study of Suffragist Cartoonist, Blanche Ames Ames* (New York: Peter Lang, 2001), pp. 79–149.

50. On Borderland, see the website of the Massachusetts Department of Conservation and Recreation: http://www.mass.gov/dcr/parks/borderland/index.htm (accessed Dec. 19, 2011).

51. Richard E. Schultes, "Oakes Ames, 1874–1950," *Rhodora: Journal of the New England Botanical Club* 53, 627, 1951, p. 70. Britton was intimately involved in the international controversies concerning protocols of plant taxonomy, and was the author of the Code of Botanical Nomenclature

that the International Botanical Congress of 1905 in Vienna did not accept, but which many American botanists did; see Dan H. Nicolson, "A History of Botanical Nomenclature," *Annals of the Missouri Botanical Garden* 78, 1, 1991, pp. 38–39.

52. Oakes Ames's career is summarized, with bibliographical references, on the website of the Harvard University Herbaria: http://www.huh.harvard.edu/libraries/archives/AMES.html (accessed Dec. 17, 2011). See also *Oakes Ames: Jottings of a Harvard Botanist, 1874–1950*, ed. Pauline Ames Plimpton (Cambridge, MA: Botanical Museum of Harvard University, 1979), p. 379.

53. Merle A. Reinikka, *A History of the Orchid* (Portland, OR: Timber Press, 1995; first published 1972), pp. 26–31.

54. John Lindley rose to secretary of the Royal Horticultural Society and professor of botany at King's College in the University of London. The herbarium he formed of approximately 7,000 orchid specimens is the acknowledged foundation of all orchid systematics, and was entered in the Royal Botanic Gardens, Kew, after his death; see the Royal Botanic Gardens website: http://www.kew.org/science/orchids/resource.html (accessed Dec. 17, 2011). His *Genera and Species of Orchidaceous Plants*, seven parts (London: J. Ridgeway, 1830–40) set the benchmark in the field.

55. Heinrich Gustav Reichenbach was, from 1863, professor of botany and director of the Botanischer Garten of the University of Hamburg. He assembled a large orchid herbarium to which orchidologists the world over sent their specimens for identification. This was the basis of his power within the orchid world, and it was bolstered not only by publications he initiated himself, but by fascicles published serially by Frederick Sander, lavishly produced with chromolithographic illustrations, most of which were by Joseph Mansell, after elaborate watercolors by the landscape and botanical artist Henry G. Moon and others, and descriptions by Reichenbach; Frederick Sander, *Reichenbachia: Orchids Illustrated and Described* (St. Albans, UK: F. Sander & Co., 1888–94). See also R. J. Ferry, "Reichenbachia," *The McAllen International Orchid Society Journal* 7, 11, 2006, pp. 5–10.

56. Robert Allen Rolfe was the founder of *The Orchid Review*. As first curator of the Orchid Herbarium at the Royal Botanic Gardens, Kew, Rolfe controlled Lindley's legacy and built upon it relentlessly, offering an alternative source of taxonomic authority to Reichenbach.

57. Oakes Ames, "Friedrich Richard Rudolf Schlechter," *American Orchid Society Bulletin* 2, 2, 1933, p. 21.

58. Oakes Ames, "The Destruction of the Schlechter Herbarium by Bombing," *American Orchid Society Bulletin* 13, 4, 1944, p. 106.

59. Schlechter, *Orchidaceae Powellianae Panamenses*, p. 35.

60. Ames, "Destruction," 1944, p. 106. Ames had himself recently proposed seven new species of Panamanian orchid; Oakes Ames, "Additions to the Orchid Flora of Panama," *Proceedings of the Biological Society of Washington* 34, 1921, pp. 149–154.

61. Ames recalled: "It was a time when my enthusiasm was reaching dizzying heights and in addition to routine determinations undertaken for numerous institutions, I was laying the groundwork of a flora of the Central American orchids in connection with C. W. Powell of the Canal Zone and C. H. Lankester of Cartago, Costa Rica"; *Jottings*, 1979, p. 69.

62. Ames, "Destruction," 1944, pp. 105–106.

63. Lorraine Daston, "Type Specimens and Scientific Memory," *Critical Inquiry* 31, 1, 2004, p. 157 (original emphasis). Daston convincingly argues that the "gradual articulation of a set of practices (publishing, labeling, traveling, referencing, compiling) centered on a collection of objects (type specimens), that is, an *art* of transmission, . . . turned the code articles on nomenclatural types into a remarkable act of applied metaphysics."

64. *Règles internationales de la nomenclature botanique adoptées par le Congrès international de botanique de Vienne, et publiées au nom de la Commission de redaction du Congrès par John Briquet* (Jena, DE: G. Fischer, 1906). The process of regulation had begun at the Paris meeting in 1867, which had resulted in the rules codified by Alphonse de Candolle; *Lois de la nomenclature botanique adoptees par le Congrès international de botanique, tenu à Paris en août 1867* (Geneva, CH: H. Georg, 1867). The Vienna rules of 1905 did not reconcile all disagreements; that would not be achieved

until 1930 or, because of circumstances, 1950 (Nicolson, "History of Botanical Nomenclature," pp. 33–56, esp. pp. 34–41). The code has continued to be modified, most recently in Melbourne in 2011; see James S. Miller, et al., "Outcomes of the 2011 Botanical Nomenclature Section at the XVIII International Botanical Congress," *PhytoKeys* 5, 2011, pp. 1–3. One of the actions was to change the title of the code to the International Code of Nomenclature for algae, fungi, and plants (lowercase denoting vernacular usage, not technical clades). For details of each progressive revision, see *Regnum Vegetabile* (Köningstein, DE: Koeltz, 1953).

65. Ames gives the history of his examination of the specimen he received from Powell, describing it as a duplicate type, and comparisons made with other species of *Epidendrum*, in Oakes Ames, F. Tracy Hubbard, and Charles Schweinfurth, *The Genus Epidendrum in the United States and Middle America* (Cambridge, MA: Botanical Museum, 1936), p. 107. However, a recent determination in the *ITIS Catalogue of Life Annual Checklist* for 2008 is that *Epidendrum lorifolium* Schltr. is a synonym for *Epidendrum flexuosum* G. Mey., which takes precedence; see http://www.catalogueoflife.org/annual-checklist/2008/show_species_details.php?record_id=4943515 (accessed Jan. 16, 2012).

66. John D. Dwyer, "Panama, Plant Collection, and the Missouri Botanical Garden," *Annals of the Missouri Botanical Garden* 51, 1/4, 1964, p. 109.

67. In 1939, the Tropical Station was relinquished to the Canal Zone Government as a public park; Dwyer, "Panama," p. 110. See also "The Tropical Station of the Missouri Botanical Garden," *Science* NS 89, No. 2310, 1939, p. 310. Two series of undated photographs from the Missouri Botanical Garden Archives of the C. W. Powell Orchid Garden and the Tropical Station, respectively, are available on the Missouri Digital Heritage website: http://cdm.sos.mo.gov/cdm4/results.php?CISOOP1=any&CISOFIELD1=CISOSEARCHALL&CISOROOT=/mobot&CISOBOX1=Panama&CISOSTART=1,1 (accessed Dec. 19, 2011).

68. But not fully conquered until 1913; see, inter alia, A. B. Feuer, *America at War: The Philippines, 1898–1913* (Westport, CT.: Praeger, 2002); see also Teodoro A. Agoncillo, *Malolos: The Crisis of the Republic* (Quezon City, Philippines: University of the Philippines, 1960).

69. The garden, founded on land owned by an American sugar cane planter, Edwin Atkins, is now called the Cienfuegos Botanical Garden and is administered by the Cuban government; Arnold Arboretum website, http://arboretum.harvard.edu/library/image-collection/cienfuegos-botanical-garden-cuba/ (accessed Dec. 19, 2011). See also Marion D. Cahan, "The Harvard Garden in Cuba—A Brief History," *Arnoldia* 51, 3, 1991, pp. 22–32.

70. "Oakes Ames (1874–1950) Papers," Harvard University Herbaria website: http://www.huh.harvard.edu/libraries/archives/AMES.html (accessed Dec. 19, 2011).

71. George Sterling, *The House of Orchids, and Other Poems* (San Francisco: A. M. Robertson, 1911), p. 35.

72. Oscar Wilde, *The Picture of Dorian Gray* (New York: Charterhouse Press, 1904; first published 1890, revised 1891), p. 287.

73. Ames, "Destruction," p. 106; the species Schlechter proffered was Rucker's Stanhopea (*Stanhopea ruckeri*).

74. See, in particular, Gregory J. Galer, "Forging Ahead: The Ames Family of Easton, Massachusetts, and Two Centuries of Industrial Enterprise, 1635–1861" (Ph.D. dissertation, Massachusetts Institute of Technology, 2002). Stonehill College, Easton, Massachusetts, houses a substantial archive on the Ames Shovel Company, and the Stonehill Industrial History Center at the college contains a collection of approximately 755 shovels.

75. Four-handled glass jar, Roman, fourth–fifth century, Semitic Museum, 1936.2.98.

76. E. M. Stern, *Roman, Byzantine, and Early Medieval Glass 10 BCE–700 CE: Ernesto Wolf Collection* (Ostfildern-Ruit, DE: Hatje Cantz Publishers, 2001), p. 133.

77. For example, a similar jar was found with traces of *cannabis* in Giv'at Sharet, Israel. Stern, 150.

78. Catalog records for 1936.2.98, Semitic Museum, Harvard University; "An Interesting Archæological Collection," *Bulletin of the American Schools of Oriental Research*, No. 4 (Sept. 1921), pp. 14–16.

79. Max Kellner, "A Day with the Neoliths," *Palestine Exploration Fund: Quarterly Statement* (1913), pp. 184–190.

80. Charles Peabody, "Notes on Prehistoric Palestine and Syria," *American Anthropologist, New Series* 17:4 (Oct.–Dec. 1915), pp. 695–707.

81. Warren J. Moulton, "Gleanings in Archaeology and Epigraphy," *The Annual of the American School of Oriental Research in Jerusalem* I (1919–1920), pp. 74–75.

82. Maximilian Lindsay Kellner, *The Assyrian monuments illustrating the sermons of Isaiah* (Boston: Dameral and Upham, 1900), p. 5.

83. *Reports of the President and Treasurer of Harvard College, 1913–1913* (Cambridge, MA: Published by the University, 1915), pp. 239–240.

84. For example, Mrs. Kellner is credited as the owner of one of the objects Moulton published in his 1919–20 article.

85. Elisabeth W. Brooks, *As the World Goes By* (Boston: Little, Brown and Co., 1905).

86. Jackson Lears, *No Place of Grace: Antimodernism and the Transformation of American Culture, 1880–1920* (New York: Pantheon, 1981).

87. Martin Eidelberg, "Tiffany's Glass Vessels," in *Tiffany Glass: A Passion for Colour* (Montreal: Montreal Museum of Fine Arts and Skira-Flammarion, 2009), pp. 116–120.

88. Scrapbook of Maximilian L. Kellner, HUA 885.44 f, Harvard University Archives.

89. Kellner also collected art. He donated his collection of Christoffel van Sichem II's series "Subjects from the New Testament" to the Fogg in 1925–26.

90. Plato, *The Republic*, 3. 406a5-b4. The MS fragment is universally known as P.Oxy.3.455 and is included in several catalogues: Bernard P. Grenfell and Arthur S. Hunt, *The Oxyrhynchus Papyri*, Part III (London, 1903), No. 455, p. 109 and plate vi; P. Mertens and R. A. Pack, *Catalogue des papyrus littéraires grecs et latins*, 3rd ed. [MP3], MS 1418; digitized and updated by the Centre de Documentation de Papyrologie Littéraire, dir. M.-H. Marganne, and online at http://promethee.philo.ulg.ac.be/cedopal/indexsimple.asp; W. Clarysse, *Leuven Database of Ancient Books*, MS 3818, online at http://www.trismegistos.org/ldab/text.php?quick=3818; and *Digital Papyri at Houghton Library*, MS GR SM3739, online at http://hcl.harvard.edu/librar ies/houghton/collections/papyrus/bibliographies.cfm.

91. Known as "A," Platonis Codex Parisinus Graecus 1807, Bibliothèque nationale de France. See Gerrit Boter, *The Textual Tradition of Plato's Republic* (Amsterdam: Free University Press, 1986), pp. 65–69, 89–117. The manuscript was acquired in the East by Johannes Lascaris, arriving in Italy around 1490. After his death, it changed hands a number of times passing through the libraries of, among others, Catherine de Medici and the King of France.

92. Boter, *Textual Tradition*, pp. 306–313, lists eleven authoritative papyri from the second and third centuries as the earliest extant.

93. Quotations taken from Plato, *The Republic*, trans. A. D. Lindsay, Everyman's Library edition (New York: Alfred A. Knopf, 1992).

94. Readers may be helped by this chronology: ca. 1575–1087 BCE, New Kingdom of Egyptian Empire; 525 BCE, Persians conquer Egypt; 332/1 BCE, Alexander the Great conquers Egypt, and many Greek immigrants follow; 323 BCE, death of Alexander and installation of his general Ptolemy I as governor and later King of Egypt (305 BCE); Ptolemaic period follows; 30 BCE, Egypt becomes a province of the Roman Empire after the Battle of Actium and suicide of Antony and Cleopatra; 324 CE, Emperor Constantine establishes imperial capital at Constantinople; 395 CE, division of Roman Empire into East and West; 639–642 CE, Arab conquest of Egypt, which then becomes a province of the Caliphate; 968–1171 CE, Fatimid Dynasty and flowering of Muslim culture in Egypt; 1250–1805, Mamluks rule; 1517, Ottoman Turks conquer Egypt; 1798–1799, Napoleanic expedition to Egypt followed by capitulation to British in 1801; first systematic survey of antiquities including discovery of Rosetta Stone; 1805, start of regime of Muhammad Ali; 1882, British occupation of Egypt; 1896–1907, Grenfell and Hunt excavate el-Behnesa (formerly known as Oxyrhynchus). From Peter Parsons, *City of the Sharp-Nosed Fish: Greek Lives in Roman Egypt* (London: Weidenfeld and Nicolson, 2007), xi–xiii.

95. Parsons, *City of the Sharp-Nosed Fish*, pp. 111, figs. 26, 29, 32, 34, 35. Other examples are found online at "POxy: Oxyrhynchus Online," http://www.papyrology.ox.ac.uk/POxy/index.html (accessed Sept. 13, 2012).

96. See correspondence in files for SM1904.8, Semitic Museum, Harvard University.

97. Plato, *Republic*, 7, pp. 514–518.

98. Mold for casting openwork ornaments, Avar people, Balkans, ca. 567–822 CE, limestone, Harvard Art Museums/Arthur M. Sackler Museum, Gift of Bruce Ferrini, 2001.270.59. David Gordon Mitten, who reluctantly retired as George M. A. Hanfmann Curator of Ancient Art at the Harvard Art Museums in 2005 on reaching the age of seventy had the imagination and determination to acquire this and a number of other Avar objects in the face of skepticism from those at the museums who regarded such fascinating things beneath their notice.

99. Falko Daim, et al., *Hunnen + Awaren: Reitervölker aus dem Osten*, exh. cat. Schloss Halbturn (Eisenstadt, DE: Amt der Burgenländischen Landesregierung, 1996), pp. 356–357, No. 5.296, ill. p. 357.

100. Nelson Goodman, *Ways of Worldmaking* (Indianapolis: Hackett, 1978), pp. 57–70.

101. A drawing proposing a reconstruction of a pair of belts found in the grave of an Avar leader at Bócsa in Hungary, excavated in 1935, reveals how an arrow quiver might be attached by cords or leather laces to a pair of such belt fittings; Gyula László, *Études archéologiques sur l'histoire de la société des Avars (Archaeologia Hungarica: Dissertationes Archaeologicae Musei Nationalis Hungarici,* Series Nova XXXIV) (Budapest: Akadémiai Kiadó, 1955), pp. 220–232. The gold belt fittings themselves, dating from the first half of the seventh century, are in the Hungarian National Museum, Budapest; Éva Garam and Attila Kiss, *Gold Finds of the Migration Period in the Hungarian National Museum* (Budapest: Helikon, and Milan: Electa, 1992), p. 46.

102. On the Avars, see, in particular, Walter Pohl, *Die Awaren. Ein Steppenvolk in Mitteleuropa, 576–822 n. Chr.* (Munich: Beck, 1988).

103. This object and those discovered with it at Nagyszentmiklós (now Sînnicolau Mare, Romania) in 1799 have been the subject of contention. See Gyula László and István Rácz, *The Treasure of Nagyszentmiklós* (Budapest: Corvina Kiadó, 1984), for a detailed account with extensive bibliography.

104. Daim, et al., *Hunnen + Awaren*, p. 232, No. 5.59, ill.

105. Gábor Kiss, "Die Mitbestattung von Pferden bei den Awaren" in Daim, et al., *Hunnen + Awaren*, pp. 387–390, discussing a gravesite at Gyenesdiás, Hungary.

106. Modern Sremska Mitrovica, Vojvodina, northern Serbia.

107. Pál Lipták, *Avars and Ancient Hungarians* (Budapest: Akadémiai Kiadó, 1983), pp. 48–52, 159.

108. Benedict Anderson, *Imagined Communities: Reflections on the Origin and Spread of Nationalism* (London: Verso, 1983).

109. Susan Reynolds, "Our Forefathers? Tribes, Peoples, and Nations in the Historiography of the Age of Migrations" in Alexander Callander Murray, ed., *After Rome's Fall: Narrators and Sources of Early Medieval History. Essays presented to Walter Goffart* (Toronto, Buffalo, and London: University of Toronto Press, 1998), p. 33.

110. Édouard Glissant, *Poétique de la relation* (Paris: Gallimard, 1990).

111. This section is excerpted from Ivan Gaskell, "After Art, Beyond Beauty," in *Inspiration and Technique: Ancient to Modern Views on Beauty and Art*, eds. John Roe and Michele Stanco (Oxford, UK, and New York: Peter Lang, 2007), pp. 311–334, and is reprinted with the permission of the publisher.

112. Bottles of chemicals marked "Medical College of Alabama," Rousseau Frères, Paris, ca. 1862, Collection of Historical Scientific Instruments, Harvard University, Inv. Nos. 4516, 4529, 4609, 4618, 4654, 4661, 4671.

113. Josiah C. Nott, "Medical Museums and Schools, with remarks on the Radical Cure of Hernia," *New Orleans Medical and Surgical Journal* 17 (1860), pp. 74ff; Willis G. Clark, *History of Education in Alabama, 1702–1889*, United States Bureau of Education Circular of Information, No. 3, 1889; Contributions to American Educational History, No. 8 (Washington, DC: Government Printing Office, 1889), pp. 147–149; Charles B. Rodning, "Medical College of Alabama in Mobile, 1859–1920: A Legacy of Dr. Josiah Clark Nott," *Southern Medical Journal* 82 (1989), pp. 53–63; Howard L. Holley, "A Century and a Half of the History of the Life of Sciences in Alabama: 'The past is never dead. It's not even past.' Dr. Josiah Clark Nott's Commencement

Address at the Medical College of Alabama, Mobile, Alabama, March 8, 1860," *Alabama Journal of Medical Sciences* 15 (1978), pp. 125–129.

114. Nott, "Medical Museums," p. 74.

115. F. W. Clarke, "Chemistry in the United States," *Science*, New Series, 5, No. 108 (1897), pp. 117–129; E. F. Smith, *Chemistry in America: Chapters from the History of Science in the United States* (New York: n.p., 1914); C. A. Browne, "The History of Chemical Education in America between the Years 1820 and 1870," *Journal of Chemical Education*, 9 (1932), pp. 705–706.

116. I. Bernard Cohen, *Some Early Tools of American Science* (Cambridge, MA: Harvard University Press, 1950), pp. 34–35.

117. Samuel Williams, "Lecture XV. On the different kinds of Air," read to undergraduates every May from 1785 to 1788, in Papers of Samuel Williams, 1752–1794, Harvard University Archives, HUM 8.

118. Cohen, *Some Early Tools*, pp. 66–95, quotes numerous archival documents in the period before Josiah P. Cooke. See also Josiah P. Cooke, "Letter of Professor Cook to President Walker" (1857), pp. 13–17, in the "Thirty-Second Annual Report of the President of Harvard College to the Overseers, Exhibiting the State of the Institution for the Academical Year 1856–57" (1858), Harvard University Archives, HU 30.10; Josiah P. Cooke, "Report of the Committee on the Chemical Laboratory," pp. 4–5, in the "Reports of the Visiting Committees of the Board of Overseers of Harvard College from February 6, 1890, to January 8, 1902 inclusive" (1902), pp. 4–5.

119. George Bemis, *Report of the case of John W. Webster…indicted for the murder of George Parkman…before the Supreme Judicial Court of Massachusetts; including the hearing on the petition for a writ of error, the prisoner's confessional statements and application for a commutation of sentence, and an appendix containing several interesting matters never before published* (Boston: Charles C. Little and James Brown, 1850). Vesuvianite from Webster's mineral collection was also exhibited in *Tangible Things*.

120. M. B., "Josiah Parsons Cooke," *Scientific American*, (Dec. 10, 1887), p. 377.

121. "Harvard University, Cambridge, Mass., Comprises the Following Departments…" [notice of schools, faculty, and dates of entrance examinations], *The Nation*, 13 No. 321 (Aug. 17, 1871), p. 136; Harvard University, *Quinquennial Catalogue of the Officers and Graduates 1636–1930, Harvard University* (Cambridge, MA: Harvard University, 1930).

122. Charles W. Eliot and Frank H. Storer, "On the Impurities of Commercial Zinc, with Special Reference to the Residue insoluble in Dilute Acids, to Sulphur, and to Arsenic," *Memoirs of the American Academy of Arts and Sciences*, New Series, 8 (1860, pp. 57ff; reviewed in *The American Journal of Science and Arts*, 2nd Series, 31 (May 1861), pp. 142–147; and Josiah P. Cooke, *Contributions from the Chemical Laboratory of Harvard College* (Cambridge, MA, 1877), pp. 12, 39.

123. Clark, *History of Education in Alabama*, pp. 148–149; Reginald Horsman, *Josiah Nott of Mobile: Southerner, Physician, and Racial Theorist* (Baton Rouge: Louisiana State University Press, 1987).

124. The new observatory in Chicago would be named the Dearborn Observatory. The famous lens and telescope are now in the Adler Planetarium. Deborah Jean Warner and Robert B. Ariail, *Alvan Clark & Sons, Artists in Optics*, 2nd ed. (Richmond, VA: Willmann-Bell, in association with the National Museum of American History, Smithsonian Institution, 1995), pp. 17, 87–88, 134; Bessie Zaban Jones and Lyle Gifford Boyd, *The Harvard College Observatory: The First Four Directorships, 1839–1919* (Cambridge, MA: Belknap Press, 1971), pp. 122–124.

125. George P. Bond to Asaph Hall, (March 2, 1863), quoted in Jones and Boyd, *Harvard College Observatory*, p. 124.

126. Elizabeth Wright Plimpton Papers, Arthur and Elizabeth Schlesinger Library on the History of Women in America.

127. For a cogent summary of efforts to secure co-education, see Sally Schwager, "Taking Up the Challenge: The Origins of Radcliffe," in *Yards & Gates: Gender in Harvard and Radcliffe History*, ed. Laurel Thatcher Ulrich (New York: Palgrave/Macmillan, 2004), pp. 87–116. A brief timeline of Radcliffe's history can be found on the website of the Radcliffe Institute

for Advanced Study at http://www.radcliffe.harvard.edu/about-us/our-history. Harvard's own website pretty much buries Radcliffe's history. See, for example, "Harvard at a Glance," at http://www.harvard.edu/harvard-glance and "Historical Facts" at http://www.harvard.edu/historical-facts.

128. "Report of the Director of the Gymnasium," in *Annual Report of Radcliffe College 1907–08* (Cambridge, MA: Radcliffe College, 1908), p. 35. On the broader history of this argument over the value of physical education, see Martha H. Verbrugge, *Active Bodies: A History of Women's Physical Education in Twentieth-Century America* (New York: Oxford University Press, 2012).

129. Dorothy Ella Howells, *A Century to Celebrate: Radcliffe College, 1879–1979* (Cambridge, MA: Radcliffe College, 1978), pp. 77–79.

130. Elizabeth A. Wright, "The Radcliffe Gymnasium" (read at the Conference of Radcliffe Representatives, June 20, 1922), *The Radcliffe Quarterly* v. VI, No. 4 (Sept. 1922), pp. 52–56 (quote on p. 53).

131. Sarah K. Fields, *Female Gladiators: Gender, Law, and Contact Sport in America*, (Urbana, IL: University of Illinois Press, 2005), pp. 132, 133.

132. Edith Plimpton's gymnasium suit almost perfectly matches the nineteenth-century instructions quoted in Patricia Campbell Warner, "Clothing the Woman for Sport and Physical Education, 1860 to 1940," Ph.D. dissertation, University of Minnesota, 1986, pp. 73–74.

133. Campbell, "Clothing the Woman," pp. 39, 40.

134. Gloria Bruce, "Radcliffe Women at Play," in *Yards and Gates: Gender in Harvard and Radcliffe History*, ed. Laurel Thatcher Ulrich (New York: Palgrave/Macmillan, 2004), pp. 142–144.

135. Field Hockey at Radcliffe College, 1910, Radcliffe Archives, TC 149-1-1.

136. Elizabeth Wright Plimpton, Scrapbook.

137. LeBaron Russell Briggs, *Girls and Education* (Boston, New York: Houghton Mifflin, 1911), pp. 105, 106, 113.

138. Radcliffe 25th Reunion Questionnaire, 1953–54, Elizabeth Plimpton Biographical File, Radcliffe Archives.

139. "At 75, she keeps family tradition," *New Tribune*, undated clipping, Elizabeth Plimpton Biographical File, Radcliffe Archives. On the 1930 census, Elizabeth's father, Henry R. Plimpton, lists himself as an "inventor." United States Census, 1930, Newton, Middlesex, Massachusetts, Roll 927, p. 11B, accessed on Ancestry.com.

140. Blanche Wiesen Cook, "Woman of the Century: Eleanor Roosevelt's Biographer Assesses the Legacy of a First Lady Who Sought Justice for All," *The Women's Review of Books*, 17, Nos. 10/11 (July 2000), p. 23.

141. 1969 Reunion Questionnaire, Elizabeth Plimpton Biographical File, Radcliffe Archives.

142. Radcliffe College Yearbook, 1929, p. 46.

143. 25th Anniversary Alumnae Questionnaire, Elizabeth Plimpton Biographical File.

CHAPTER 2

1. Harvard student's summer gown, ca. 1834, Harvard University Archives, gift of Mrs. F. Parker, HUD 837.87.

2. *Norma* and *Normman*, Abram Belskie, USA, ca. 1945, Warren Anatomical Museum in the Francis A. Countway Library of Medicine, WAM 20519 and 20520.

3. "Blondie goes to Leisureland: a Westinghouse game," USA, ca. 1940, Baker Library, Baker Old Class RFCW.66 W52.

4. Tiger cranium and jaw (*Felis tigris tigris*), Mammalogy Collection, Museum of Comparative Zoology, 46407.

5. Parasitic tapeworms (*Taenia* sp.), Boston, 1893, Department of Invertebrates, Museum of Comparative Zoology, 37376.

6. Unidentified text written on palm leaves and bound accordion-style between wood, Indonesia, Houghton Library, MS Indo 2.

7. Quirt handle, Omaha or Ponca peoples, Nebraska, ca. 1870–90, General Artemas Ward House Museum, HU 4175. This was the subject of Sigurd Østrem's seminar paper in fall 2006.

8. Enju School short sword, cut down from longer blade, Higo Province, Kyushu, Japan, ca. 1530, Harvard Art Museums/Arthur M. Sackler Museum, Gift of Professor Albert Bushnell Hart, Class of 1880, 1936.126.B.

9. Transatlantic telegraph cable section, UK, ca. 1866, General Artemas Ward House Museum, HU 3334.

10. Letter stick announcing the death of a relative, Mary River, Kimberley, Western Australia, 1922 or earlier, Peabody Museum of Archaeology and Ethnology, Gift of Mrs. Walter Badenach, 22-29-70/D1699.

11. Tortilla made from (*Zea mays*), Mexico, 1897, Economic Botany Herbarium of Oakes Ames, Harvard University Herbaria, cat. 8535.

12. Deborah Phillips Chodoff, *Little Chaos* (Katonah, NY, 1996), from an edition of four, Houghton Library, TypZ 970.97.278.

13. Samples of so-called "Negro cloth," Rhode Island, 1839–50, Peace Dale Collection, Baker Library, unnumbered.

14. Albert Bushnell Hart, *The Obvious Orient* (New York: D. Appleton, 1911), pp. 4, 5.

15. Samuel Eliot Morison, "Albert Bushnell Hart," *Proceedings of the Massachusetts Historical Society*, Third Series, Vol. 66 (Oct. 1936–May 1941), pp. 434–438; Albert Bushnell Hart, "Brother Jonathan's Colonies: A Historical Account," *Harper's Magazine*, 98 (1898–99), pp. 319, 327. Gary Marotta, "The Academic Mind and the Rise of U.S. Imperialism: Historians and Economists as Publicists for Ideas of Colonial Expansion," *American Journal of Economics and Sociology* 43 (1983), pp. 219–233. "Imagination in History," American Historical Association Presidential Address, *American Historical Review* 15, No. 2 (Jan. 1910), pp. 227–251. Sam Stupak, final paper in History 2404, Dec. 2009.

16. *Apollo 10 View of Earth*, May 18, 1969, printed later, Harvard Art Museums/Fogg Museum, on loan from the Carpenter Center for the Visual Arts, 2.2002.2158.

17. Medal of Livio I Odescalchi (1652–1713), Giovanni Martino Hamerani, Rome, 1689, Harvard Art Museums/Fogg Museum, Gift of Edward W. Forbes, by exchange, 1996.220.

18. Ostracon concerning textiles from vicinity of the First Cataract of the Nile, Egypt, ca. 100–200, Houghton Library (transferred from the Fogg Art Museum), MS Ostraca 3152.

19. Pieced quilt with inscriptions, Sarah Henshaw Ward Putnam, Shrewsbury, MA, 1881, General Artemas Ward House Museum, HU 3681.

20. Sash of blue watered-grosgrain ribbon worn by George Washington, France (?), ca. 1775–83, Peabody Museum of Archaeology and Ethnology, Gift of the Heirs of David Kimball, 979-13-10/58761.

21. Bedspread (black, tan, and red) for Harvard Graduate Center, Anni Albers, Cambridge, MA, 1949, Harvard Art Museums/Busch-Reisinger Museum, Gift of Anni Albers, BR67.20.

22. Stamps of authenticity from the silk industry, China, late nineteenth century, Baker Library.

23. The personal seal of ᵈSin-Ishme-anni, an administrator, and its impression, Mesopotamia, Old Babylonia, Semitic Museum, 1899.2.514.

24. Fragment of a papyrus manuscript of Plato, *The Republic*, Oxyrhynchus, Egypt, ca. 250–300, Houghton Library (transferred from Harvard Semitic Museum, gift of the Egypt Exploration Fund, 1904), MS Gr SM3739.

25. Playing cards related to the South Sea Bubble, printed for Carington Bowles, London, 1721, Baker Library, Kress Collection 06054.62-1.

26. Judah Monis, *Short nomenclator or vocabulary in English and Hebrew*, ca. 1735, Harvard University Archives, HUC 8635.235.

27. Pencil that belonged to Henry David Thoreau, Concord, MA, ca. 1850s, Houghton Library, *47Z-7.

28. Tombstone, Cairo, Abbasid Caliphate (Egypt), ninth century, Semitic Museum, 1947.6.1.

29. Transatlantic telegraph cable section, UK, ca. 1866, General Artemas Ward House Museum, HU 3334.

30. Slate with "spirit writing," Herrick-Chapman Family Papers, Arthur and Elizabeth Schlesinger Library on the History of Women in America, 2007-M7.

31. Quizzing glass owned by Ebenezer Storer, UK, late eighteenth century, Harvard University Archives, Ebenezer Storer Collection, HUG 1808.1000.1.

32. Camera lucida, William & Samuel Jones, London, ca. 1815, Collection of Historical Scientific Instruments, 1994-1-0001.

33. Louis Agassiz's drum microscope, Georges Oberhaeuser, Paris, ca. 1845–1846, Collection of Historical Scientific Instruments, 1117; Mark Twain's compound microscope and accessories, Negretti and Zambra, London, ca. 1880, Collection of Historical Scientific Instruments, 1113.

34. Colorless quartz sphere, Mineralogical Museum, 122838.

35. Project Moonwatch telescope belonging to Fred Whipple, Micronta, Japan, ca. 1957, Collection of Historical Scientific Instruments, 2006-1-0119.

36. Henry David Thoreau, *Walden and Other Writings of Henry David Thoreau*, ed. Brooks Atkinson (New York: Modern Library, 1992), p. 212.

37. Spoon carved with a human hand, Luanda, Angola, 1857 or earlier, Peabody Museum of Archaeology and Ethnology, Gift of Mrs. John D. Sparhawk, 83-14-50/30212.

38. Beetle necklace or bracelet, Naga people, India or Myanmar, 1913 or earlier, Peabody Museum of Archaeology and Ethnology, 13-24-60/D2145.

39. Vellum manuscript with watercolor drawings and inscriptions, bound in quilted satin, with a letter to the recipient of the Gift, Frances Lady Douglas, by Sarah Ponsonby and Eleanor Butler, Wales, 1788, Houghton Library, MS Eng 1225.

40. *Memorandums of a Cottage*, gift of Sarah Ponsonby (1755–1832) and Eleanor Butler (1739–1829) to Frances Lady Douglas, vellum manuscript with watercolor drawings, bound in satin and stored with a reticule purse in a silk pocket book, with a letter to the recipient of the Gift, Wales, 1788, Houghton Library.

41. *A Year with the Ladies of Llangollen*, ed. Elizabeth Mavor (New York: Penguin, 1986), p. 109 (June 4, 1787), p. 49 (Feb. 3, 1794), pp. 51, 52 (Feb. 4, 1796), p. 194 (Oct. 25, 1793); Elizabeth Mavor, *The Ladies of Llangollen: A Study in Romantic Friendship* (London: Michael Joseph, 1979), pp. 68, 71, 108, 117; Jill H. Casid, *Sowing Empire: Landscape and Colonization* (Minneapolis: University of Minnesota Press, 2005), pp. 175, 176; Douglas Archives, a collection of historical and genealogical records: http://www.douglashistory.co.uk/history/francesla dydouglas.htm.

42. Martha Vicinus, "'They Wonder to Which Sex I Belong': The Historical Roots of the Modern Lesbian Identity," *Feminist Studies* 18 (1992), pp. 467–497; Susan S. Lanser, "Befriending the Body: Female Intimacies as Class Acts," *Eighteenth-Century Studies* 32 (Winter 1998/99), pp. 179–199, and "Bluestocking Sapphism and the Economy of Desire," *Huntington Library Quarterly* 65, No. 1/2 (2002), pp. 257–275; Rebecca Jennings, *A Lesbian History of Britain: Love and Sex between Women since 1500* (Oxford, UK, and Westport, CT: Greenwood World Publishing, 2007), chap. 3.

43. Vicinus, "They Wonder," p. 479.

44. John Lockhart to his wife, (Aug. 24, 1825), Mavor, *Year*, p. 162.

45. Charles Mathew to Mrs. Mathew, (Sept. 4, 1820), Mavor, *Year*, pp. 178–179.

46. Mavor, *Year*, p. 219 (Dec. 4, 1785), p. 184 (Oct. 25, 1785). On the complexity of their relationship, see, in addition to the above, Mavor's *Ladies of Llangollen*, pp. 86–105.

47. Mavor, *Year*, p. 24 (Jan. 1, 1788), p. 31 (Jan. 2, 1790).

48. C. C. L. Hirschfeld, *Theorie de L'art Des Jardins* (Leipzig, DE: n.p., 1779), pp. 50, 54, who took the poem from Claude-Henri Watelet, *Essai sur les jardins* (Paris: Prault, 1774), pp. 149, 151, 159. Thanks to Janet Polasky for helping me identify the poem.

49. Christian Cajus Lorenz Hirschfeld, *Theory of Garden Art*, ed. and trans. Linda B. Parshall (Philadelphia: University of Pennsylvania Press, 2001), p. 92. Translations for the other two stanzas in the order in which they appear in the manuscript can be found on pp. 4 and 87. An English translation of Watelet's text can be found in Claude-Henry Watelet, *Essay on Gardens: A Chapter in the French Picturesque*, ed. and trans. Samuel Danon (Philadelphia: University of Pennsylvania Press, 2003), pp. 71–78.

50. Casid, *Sowing Empire*, pp. 175, 176, 186.

51. Nicole Reynolds, "Cottage Industry: The Ladies of Llangollen and the Symbolic Capital of the *Cottage Ornée*," *The Eighteenth Century* 51 (Spring/Summer 2010), pp. 211–259.

52. Anna Seward to The Rev. Henry White of Lichfield, Barmouth, (Sept. 7, 1795), in Mavor, *Year*, pp. 172–174.

53. Mavor, *Year*, p. 37 (Jan. 26, 1802), p. 67 (March 22, 1802).

54. Mavor, *Year*, p. 219 (Dec. 3, 1785); *The Hamwood Papers of the Ladies of Llangollen*, ed. Mrs. G. H. Bell (London: Macmillan, 1930), p. 104.

55. Mavor, *Year*, p. 58 (March 13, 1788), p. 61 (March 28, 1789), p. 60 (March 20, 1789); *Ladies of Llangollen*, p. 152, 153.

56. Mavor, "Sarah Ponsonby to Mrs. Parker," *Year*, p. 69.

57. Susan S. Lanser, "'Put to the Blush': Romantic Irregularities and Sapphic Tropes," Praxis Series, http://www.rc.umd.edu/praxis/sexuality/lanser/lanser.html (accessed Aug. 7, 2012). Wordsworth's poem originally appeared in *Miscellaneous Sonnets* (1827) and is now available in *Poetical Works of William Wordsworth*, ed. William Knight (London and New York: Macmillan, 1896), VII, pp. 128–129.

58. Mavor, *Ladies of Llangollen*, p. 211.

59. "Provenance," MS Eng 1225, Houghton Library, Harvard University; "Amy Lowell's Library is Left in Will to Harvard," *Harvard Crimson*, (May 16, 1925), http://www.thecrimson.com/article/1925/5/16/amy-lowells-library-is-left-in/. On Amy Lowell's self-presentation, see Melissa Bradshaw, "Outselling the Modernism of Men: Amy Lowell and the Art of Self-Commodification," *Victorian Poetry* 38 (2000), pp. 141–169.

60. *Testudo nigra* holotype marked "Ship Abigail," collected ca. 1834 from the Galapagos Islands, Ecuador, Herpetology R-11064, Museum of Comparative Zoology, Harvard University. For full record, see http://mczbase.mcz.harvard.edu/guid/MCZ:Herp:R-11064.

61. Ortelius's 1570 world map labels them as *Insulae de los Galopegos*.

62. Salvator R. Tarnmoor [pseudonym of Herman Melville], "The Encantadas, or Enchanted Isles," *Putnam's Monthly Magazine of American Literature, Science, and Art* 3 (1854), pp. 311–319, 345–355, 460–466, quotation on p. 311.

63. Melville, "Encantadas," 312.

64. Ibid., 311.

65. William Dampier, *A New Voyage Round the World*, 4th ed. (London, 1697), pp. 102, 109, 110; John van Denburgh, "The gigantic land tortoises of the Galapagos archipelago," *Proceedings of the California Academy of Sciences*, Fourth Series, 2 (1914), pp. 203–374; see esp. pp. 209–210.

66. K. Thalia Grant and Gregory B. Estes, *Darwin in Galápagos* (Princeton, NJ: Princeton University Press, 2009), pp. 70, 78.

67. James Colnett, *A Voyage to the South Atlantic and Round Cape Horn into the Pacific Ocean for the Purpose of Extending the Spermaceti Whale Fisheries, and other objects of commerce* (London, 1798), p. 156.

68. Charles Haskins Townsend, "The Galapagos Islands Revisited," *Bulletin of the New York Zoological Society* 31, No. 5 (1928), p. 159.

69. Lance E. Davis, Robert E. Gallman, and Karin Gleiter, "Data Sets and Sources," pp. 57–130, in *In Pursuit of Leviathan: Technology, Institutions, Productivity, and Profits in American Whaling, 1816–1906*, eds. Lance E. Davis, Robert E. Gallman, and Karin Gleiter (Chicago: University of Chicago Press, 1997); chapter is online courtesy of the National Bureau of Economic Research at http://www.nber.org/chapters/c8278.

70. Colnett, *Voyage*, pp. 157, 158.

71. Charles Darwin, *Journal of Researches into the Geology and Natural History of the Various Countries Visited by H.M.S. Beagle, Under the Command of Captain Fitzroy, R.N. from 1832 to 1836* (London, 1840), p. 459. Originally published as Vol. 3 ("Journal and Remarks, 1832–1836") of Robert FitzRoy, *Narrative of the Surveying Voyages of His Majesty's Ships Adventure and Beagle, Between the Years 1826 and 1836, Describing Their Examination of the Southern Shores of South America, and the Beagle's Circumnavigation of the Globe* (London, 1839).

72. Recollection of a sailor onboard the *Apollo* of Edgartown (Captain Daggett, master) on a whaling voyage to the Pacific in 1816; quoted at length in Charles Haskins Townsend, "The Galapagos Tortoises in Their Relation to the Whaling Industry: A Study of Old Logbooks," *Zoologica* 4, No. 3 (1925), pp. 55–135. See also G. Baur, "The Gigantic Land Tortoises of the Galapagos Islands," *American Naturalist* 23, No. 276 (Dec. 1889), pp. 1039–1057.

73. Herman Melville to Harper & Brothers, Nov. 24, 1853, Pittsfield, MA, in *The Writings of Herman Melville*, Vol. 14, "Correspondence," ed. Lynn Horth (Evanston, IL: Northwestern University Press and the Newberry Library, 1993), p. 250.

74. Hershel Parker, *Herman Melville: A Biography*, Vol. 2, 1851–1891 (Baltimore, MD: Johns Hopkins University Press, 2005), pp. 186–188, 209–213, 219, 223.

75. Melville, "Encantadas," p. 314.

76. Ibid.

77. Townsend, "Galapagos Tortoises."

78. Grant and Estes, *Darwin*, pp. 44, 100, 101.

79. Ship *Abigail* of New Bedford, Benjamin Clark, master, logbook, June 2, 1832, quoted in Townsend, "Galapagos Tortoises."

80. Melville, "Encantadas," p. 314.

81. Ibid., p. 312.

82. Townsend, "Galapagos Tortoises."

83. Nicholas Lawson, cited in *Charles Darwin's Beagle Diary*, ed. Richard D. Keynes (Cambridge, UK: Cambridge University Press, 1988), 356.

84. Ship *Abigail* logbook, 1831–1835, Whaling Log Collection, box D21, folder 1, New Bedford Free Public Library, New Bedford, MA. See p. 164 for entries headed "Ship Abigail of New Bedford at the Gallipagus Islands," and p. 165 for entries headed "Cruising for Sperm Whales All Round the Coast."

85. Townsend, "The Galapagos Islands Revisited"; Townsend, "Galapagos Tortoises"; Baur, "Gigantic Land Tortoises"; Grant and Estes, *Darwin*, pp. 84, 85.

86. Nora Barlow, ed., "Darwin's Ornithological Notes," *Bulletin of the British Museum (Natural History)* 2, Part 7 (1963), pp. 201–278, see esp. p. 262; Grant and Estes, *Darwin*, pp. 122, 123.

87. Barlow, "Darwin's Ornithological Notes," p. 262. By the time Darwin prepared the 1845 edition of his *Journal of Researches into the Natural History and Geology of the Countries Visited During the Voyage of H.M.S. Beagle Round the World under the Command of Capt. FitzRoy, R.N.*, 2nd ed. (London: John Murray, 1845), he had further confirmation of the morphological differences observed in tortoises from different islands in the report of Captain David Porter, *Journal of a Cruise made to the Pacific Ocean … in the United States Frigate, ESSEX, in the years 1812, 1813, and 1814. Containing Descriptions of the … Galapagos Islands* (Philadelphia: Bradford and Inskeep, 1815), chap. 9.

88. *Voyage autour du monde: entrepris par ordre du roi … exécuté sur les corvettes de S. M. l'Uranie et la Physicienne, pendant les années 1817, 1818, 1819 et 1820 … par M. Louis de Freycinet, capitaine de vaisseau … Zoologie, par MM. Quoy et Gaimard, Médecins de l'Expédition* (Paris, 1824), p. 174, plate 40.

89. Baur, "Gigantic Land Tortoises"; Denburgh, "Gigantic Land Tortoises."

90. P. C. H. Pritchard, *The Galapagos tortoises: Nomenclatural and survival status* (Lunenburg, MA: Chelonian Research Foundation, 1996); Nikos Poulakakis, et al., "Historical DNA analysis reveals living descendents of an extinct species of Galapagos tortoise," *Proceedings of the National Academy of Sciences* 105, No. 40 (Oct. 7, 2008), pp. 15464–15469: www.pnas.org/cgi/doi/10.1073/pnas.0805340105. Private communication by author with José Rosado, curatorial associate in herpetology, Museum of Comparative Zoology, Harvard University, Sept. 27, 2013.

91. See ledger entry MCZ Herpetology Reptiles 008001-014025, p. 123; Samuel Garman, "The Galapagos Tortoises," *Memoirs of the Museum of Comparative Zoology at Harvard College* 30, No. 4 (1917), pp. 286–290, with R-11064 specifically discussed on pp. 289 and 290, and plate 35 showing dorsal, lateral, and ventral views.

92. Poulakakis, et al., "Historical DNA analysis," 15465; and Poulakakis, et al. 10.1073/pnas.0805340105, "Supporting Information: Materials and Methods," published online at http://www.pnas.org/cgi/content/full/0805340105/DCSupplemental.

93. Melville, "Encantadas," p. 313.

94. Peabody Museum of Archaeology and Ethnology 83-14-50/30212.

95. Monni Adams, "Formal Public Titles for Wè/Guéré Women, Côte d'Ivoire," *Anthropos* 86 (1991), pp. 463–485.

96. Polly Buck Stone, *Adopted Son of Salem: Dominick Lake Marsins, 1827–1899* (Peterborough, NH: Noone House, 1971), pp. 60–68; *Collecção das Leis do Imperio do Brazil de 1850*: Descretion 698 "Tomo XI, Parte I (Rio De Janeiro: Imprensa Nacional, 1885) pp. 113-114."

97. Gerald Horne, *The Deepest South: The United States, Brazil, and the African Slave Trade* (New York: NYU Press, 2007), pp. 9, 19, 260, n. 52; I have not been able to firmly link Mary Willis Sparhawk to his supposed business partner John Willis because of their ubiquitous first names; however, some kind of family connection is likely. Mary Willis was Sparhawk's second wife, a relationship formed after he first returned from Brazil.

98. Personal communication with Roquinaldo Ferreira of Brown University, Feb. 18, 2014. The author is grateful to Professor Ferreira for sharing his research.

99. "The Sparhawk–Marsins Agreement, Fernando Po, 1865," in Stone, pp. 110–113.

100. John B. Sparhawk Passport Application, June 9, 1864, NARA, Passport Applications, 1795–1905; Collection number: ARC Identifier 566612/MLR Number A1 508; NARA Series: M1372; Roll 123, accessed via Ancestry.com; Stone, p. 67.

101. *Reports of the Peabody Museum Vol. 3* (1887), p. 359.

102. *Dedication of the Monument on Boston Common Erected to the men of Boston who died in the Civil War* (Boston: Printed by Order of the City Council, 1877), p. 11.

103. Robert F. Erickson, "Joseph Nelson Rose," *American National Biography Online*: http://www.anb.org.ezp-prod1.hul.harvard.edu/articles/13/13%2001426.html?a=1&g=m&n=Rose%2C%20Joseph&ia=-at&ib=-bib&d=10&ss=0&q=1; R. S. Cowan and F. A. Stafleu, "Rose and Britton: From Brittonrosea to Cassia," *Brittonia* 33, No. 3 (1981), pp. 285–293; J. N. Rose, "Notes on Useful Plants of Mexico," *Contributions from U.S. National Herbarium,* Vol. V, No. 4 (Washington, DC: Government Printing Office, 1899), pp. 209–211.

104. "The Economic Botany Herbarium of Oakes Ames," http://www.huh.harvard.edu/collections/economic.html.

105. Rose, "Notes on Useful Plants," plate XXVIII, fig. 2. The photograph shows a single tortilla with a pile of tamarinds and tomatillos, which Rose called "tomatoes."

106. Robert A. Bye, "An 1878 Ethnobotanical Collection from San Luis Potosí: Dr. Edward Palmer's First Major Mexican Collection," *Economic Botany* 33: 2 (1979), pp. 135–162; Richard I. Ford, "Anthropological Perspective of Ethnobotany in the Greater Southwest," *Economic Botany* 39(4) (1985), pp. 401–403; Ralph W. Dexter, "The F. W. Putnam-Edward Palmer Relations in the Development of Early American Ethnobotany," *Journal of Ethnobotany* 10(1), (1990), pp. 35–41.

107. Bye, appendix III, pp. 155, 156.

108. Ibid.

109. Ibid.

110. Rose, pp. 209–211.

111. Edgar Anderson, "Uneconomic Botany," in *Plants, Man and Life* (Boston: Little, Brown, 1952), pp. 124–135. On Anderson, see Kim Kleinman, "His Own Synthesis: Corn, Edgar Anderson, and Evolutionary Theory in the 1940s," *Journal of the History of Biology* 32, No. 2 (Autumn 1999), pp. 293–320.

112. Oakes Ames, *Germiniae. Zea Mays* L. 102, MS, Harvard University Herbarium.

113. On the latter point, see Jeffrey M. Pilcher, "Was the Taco Invented in Southern California?," *Gastronomica: The Journal of Food and Culture* Vol. 8, No. 1 (Winter 2008), pp. 26–38; and The Kitchen Sisters, "The Birth of the Frito," *NPR Morning Edition*, Oct. 18, 2007: http://www.

npr.org/templates/story/story.php?storyId=15377830 or http://thekitchensisters.blogspot.com/2007/11/birth-of-frito-another-texas-hidden.html.

114. Jeffrey M. Pilcher, *"Que vivan los tamales!": Food and the Making of Mexican Identity* (Albuquerque: University of New Mexico Press, 1998), p. 77; Meredith E. Abarca, *Voices in the Kitchen: Views of Food and the World from Working-Class Mexican and Mexican American* Women (College Station, TX: Texas A&M University Press, 2006), pp. 92–100.

115. Pilcher, pp. 93–97.

116. Abarca, *Voices*, pp. 12, 13, 80, 81. On the persistence of hand grinding over the centuries, see Arnold J. Bauer, "Millers and Grinders: Technology and Household Economy in Meso-America," *Agricultural History* 64 (Winter 1990), pp. 1–17.

117. Fall 2010 seminar student Alexandra Jumper researched this object for her final paper. Jesse Feiman, my graduate student research assistant while I was a fellow at the Clark Art Institute in fall 2011, undertook further research. I am grateful to both of them.

118. Roland B. Dixon, "Some Aspects of North American Archaeology," *American Anthropologist,* NS 15 (1913), pp. 549–566.

119. Alison Wylie, *Thinking from Things: Essays in the Philosophy of Archaeology* (Berkeley, CA, Los Angeles, and London: University of California Press, 2002), pp. 28, 29.

120. A. M. Tozzer, "Roland Burrage Dixon," *American Anthropologist* NS 38, 2 (1936), p. 292. Information about Dixon is derived from this obituary article and the one by Alfred Kroeber that immediately follows it.

121. James C. Scott, *The Art of Not Being Governed: An Anarchist History of Upland Southeast Asia* (New Haven and London: Yale University Press, 2009).

122. Ajay Skaria, "Shades of Wildness: Tribe, Caste, and Gender in Western India," *Journal of Asian Studies* 56, 3 (1997), p. 727. See also Erin L. Hasinoff, *Confluences: An American Expedition to Northern Burma, 1935* (New York: Bard Graduate Center; New Haven and London: Yale University Press, 2013).

123. H. K. Barpujari, *Problem of the Hill Tribes: North-East Frontier; a Critical Analysis of the Problems and Policies of the British Government towards the Hill Tribes of the Frontier,* 3 Vols. (Guwahati, IN: Lawyers Book Stall, 1970–81), I, p. 180.

124. Tapati Guha-Thakurta, "The Museumized Relic: Archaeology and the First Museum of Colonial India," *Indian Economic and Social History Review* 34, 1 (1997), pp. 21–51.

125. Sanghamitra Misra, "The Nature of Colonial Intervention in the Naga Hills, 1840–80," *Economic and Political Weekly* 33, 51 (1998), pp. 3273–3279.

126. H. K. Barpujari, *The American Missionaries and North-East India (1836–1900 A.D.): A Documentary Study* (Guwahati and Delhi, India: Spectrum, 1986), pp. xiv–xvi.

127. See, for example, the report of Nathan Brown to the Executive Committee, Sibsagor, April 29, 1850: "Of the principal officers in Assam (there may be about 20 civil and military officers of the First Class) there is not one who Dissents or Dissenters with the slightest cordiality or approbation much less Baptists.... There are very few of them who believe in communion in our sense of the term, very few who have any higher idea of missions than as a means of civilization, and still further many of these also stand foremost in the ranks of civilization and improvement are themselves persons of open and known immorality"; Barpujari, *The American Missionaries*, p. 92.

128. Shibani Kinkar Choube, *Hill Politics in North-East India* (Bombay: Orient Longman, 1973), pp. 57, 58.

129. Inventory in Accession File 13–24, Peabody Museum of Archaeology and Ethnology.

130. Milada Ganguli, *Naga Art* (New York: International Science Publisher, 1993), pp. 28, 82.

131. Michael Oppitz, et al., *Naga Identities: Changing Local Cultures in the Northeast of India* (Ghent, BE: Snoeck, 2008), p. 349.

132. Peabody Museum of Archaeology and Ethnology, 46-78-60/8781, collected by Ernest T. Jackson and donated by Patrick T. Jackson, described as being from South Asia.

133. The tea cozy is in the collections of the Hampshire Museums Service at the Red House Museum and Gardens, Christchurch, Dorset, UK; see http://www3.hants.gov.uk/museum/dress-and-textiles/beetlewing.htm (accessed Nov. 17, 2011).

134. Recently conserved, Ellen Terry's dress is in the collection at her house, Smallhythe Place, Kent, UK (National Trust); see http://www.nationaltrust.org.uk/main/w-vh/w-visits/w-findaplace/w-smallhytheplace/w-smallhythe-beetle-wing-dress-exhibition.htm (accessed Nov. 17, 2011).

135. John Singer Sargent, *Ellen Terry as Lady Macbeth*, 1889, oil on canvas, Tate Britain, London.

136. Alan Macfarlane, *The Nagas: Hill People of Northeast India*, http://www.alanmacfarlane.com/bamboo_naga_front/T12.htm (accessed Nov. 17, 2011), originally published as *The Naga Videodisc*, Department of Social Anthropology, Cambridge University, 1989.

137. R. B. Dixon, review of J. P. Mills, *The Lhota Nagas* (1922), in *American Anthropologist* 25, 3 (1923), pp. 419–421.

138. Westinghouse advertisement, *Hardware Age* 146 (Sept. 19, 1940), p. 140.

139. Dean Young and Melissa Ryzik, *Bumstead Family History* (Nashville, TN: Thomas Nelson, 2007).

140. William W. Savage Jr., "Young, Chic," *American National Biography Online*, (Feb. 2000), http://www.anb.org.ezp-prod1.hul.harvard.edu/articles/20/20-01429.html (accessed June 19, 2011).

141. *Blondie Gets Married, Comic Strips by Chic Young*, Library of Congress exhibition, June 22–Sept. 16, 2000, http://www.loc.gov/rr/print/swann/blondie/ (accessed June 18, 2011).

142. Westinghouse advertisement, *Hardware Age* 146 (July 25, 1940), p. 720.

143. Susan Strasser, *Never Done: A History of American Housework* (New York: Owl Books, 2000), pp. 263–281.

144. "The night shift," Sept. 5, 1933 and "It's the ostrich in him!," Jan. 25, 1952, from *Blondie Gets Married, Comic Strips by Chic Young*, Library of Congress exhibition, June 22–Sept. 16, 2000, http://www.loc.gov/rr/print/swann/blondie/ (accessed June 18, 2011).

145. Louis M. Heil and Joe Musial, "Splitting the Atom—Starring Dagwood and Blondie, How it Developed," *Journal of Educational Sociology* 22: 5 (Jan. 1949), pp. 331–336 (http://www.jstor.org/stable/2263616); Paul Boyer, "Some Sort of Peace: President Truman, the American people and the Atomic Bomb," in *The Truman Presidency*, ed. Michael James Lacey (Cambridge, UK: Cambridge University Press, 1991), pp. 174–204; see esp. p. 189.

146. Three sheep or goat knucklebones, West Asia, Iron Age, Semitic Museum, on deposit from the Department of Archaeology, University of Edinburgh, L3657, L5059, and L4507.

CHAPTER 3

1. See http://itunes.apple.com/us/itunes-u/tangible-things/id439654236 (accessed June 19, 2012). Commentaries are similarly available for eleven items that were in the core exhibit.

2. Calculus formed from oxalate of lime, uric acid, and phosphate of lime, USA, 1809, Warren Anatomical Museum in the Francis A. Countway Library of Medicine, Gift of Buckminster Brown, WAM 04089.

3. Pencil that belonged to Henry David Thoreau, Concord, Massachusetts, ca. 1850s, milled graphite and softwood, Houghton Library, *47Z-7.

4. "H.D. Thoreau: Engineer," *Invention and Technology*, vol. 5, issue 3 (1989), at http://www.innovationgateway.org/content/h-d-thoreau-engineer-1?page=2 (accessed June 24, 2014); Henry David Thoreau, *Walden* (Boston: Houghton Mifflin, 1957), p. 35.

5. Patent medicine bottle, "Macamoose, The Great Indian Tonic," containing the desiccated body of a house mouse (*Mus musculus*), USA, ca. 1865, General Artemas Ward House Museum, HU 2072 (the subject of Julia Bonnheim's seminar paper in fall 2005).

6. Dog paw print in a mud brick, Nuzi, Mesopotamia, 1500–1300 BCE, Semitic Museum, 1930.13B.2.

7. Floriform vase, Louis Comfort Tiffany, Corona, NY, ca. 1900, Harvard Art Museums/Fogg Museum, Gift of Murray Anthony and Bessie Lincoln Potter, 1957.43. This was the subject of Audrey Boguchwal's seminar paper in spring 2003.

8. Miniature globe, James Ferguson, ca. 1757, Ebenezer Storer Collection, Harvard University Archives, HUG 1808.1000.1. This was the subject of Eduardo Contreras's seminar paper in fall 2009.

9. Among his many positions of social responsibility, Storer was a trustee of the Massachusetts Society for Propagation of Christian Knowledge among the Indians of North America; see the online finding aid for the Ebenezer Storer Collection by Juliana Kuipers, 2011: http://oasis.lib.harvard.edu/oasis/deliver/~hua61011 (accessed June 20, 2012).

10. Campfire-style dress, belt, and beads by Sarah Jenney Gilbert Kerlin, 1947–1950, Arthur and Elizabeth Schlesinger Library on the History of Women in America, Gift of Catharine Wilder Guiles (Radcliffe, 1959), 2006-M88. This was the subject of Marcella Marsala's seminar paper in fall 2010.

11. See, in particular, Philip J. Deloria, *Playing Indian* (New Haven: Yale University Press, 1998).

12. Silver band for a Passamaquoddy (Peskotomuhkati) woman's hat, Maine, USA, or New Brunswick, Canada, ca. 1875, Peabody Museum of Archaeology and Ethnology, 985-27-10/60273A. This was the subject of Rachel Bennett's seminar paper in fall 2010.

13. Anna E. Hardy, Portrait of "Sarah Molasses," ca. 1886, oil on canvas, Peabody Museum of Archaeology and Ethnology, 47-36-10/74685. The sitter was the daughter of Bungawarrawit, known as John Neptune (1767–1865) of the Penobscot people, and Mary Pelagie, known as Molly Molasses (1775–1867), of the Peskotomuhkati people.

14. Jacob Bodendeich, sideboard dish with Hercules drawing his bow on Nessus abducting Deianira, 1676 or 1677, silver, Harvard Art Museums/Fogg Museum, Paul Clarke Stauffer Fund, 2003.278.

15. John Coney, Stoughton cup, 1701, silver, Harvard Art Museums/Fogg Museum, loan from Harvard University; Gift to Harvard College from the Honorable William Stoughton, 1701, 877.1927.A-B.

16. Mounted carved coconut goblet decorated with scenes from the story of Samson, Hans Peter Müller, Breslau, Germany, ca. 1600, coconut and gilt silver, Harvard Art Museums/Busch-Reisinger Museum, purchased in memory of Eda K. Loeb, BR61.58.A-B. This was the subject of Danielle Charlap's senior thesis in 2009.

17. Framed dress fragment said to have belonged to Priscilla Mullins, seventeenth century, Radcliffe Picture Collection, Arthur and Elizabeth Schlesinger Library on the History of Women in America. This was the subject of Whitney Martinko's seminar paper in spring 2003.

18. John Downame, *The Christian Warfare against the Devil, World, and Flesh* (London: William Stansby, 1634), Houghton Library, Houghton f STC 7137, lobby V.3.3. The author's name is alternatively spelled Downham.

19. President's chair, turned three-square great chair, Britain ca. 1550–1600, with later American handgrips, wood, Harvard Art Museums/Fogg Museum, loan from the President and Fellows of Harvard College, 979.1933.

20. John Singleton Copley, Edward Holyoke, ca. 1759–61, oil on canvas, Harvard University Portrait Collection, Gift of Mrs. Turner and Mrs. Ward, granddaughters of Edward Holyoke, 1829, H6.

21. Corncob pipe, USA, 1919, Economic Botany Herbarium of Oakes Ames, Harvard University Herbaria, #00200162.

22. Skull of a helmeted hornbill (*Rhinoplax vigil*), Sumatra, Borneo, or the Malay Peninsula, casque carved in China, nineteenth century, Museum of Comparative Zoology.

23. Palette used by John Singer Sargent (1856–1925), Harvard Art Museums/Fogg Museum, gift of Miss Emily Sargent and Mrs. Francis Ormond in memory of their brother, John Singer Sargent (through Thomas A. Fox, Esq.), 1933.49.

24. Walking plow, Massachusetts (?), late eighteenth or early nineteenth century, General Artemas Ward House Museum, HU 4070.

25. Palette used by John Singer Sargent, American (1856–1925), oil on wood, 56.5 x 38 cm (22 1/4 x 14 15/16 in.), Harvard Art Museums/Fogg Museum, Gift of Miss Emily Sargent and Mrs. Francis Ormond in memory of their brother, John Singer Sargent (through Thomas A. Fox, Esq.), 1933.49.

26. Lucy Davies, "Why Preserve Van Gogh's Palette?" April 14, 2010, http://blogs.telegraph. co.uk/culture/lucydavies/100007607/why-preserve-van-goghs-palette/ (accessed June 17, 2011).

27. John Ruskin, *Elements of Drawing* (London: n.p., 1857), 197.

28. *Henry James* portrait by John Singer Sargent, published in the *Yellow Book*, 1886; *Henry James*, John Singer Sargent, 1912, charcoal, 24 1/2 x 16 in. (61.8 x 41.0 cm), presented by the artist to King George V, March 1916, Royal Library at Windsor Castle, RL 13682, with history online at http://www.royalcollection.org.uk/eGallery/object.asp?searchText=henry+ james&x=0&y=0&pagesize=20&object=913682&row=0&detail=about (accessed June 20, 2010); *Henry James*, by John Singer Sargent, 1913, oil on canvas, 33 1/2 in. x 26 1/2 in. (851 mm x 673 mm), Bequeathed by Henry James, 1916, National Portrait Gallery, London, NPG 1767.

29. *Alice Runnells James (Mrs. William James)*, John Singer Sargent, 1921, watercolor over graphite pencil on paper, sheet: 53.5 x 34.3 cm (21 1/16 x 13 1/2 in.), gift of the sitter's husband, William James Jr., December 15, 1977, Museum of Fine Arts, Boston, 1977.834.

30. Henry James, "John S. Sargent," *Harper's Magazine* (Oct. 1887), pp. 683–691.

31. Hugo Munsterberg, *Psychological Laboratory of Harvard University* (Cambridge, MA: Harvard University, 1893); Herbert Nichols, "The Psychological Laboratory at Harvard," *McClure's Magazine* (1893), pp. 399–409.

32. William James, *Principles of Psychology* (New York: Henry Holt & Co., 1890); Henry Smith Williams, "The Century's Progress in Experimental Psychology," *Harper's New Monthly Magazine*, No. 592 (Sept. 1899), pp. 512–527.

33. Nichols, pp. 399.

34. Sara J. Schechner, curator, *Time, Life & Matter: Science in Cambridge*, a permanent exhibition in the Putnam Gallery of the Collection of Historical Scientific Instruments, Harvard University, 2005–present.

35. *Sargent in the Studio: Drawings, Sketchbooks, and Oil Sketches*, an exhibition at the Harvard Art Museums, June 10, 1999–Sept. 26, 1999.

36. The ophthalmotrope, Max Kohl, Chemnitz, Germany, ca. 1893, demonstrated how muscles controlled ocular motion; oversized clastic model of the human eye, Cambridge Botanical Supply Co., Waverley, MA, ca. 1925; wooden model of the eye showing how the lens projects an image on the retina, unsigned, ca. 1840; oversized clastic model of the human eye, Louis Thomas Jérôme Auzoux, Paris, 1891; all from the Collection of Historical Scientific Instruments (hereafter CHSI), accession numbers WJ0002, 1996-1-0613, DW0855, WJ0174.

37. Zoetrope, Max Kohl, Chemnitz, Germany, ca. 1875, with reversible movie strip entitled "Magic Ocean" and "Chewing Gum" and a second movie strip with "Baseball" and "Raining Pitchforks." CHSI, WJ0049, WJ0049b-c.

38. Holmes-type refracting stereoscope, American, ca. 1870, CHSI, WJ0097.

39. Waterfall illusion, built by William James in the Harvard Psychology Laboratory, ca. 1885, CHSI, WJ0216.

40. Titchener's color pyramid, Harvard Psychology Laboratory, ca. 1924, CHSI, WJ0102.

41. Munsell's color globe, A. H. Munsell, Boston (?), ca. 1900, CHSI, WJ0104.

42. Silbermann-type heliostat, Louis Jules Duboscq & Philibért François Pellin, Paris; clockwork by Paul Garnier, Paris, ca. 1885, CHSI, 1997-1-1587; mirrors for recombining wavelengths of light in solar spectrum, Max Kohl, Chemnitz, Germany, ca. 1890, CHSI, WJ0032.

43. Holmgren's test for color blindness, ca. 1890, CHSI, WJ1151.

44. John Law and Michael Lynch, "Lists, Field Guides, and the Descriptive Organization of Seeing: Birdwatching as an Exemplary Observational Activity," *Human Studies* 11, No. 2/3 (April–July 1988), pp. 271–303.

45. Chester Albert Reed, *Bird Guide: Land Birds East of the Rockies from Parrots to Bluebirds* (Garden City, NY: Doubleday, 1909), p. 208.

46. Mark Barrow, *A Passion for Birds: American Ornithology after Audubon* (Princeton, NJ: Princeton University Press, 1998).

47. As an adult, Katharine Lane Weems achieved renown as an animal sculptor. In 1937, she created two rhinoceroses, door panels with insects, and brick reliefs that included pelicans in flight for the Biological Laboratories at Harvard. See Katharine Lane Weems as told to Edward Weeks, *Odds Were Against Me: A Memoir* (New York: Vantage Press, 1985), pp. 84–97.

48. Frank M. Chapman, "Birds and Bonnets," letter to the editor, *Field and Stream* 26 (Feb. 25, 1886, p. 84; Robin W. Doughty, *Feather Fashions and Bird Preservation: A Study in Nature Protection* (Berkeley, CA: University of California Press, 1975), pp. 16, 17; Jennifer Price, *Flight Maps: Adventures with Nature in Modern America* (New York: Basic Books, 1999), pp. 57, 58.

49. François Vuilleumier, "Dean of American Ornithologists: The Multiple Legacies of Frank M. Chapman of the American Museum of Natural History," *The Auk: A Quarterly Journal of Ornithology* 122 (April 2005), p. 395.

50. *Flight Maps*, p. 59.

51. Celia Thaxter, *Woman's Heartlessness* (Boston, 1886; reprinted for the Audubon Society of the State of New York, 1899) in National Audubon Society records, 1883–1991, Manuscript and Archives Division, Humanities and Social Library of the New York Public Library, Section C (Box C32, New York State Audubon Society folder): http://www.seacoastnh.com/Famous_People/Celia_Thaxter/Celia_Thaxter_Attacks_Heartless_Women_Wearing_Birds_as_Fashion/ (accessed June 23, 2012).

52. *Flight Paths*, pp. 62–64.

53. Mark V. Barrow Jr. "The Specimen Dealer: Entrepreneurial Natural History in America's Gilded Age," *Journal of the History of Biology* 33 (2000), pp. 493–534.

54. Madelyn Holmes, *American Women Conservationists: Twelve Profiles* (Jefferson, NC: McFarland, 2004), p. 40; Spencer Schaffner, *Binocular Vision: The Politics of Representation in Birdwatching Field Guides* (Boston: University of Massachusetts Press, 2011), p. 22.

55. Schaffner, *Binocular Vision*, pp. 29–49.

56. Mabel Osgood Wright, *Birdcraft: A Field Book of Two Hundred Song, Game, and Water Birds* (New York: Macmillan, 1895), p. 67.

57. Carolyn Merchant, "Women of the Progressive Conservation Movement: 1900–1916," *Environmental Review*, Vol. 8 (1984), pp. 70–76.

58. Schaffner, *Binocular Vision*, pp. 18, 19.

59. Mabel Osgood Wright and Elliott Coues, *Citizen Bird: Scenes from Bird-Life in Plain English for Beginners* (New York and London: Macmillan, 1897), p. 95.

60. Florence A. Merriam, *Birds Through An Opera Glass* (Boston and New York: Houghton, Mifflin and Company, 1896), p. 14.

61. Sharon Hartman Strom, "Leadership and Tactics in the American Woman Suffrage Movement: A New Perspective from Massachusetts," *Journal of American History*, Vol. 62, No. 2 (Sept. 1975), pp. 296–315; quotation from *Boston Transcript* [this is a newspaper name] on page 310. For more on Foley and her complex relationship with the women's movement, see James J. Kenneally, "Catholic and Feminist: A Biographical Approach," *U.S. Catholic Historian* 3, No. 4 (Spring 1984), pp. 245–253; and Sarah Deutsch, *Women and the City: Gender, Space, and Power in Boston, 1870–1940* (New York: Oxford University Press, 2000), pp. 222–228.

62. *The History of Woman Suffrage*, Vol. VI, ed. Ida Husted Harper (Boston: National American Woman Suffrage Association, 1922), pp. 285–290. Many of the suffrage birds survive, some in private hands, others in women's rights collections and libraries around New England. See, for example, Massachusetts Woman Suffrage Association, tin bluebird, "Votes for Women Nov. 2," Smith College Library, http://www.smith.edu/libraries/libs/ssc/captions.html; and woman's suffrage: Massachusetts die-cut tin blue bird, Heritage Auctions, lot 47126, in a 1088 December Grand Format Americana Auction #6006 (http://historical.ha.com/c/item.zx?saleNo=6006&lotNo=47126); and die-stamped metal window hanger, Second Life Books (http://www.secondlifebooks.com/shop/secondlife/49048) (accessed June 18, 2012).

63. "Maurice Maeterlinck, Nobel Prize in Literature 1911," http://www.nobelprize.org/nobel_prizes/literature/laureates/1911/; "Maeterlinck, Maurice," *The Oxford Companion to English Literature*, ed. Dinah Birch, Oxford Reference Online (http://www.oxfordreference.com/views/ENTRY.html?subview=Main&entry=t113.e4762).

64. *The History of Woman Suffrage*, pp. 285–290.

65. "Voters Deny Massachusetts Women the Vote," Massachusetts Humanities Council website at http://massmoments.org/moment.cfm?mid=316 (accessed June 26, 2012); also see Louise Stevenson, "Women Anti-suffragists in the 1915 Massachusetts Campaign," *New England Quarterly* 52, (March 1979), pp. 80–93.

66. *The Complete Poems of Emily Dickinson*, ed. Thomas H. Johnson (Boston and Toronto: Little, Brown, 1960, p. 598, #1395; also see p. 535, #1213; p. 620, #1465; p. 640, #1530.

67. Walking plow, Massachusetts (?), late eighteenth century, General Artemas Ward House Museum, HU 4070.

68. The Semitic Museum exhibition *The Houses of Ancient Israel: Domestic, Royal, Divine* is based on the book *Life in Biblical Israel* by Philip J. King and Lawrence E. Stager (Louisville, KY: John Knox/Westminster Press, 2001).

69. Andrew Baker and Frank G. White, "The Impact of Changing Plow Technology in Rural New England in the Early 19th Century," OSV research paper (Jan. 1990), https://osv.org/explore_learn/document_viewer.php?DocID=715 (accessed June 14, 2011).

70. Rebecca Goetz, "General Artemas Ward: A Forgotten Revolutionary Remembered and Reinvented, 1800–1938," *Proceedings of the American Antiquarian Society* 113:1 (2003), pp. 103–134.

71. Livy, *History of Rome by Titus Livius, the first eight Books, literally translated, with notes and illustrations*, trans. D. Spillan (London: Henry G. Bohn, 1857), p. 3.26; http://www.perseus.tufts.edu/hopper/ (accessed June 14, 2011).

72. "Rhode Island, 3 pounds, 1786," Baker Library, Harvard Business School, Historical Collections, 1-42/4, MS:78 C 1709-1868 976.

73. David R. Foster and John F. O'Keefe, *New England Forests through Time: Insights from the Harvard Forest Dioramas* (Cambridge, MA: Harvard University Press, 2000).

74. Ivan Gaskell, "The Riddle of the Riddle," *Contemporary Aesthetics* 6 (2006).

75. "Hassanamisco Indian Museum History," http://nipmucmuseum.org/history (accessed June 14, 2011).

76. Our thanks to Jeremiah Trimble, curatorial associate and collection manager of the Ornithology Department, Museum of Comparative Zoology, who drew our attention to the helmeted hornbill skull, the gift of Mrs. Edward J. Dimock in 1975. He generously facilitated its loan and oversaw its installation at the Arthur M. Sackler Museum.

77. Ulisse Aldrovandi, *Ornithologiae hoc est de avibvs historiae libri XII* (Bologna, IT: Francesco de Francesco Senese, 1599–1603), Vol. 1, p. 833.

78. George Edwards, *Gleanings of Natural History, Exhibiting Figures of Quadrupeds, Birds, Insects, Plants, &c. Most of Which have not, till Now, been either Figured or Described* (London: Printed for the author, at the Royal College of Physicians, 1758), Vol. 2, pp. 151–153, plate 281, "Beaks of exotic birds drawn from nature," fig. C.

79. Georges-Louis Leclerc, Comte de Buffon, *Histoire naturelle des oiseaux*, Vol. 7 *(Histoire naturelle, générale et particulière, avec la description du Cabinet du Roi*, Vol. 22) (Paris: L'Imprimerie royale, 1780), pp. 159–161.

80. Johann Reinhold Forster, *Indische Zoologie; oder, Systematische Beschreibungen seltener und unbekannter Thiere aus Indien* (Halle, DE: J. J. Gebauer, 1781), p. 40.

81. Joseph Needham, "Physics and Physical Technology," *Science and Civilization in China*, Vol. 4, Part 1 (Cambridge, UK: cambridge University Press, 1962), p. 537.

82. Schuyler Cammann, *Substance and Symbol in Chinese Toggles: Chinese Belt Toggles from the C. F. Bieber Collection* (Philadelphia: University of Pennsylvannia Press, 1962), p. 66. See also Schuyler Camman, "The Story of Hornbill Ivory," *University Museum Bulletin* 15, 2 (1950), pp. 19–47.

83. Jiang's advice to King Wen was recorded and later codified as the *Liu Tao (Six Secret Teachings)*, incorporated in the influential *Wu ching ch'i shu (Seven Military Classics)* in the eleventh century: *The Seven Military Classics of Ancient China*, eds. and trans. Ralph D. Sawyer and Mei-chün Sawyer (Boulder, CO: Westview Press, 1993). The scene was identified when the skull was received by the collection in 1975; Raymond A. Paynter Jr., "Bird Department Receives

Unusual Gift," *Museum of Comparative Zoology Newsletter* 15, 1 (1975). I owe this reference to Jeremiah Trimble.

84. See Tom Harrisson, "Birds and Men in Borneo," in Bertram E. Smythies, *The Birds of Borneo*, 4th ed. revised by Geoffrey W. H. Davison (Kota Kinabalu, MY: Natural History Publications, 1999), pp. 45–74.

85. Jean-Baptiste Oudry, *Avian Album*, black ink and watercolor on eighty-three leaves of off-white antique paper, Harvard Art Museums/Fogg Museum, anonymous gift, 1953.75. Fall 2009 graduate seminar student and 2010 summer fellow David Pullins researched the *Avian Album* as the subject of his final paper and for a digital archive for the spring 2011 undergraduate course.

86. Mme Jean-Baptiste Oudry, née Marie-Marguerite Froissé, after Nicolas de Largillière, *Jean-Baptiste Oudry*, etching, Harvard Art Museums/Fogg Museum, Gift of Belinda L. Randall from the collection of John Witt Randall, R9302.

87. Jacques-Charles Oudry, *Still Life with Woodcock and Quail*, 1769, oil on canvas, Harvard Art Museums/Fogg Museum, Alpheus Hyatt Purchasing Fund, 1945.16.

CHAPTER 4

1. John Downame, *The Christian Warfare against the Devil, World, and Flesh* (London: William Stansby, 1634), Houghton Library, Houghton f STC 7137, lobby V.3.3. The author's name is alternatively spelled Downham.

2. Framed dress fragment said to have belonged to Priscilla Mullins, seventeenth century, Radcliffe Picture Collection, Arthur and Elizabeth Schlesinger Library on the History of Women in America. This was the subject of Whitney Martinko's seminar paper in spring 2003.

3. Sash of blue watered-grosgrain ribbon worn by George Washington, France (?), ca. 1775–83, Peabody Museum of Archaeology and Ethnology, gift of the heirs of David Kimball, 979-13-10/58761.

4. Louis Agassiz's drum microscope, Georges Oberhaeuser, Paris, ca. 1845–46, Collection of Historical Scientific Instruments, 1117.

5. Pencil that belonged to Henry David Thoreau, Concord, MA, ca. 1850s, milled graphite and softwood, Houghton Library, *47Z-7.

6. Bow, known as the Sudbury bow, hickory wood, Peabody Museum of Archaeology and Ethnology, Gift of the American Antiquarian Society, 95-20-10/49340. The bow was displayed among European and Euro-American objects in the Arthur M. Sackler Museum of the Harvard Art Museums in an installation called *Re-View* between 2008 and 2011 as an experimental forerunner of the guest objects in *Tangible Things*. See Ivan Gaskell, "Museum display, an Algonquian bow, and the Ship of Theseus," in *Cultural Histories of the Material World*, ed. Peter N. Miller (Ann Arbor: University of Michigan Press, 2013), pp. 59–73.

7. *The Prodigal Daughter Revived*, Peter Fleet, Boston, MA, 1736, Harvard Art Museums/Fogg Museum, gift of Rona Schneider, M23577. This was the subject of Gloria Whiting's seminar paper in fall 2010.

8. Silver teapot by John Parker and Edward Wakelin, 1765 belonging to Samuel Johnson, with later inscription and inscribed stand, England, Donald and Mary Hyde Collection of Dr. Samuel Johnson, Houghton Library, *2003JM-63.

9. Samples of so-called "Negro" cloth, Rhode Island, 1839–50, Peace Dale Collection, Baker Library, unnumbered.

10. The original daguerreotypes in the archive of the Peabody Museum could not be shown because of their fragility, but were represented by a copy of Molly Rogers, *Delia's Tears: Race, Science, and Photography in Nineteenth-Century America* (New Haven, CT: Yale University Press, 2010) in which they are illustrated.

11. Quirt handle, Omaha or Ponca peoples, Nebraska, ca. 1870–90, General Artemas Ward House Museum, HU 4175. This was the subject of Sigurd Østrem's seminar paper in fall 2006.

12. Sixty-four duplicate plaster busts of Plains Indians, Peabody Museum, 78-1-10/13848.1, 78-1-10/13848.2, 78-1-10/13849-50, 78-1-10/13851.1, 78-1-10/13851.2, 78-1-10/13852-59, 78-1-10/13860.1, 78-1-10/13860.2, 78-1-10/13861-74, 78-1-10/13875.1, 78-1-10/13875.2, 78-1-10/13876.1, 78-1-10/13876.2, 78-1-10/13877.1, 78-1-10/13877.2, 78-1-10/13878.1, 78-1-10/13878.2, 78-1-10/13879.1, 78-1-10/13879.2, 78-1-10/13880-89, 78-1-10/13890.1, 78-1-10/13890.2, 78-1-10/13891-95, 78-1-10/13896.1, 78-1-10/13896.2, 78-1-10/13897, 78-1-10/13898.1, 78-1-10/13898.2, 78-1-10/13899-905, 78-1-10/13906.1, 78-1-10/13906.2, 78-1-10/13907, 78-1-10/13908.1, 78-1-10/13908.2, 78-1-10/13910. These were the subject of Lisa May's seminar paper in spring 2003 and of Lindsay Grant's seminar paper in fall 2009.
13. Pottery plate painted by Nock-ko-ist (Bear's Heart), Southern Tsistsistas (Cheyenne people), ca. 1887–94, Peabody Museum of Archaeology and Ethnology, Gift of the Hemenway heirs, 44-35-10/27481.
14. John Cocks, *Algarum Fasciculi; or A Collection of British Sea-weeds, Carefully Dried and Preserved, and correctly named after Dr. Harvey's "Phycologia Britannica,"* Fascicle 1 (Dublin: M. H. Gill, 1855), Farlow Herbarium of Cryptogamic Botany, Harvard University Herbaria.
15. Emily Dickinson Herbarium, ca. 1839–46, Houghton Library, MS Am 1118.11, Gift of Gilbert H. Montague, 1950.
16. Brenda Wineapple, *White Heat: The Friendship of Emily Dickinson and Thomas Wentworth Higginson* (New York: Knopf, 2008).
17. Cat Lea Holbrook's transcription of the spirit writing slates from the Papers of the Herrick-Chapman Family, 1857–1966, unprocessed collection, Schlesinger Library, Radcliffe College.
18. Eva Payne, "Slate Tablet with Spirit Writing, Elmira, New York," unpublished paper, 2010.
19. *Clasped Hands of Robert and Elizabeth Barrett Browning*, Harriet Hosmer, Rome, original cast, 1853, Harriet Hosmer Papers, A-162, Schlesinger Library, Radcliffe Institute, Harvard University.
20. Nathaniel Hawthorne, *The Marble Faun, or the Romance of Monte Beni* (Boston: Houghton Mifflin, 1860), p. 136.
21. "History of the Browning clasped hands, Chicago, March 12, 1896," Hosmer Papers, Series 1, Box 28.
22. Divination basket on a gourd base, containing fifty-four items of assorted materials, Chokwe people, Benguela Highlands, Angola, twentieth century, Peabody Museum of Archaeology and Ethnology, 39-64-50/3459.
23. Records of the Peabody Museum of Archaeology and Ethnology, Harvard University.
24. Sónia Silva, *Along an African Border: Angolan Refugees and Their Divination Baskets* (Philadelphia: University of Pennsylvania Press, 2011), p. 1.
25. Luvale is similar to the language spoken by the Chokwe peoples, the culture that the Peabody Museum of Archaeology and Ethnology has associated with this basket. Sónia Silva, *Along an African Border: Angolan Refugees and Their Divination Baskets* (Philadelphia: University of Pennsylvania Press, 2011).
26. Hosmer Papers, Folder 175f.
27. Edward Lamson Henry (1841–1919), *The Message*, 1893, 23.5 x 30.5 cm (9 1/4 x 12 in.), Harvard Art Museums/Fogg Museum, Gift of Theodore E. Stebbins, Jr., 2003.279.
28. Amy Kurtz Lansing, *Historical Fictions: Edward Lamson Henry's Paintings of Past and Present* (New Haven, CT: Yale University Art Gallery, 2005), pp. 7–10, 30–33.
29. Note on reconstruction. Frederick Douglass, "Introduction," *The Reason Why the Colored American is not in the World's Columbian Exposition* (Chicago: privately published, 1893), p. 9.
30. Judy Sund, "Columbus and Columbia in Chicago, 1893: Man of Genius Meets Generic Woman," *Art Bulletin*, Vol. 75, No. 3 (Sept. 1993), pp. 448–451, quotation on p. 450.
31. Anders Leonard Zorn, Mrs. Potter Palmer, Chicago, 1993. Art Institute of Chicago, Potter Palmer Collection, 1922.450. The painting can be seen at http://www.artic.edu/aic/collections/artwork/81576.
32. Tracey Jean Boisseau. *White Queen: May French-Sheldon and the Imperial Origins of American Feminist Identity* (Bloomington, IN: Indiana University Press, 2004), pp. 4–10. For a sample

of Sheldon's own prose, see *Sultan to Sultan: Adventures among the Masai and other tribes of East Africa*, available in Google books.

33. Mrs. May French Sheldon, "An African Expedition," *The Congress of Women*, ed. Mary Kavanaugh Oldham Eagle (Chicago and Philadelphia: Monarch Book Company, 1894), pp. 131–134.

34. Louise Michelle Newman, *White Women's Rights: The Racial Origins of Feminism in the United States* (New York: Oxford University Press, 1999), pp. 103, 104.

35. Robert C. Smith, "Liberty Displaying the Arts and Sciences: A Philadelphia Allegory by Samuel Jennings," *Winterthur Portfolio* 2 (1965), pp. 85–105. The painting is owned by the Library Company of Philadelphia and can be seen on its website at http://www.librarycompany.org/artifacts/painters_jennings.htm (accessed Aug. 10, 2012). For more on the iconography of liberty and its relationship to race and gender, see Laurel Thatcher Ulrich, *Well-behaved Women Seldom Make History* (New York: Knopf, 2007), pp. 105–142.

36. Curtis M. Hinsley, "The World as Marketplace: Commodification of the Exotic at the World's Columbian Exposition, Chicago, 1893," in *Exhibiting Culture: The Poetics and Politics of Museum Display*, eds. Ivan Karp and Steven D. Lavine (Washington, DC: Smithsonian institution Press, 1991), pp. 344-365. More recent scholarship has begun to look at these exhibits in more detail, discovering the sometimes "entrepreneurial exotics" who created them. See Mae M. Ngai, "Transnationalism and the Transformation of the 'Other,'" *American Quarterly* 57 (2005), pp. 61–64.

37. "Johnson Family in the Kentucky Building," *Harper's Illustrated Weekly* (Nov. 4, 1893).

38. Jo-Ann Morgan, "Mammy the Huckster: Selling the Old South for the New Century," *American Art*, Vol. 9, No. 1 (Spring 1995), pp. 86–109.

39. A digital text of the cookbook can be found at "Feeding America: The Historic American Cookbook Project," Michigan State University Library, http://digital.lib.msu.edu/projects/cookbooks/html/books/book_35.cfm (accessed Aug. 10, 2012).

40. Rafia Zafar, "What Mrs. Fisher Knows About Old Southern Cooking," *Gastronomica: The Journal of Food and Culture* 1 (2001), pp. 88–90.

41. John Winthrop, "Observation of the Transit of Venus, June 6, 1761, at St. John's Newfoundland," *Philosophical Transactions* 54 (1764), pp. 279–283, quotation on p. 279.

42. Meeting of the President and Fellows of Harvard College, May 5, 1761; Corporation Records, 2:142, Harvard University Archives, UAI 5.30.2.

43. For details of the transit-of-Venus expeditions, see Harry Woolf, *The Transit of Venus: A Study of Eighteenth-Century Science* (Princeton, NJ: Princeton University Press, 1959); Eli Maor, *Venus in Transit* (Princeton, NJ: Princeton University Press, 2004); William Sheehan and John Westfall, *The Transits of Venus* (Amherst, NY: Prometheus Books, 2004).

44. *Monthly Review* 29 (1763), pp. 22–26, speaking about a volume of poems issued in 1761 by Harvard College in commemoration of the death of George II and the accession of George III.

45. John Winthrop to James Bowdoin, Cambridge, Jan. 18, 1769; published in *The Bowdoin and Temple Papers*, Collections of the Massachusetts Historical Society, Sixth Series, Vol. 9 (Boston: Massachusetts Historical Society), p. 116. See also reference to "Papers respecting Professor Winthrop's going to Newfoundland to observe the Transit of Venus, April 10, 1761" listed in "Papers found in State Office relating to Harvard College" [1838], in College Papers, Second Series, 8:309, Harvard University Archives, UAI 5.131.10.

46. "Extract from the Votes of the Hon. House of Representatives," appended to John Winthrop, *Relation of a Voyage from Boston to Newfoundland, for the Observation of the Transit of Venus, June 6, 1761* (Boston: n.p., 1761), pp. 22, 23.

47. "A list of all Grants made to Harvard College by the Colony and State of Massachusetts from 1636 to 1846," folio 2v; found in the Supplement to the Harvard College Papers, 1:4, Harvard University Archives, UAI 5.110 mf. On Winthrop's payment in 1764, see "Papers found in State Office relating to Harvard College" [1838], in College Papers, Second Series, 8:309, Harvard University Archives, UAI 5.131.10. On Winthrop's salary, see the Corporation Records: Minutes, 1643–1989, First Series, Vol. 2, Sept. 17, 1750–April 23, 1778, Harvard University Archives, UAI 5.30, Box 2.

48. Winthrop, *Relation of a Voyage*, p. 8.
49. Meeting of the President and Fellows of Harvard College, May 5, 1761; Corporation Records, 2:142, Harvard University Archives, UAI 5.30.2.
50. John Winthrop, Meteorological Journal, 1761, Harvard University Archives, HUG 1879.207.5mfP; *Halifax Gazette*, May 28, 1761, p. 2. For dates of departure and arrival, see Winthrop, *Relation of a Voyage*, p. 9; Winthrop, "Observation of the Transit of Venus, June 6, 1761," p. 280.
51. Winthrop, *Relation of a Voyage*, pp. 7, 8. The clock survives in the CHSI, inv. no. 0069.
52. Winthrop, *Relation of a Voyage*, p. 10.
53. Meeting of the President and Fellows of Harvard College, April 6, 1761, Corporation Records, 2: 141, Harvard University Archives. The Martin telescope survives in the Science Museum, London (SM-1911-283) and is on long-term loan to CHSI.
54. Corporation Records, 2:142, Harvard University Archives.
55. John Singleton Copley, *John Winthrop*, oil on canvas, ca. 1773, Harvard Portrait Collection. See also Brandon Brame Fortune with Deborah Jean Warner, *Franklin & His Friends: Portraying the Man of Science in Eighteenth-Century America* (Washington, DC, and Philadelphia: Smithsonian Institution, National Portrait Gallery, in association with University of Pennsylvania Press, 1999).
56. "An Account of the Fire at *Harvard-College*, in *Cambridge*; with the Loss sustained thereby," broadsheet, Boston, Jan. 25, 1764.
57. Benjamin Franklin to John Winthrop, Philadelphia, July 10, 1764, in *The Papers of Benjamin Franklin*, eds. Leonard W. Labaree, et al. (New Haven, CT: Yale University Press, 1959), 11: pp. 254, 255.
58. The invoices are in the Corporation Papers, 1765 and later, Harvard University Archives.
59. Benjamin Franklin to John Winthrop, London, July 2, 1768, *The Papers of Benjamin Franklin*, 15: p. 167.
60. John Winthrop to James Bowdoin, Cambridge, Jan. 18,1769, *The Bowdoin and Temple Papers*, Collections of the Massachusetts Historical Society, Sixth Series, Vol. 9 (Boston: Massachusetts Historical Society), pp. 116–118.
61. James Bowdoin to Thomas Gage, Boston, Jan. 23, 1769 and Feb. 26, 1769, *The Bowdoin and Temple Papers*, pp. 119, 127.
62. Frank E. Manuel and Fritzie P. Manuel, *James Bowdoin and the Patriot Philosophers* (Philadelphia: American Philosophical Society, 2004), chap. 5.
63. John Winthrop to James Bowdoin, Cambridge, Feb. 27, 1769, *The Bowdoin and Temple Papers*, pp. 127, 128.
64. Thomas Gage to James Bowdoin, New York, Jan. 30, 1769, and James Bowdoin to Thomas Gage, Boston, March 1, 1769 and March 27, 1769, *The Bowdoin and Temple Papers*, pp. 120, 121, 130.
65. John Winthrop, "Observations of the Transit of Venus over the Sun, June 3, 1769," *Philosophical Transactions* 59 (1769), pp. 351–358, esp. pp. 351, 352; Benjamin Franklin to John Winthrop, London, July 2, 1768 and March 11, 1769, *The Papers of Benjamin Franklin*, 15: pp. 166–172, and 16: p. 65.
66. Regulator clock, John Ellicott, ca. 1764 (CHSI 0070); astronomical quadrant, Jeremiah Sisson, ca. 1765 (CHSI 0061); brass octant, Benjamin Martin, 1764 (CHSI 0007), astronomical transit, John Bird, ca. 1767 (CHSI 0058), three reflecting telescopes of 1-, 2-, and 4-foot lengths, James Short, ca. 1758, 1763, and 1767 (CHSI 0053, 0002, 0001 respectively); two split object-glass micrometers, Dollond, ca. 1758–64 (CHSI 0002 and 0059).
67. John L. O'Sullivan, "Annexation," *United States Magazine and Democratic Review* 17, 85 (July/Aug 1845), pp. 5–10 (propounding the annexation of the Republic of Texas by the United States) and used by him influentially to deride British claims to the Oregon country later that year (*New York Morning News*, Dec. 27, 1845).
68. The most prominent example of hostility to revisionist historical accounts is that of the vituperative response by certain U.S. senators and others to the exhibition *The West as*

America: Reinterpreting Images of the Frontier, 1820–1920 at the National Museum of American Art, Washington, DC, in 1991. See the website by Mary Wood, University of Virginia: http://people.virginia.edu/~mmw3v/west/home.htm (accessed June 7, 2012).

69. The Mashantucket Pequot Tribal Nation gained federal recognition by an act of Congress (the Connecticut Indian Land Claims Settlement Act) in 1983, rather than by application to the Bureau of Indian Affairs. A high-stakes bingo hall preceded the resort casino in 1986. In 1978, the Bureau of Indian Affairs published final rules and procedures by which qualified

70. See the account by one of the Native scholars who worked on the project: Jolene Rickard, "Absorbing or Obscuring the Absence of a Critical Space in the Americas for Indigeneity: The Smithsonian's National Museum of the American Indian," Editorial: "Museums—Crossing Boundaries," eds. Ivan Gaskell and Jeffrey Quilter, *Res: Anthropology and Aesthetics* 52 (2007), pp. 85–92. She describes the creation of the NMAI as a "first safe space to begin to reconnect with the Indigenous peoples of the Americas," and concludes that the "NMAI cannot stand in for the political and legal infrastructure necessary to sustain Indigenous America, but it reminds the nerve center of the most powerful country in the world to rethink its ongoing colonizing encounters" (p. 92).

71. Judy Kertész and Lauren Brandt, *History of the Indian College*, 2005: http://www.fas.harvard.edu/~amciv/HistoryofIndianCollege.htm (accessed June 8, 2012).

72. See the online version: http://www.peabody.harvard.edu/DV-online (accessed June 8, 2012). *Veritas* (truth) appears on the university's armorial device and is usually (though incorrectly from a strictly heraldic point of view) described as its motto.

73. *The Holy Bible: Containing the Old Testament and the New. Translated into the Indian Language* (Cambridge, MA: Samuel Green and Marmaduke Johnson, 1663). Other pieces of type had been found during excavations in Harvard Yard in 1979 and 1980. All are in the Peabody Museum; see "Printing Type and the Eliot Bible": http://www.peabody.harvard.edu/node/499 (accessed June 8, 2012).

74. See the Wôpanâak Language Reclamation Project website: http://wlrp.org/index.html (accessed June 8, 2012).

75. Small bag, Peabody Museum 90-17-50/49302. The bag was the subject of the final research paper for the spring 2002 seminar by Claire Eager, "Settlers, Slaves, and 'Salvages': The American Fabric of History and Value in an African 'Indian' Bag."

76. Monni Adams and T. Rose Holdcraft, "Dida Woven Raffia Cloth from Côte d'Ivoire," *African Arts* 25, 3 (1992), pp. 42–51, 100, 101. A note in the museum registration ledger states, "Probably African Mfg." and the bag was indeed placed in an unrecorded location among the African textiles from perhaps the 1930s until its rediscovery in 1997.

77. See Lorie M. Graham and Peter R. Golia, "In Caleb's Footsteps: The Harvard University Native American Program," in *Native American Studies in Higher Education: Models for Collaboration between Universities and Indigenous Nations*, eds. Duane Champagne and Jay Stauss (Walnut Creek, CA: AltaMira, 2002), pp. 123–144.

78. Notice announcing a lecture by Geraldine Brooks, Sept. 24, 2009: http://www.peabody.harvard.edu/node/532 (accessed June 8, 2012).

79. Eager, 2002, p. 20.

80. Half Moon Ledger Book (MS Am 2337), Houghton Library, Harvard University, gift of Harriet J. Bradbury, 1930. It was rebound with an introduction by James Howard (writing as Phocion Howard) as *The Pictorial Autobiography of Half Moon, an Uncpapa Chief.* A facsimile is available online: http://nrs.harvard.edu/urn-3:FHCL.HOUGH:1385758 (accessed June 11, 2012). See also Lewis O. Saum, "James William 'Phocion' Howard of the *Chicago Tribune* Reports the Aftermath of the Little Big Horn Disaster," *Journal of Illinois History* 9 (2006), pp. 82–94, for an account of Howard's journey by steamboat up the Missouri River with relief troops; and Castle McLaughlin, *A Lakota War Book from the Little Big Horn: "The Pictorial Autobiography of Half Moon"* (Houghton Library Studies; Cambridge, MA: Houghton Library and Peabody Museum Press, 2013).

81. Pottery plate painted by Nock-ko-ist (Bear's Heart), Southern Tsistsistas (Cheyenne people), ca. 1878–82, Peabody Museum of Archaeology and Ethnology, Gift of the Hemenway heirs, 44-35-10/27481.

82. Pratt was a leading proponent of the forced cultural assimilation of Indians and others, and was the founder of the Carlisle Indian Industrial School in Carlisle, PA. See Richard Henry Pratt, *Battlefield and Classroom: Four Decades with the American Indian, 1867–1904*, ed. Robert M. Utley (New Haven, CT: Yale University Press, 1964).

83. Harriet Beecher Stowe, "The Indians at St. Augustine," *Christian Union* 15, 16, April 18, 1877, p. 345; 15, 17, April 25, p. 372. She concludes: "Might not the money now constantly spent on armies, forts and frontiers be better invested in educating young men who shall return and teach their people to live like civilized beings?"

84. *The Bear's Heart Ledger Book*, Nock-ko-ist (Bear's Heart), ca. 1875, National Museum of the American Indian, Washington, DC. See Karen Daniels Petersen, *Plains Indian Art from Fort Marion* (Norman, OK: University of Oklahoma Press, 1971).

85. "Buffalo Chase and Encampment" in *The Bear's Heart Ledger Book* (n. 19).

86. Petersen, *Plains Indian Art from Fort Marion*, p. 104.

87. See Petersen, *Plains Indian Art from Fort Marion*, pp. 97–109, for a detailed biography; see also *Keeping History: Plains Indian Ledger Drawings*, National Museum of American History, Washington, DC, 2009–10, online version: http://americanhistory.si.edu/documentsgallery/exhibitions/ledger_drawing_6.html# (accessed June 11, 2012).

88. Duplicate cast of Nock-ko-ist, Bear's Heart, Cheyenne warrior, Peabody Museum 78-1-10/13856. Two of the busts were not of prisoners but of a Comanche woman, Pe-ah-in, and her young daughter, Ah-kes (duplicate cast, Peabody Museum 78-1-10/13910; the Peabody's duplicate cast of Pe-ah-in is untraced). Fall 2003 seminar student Lisa May researched the busts for her final paper, as did fall 2009 graduate seminar student Lindsay Grant who, as a 2010 summer fellow, produced a digital archive for the spring 2011 undergraduate course.

89. See Robin Ridington, *Blessing for a Long Time: The Sacred Pole of the Omaha Tribe* (Lincoln, NE: University of Nebraska Press, 1997), for the return of Umon'hon'ti from the Peabody Museum to Omaha in 1989.

90. Daniel K. Richter, *Facing East from Indian Country: A Native History of Early America* (Cambridge, MA: Harvard University Press, 2001).

About the Authors

Laurel Thatcher Ulrich is the 300th Anniversary University Professor at Harvard. She is best known for *A Midwife's Tale: The Life of Martha Ballard Based on Her Diary, 1785–1812*, which won the Pulitzer Prize for History in 1991. Working on a PBS documentary based on the book reinforced Ulrich's longstanding interest in material culture. In *The Age of Homespun* (2001), she experimented with object-centered history by focusing each chapter on a different object, including Indian baskets and a painted cupboard, as well as a variety of homespun textiles. She is also known for coining a slogan that ended up on T-shirts, bumper stickers, and coffee mugs, and that became the title of her 2007 book, *Well-behaved Women Seldom Make History*.

Ivan Gaskell is Professor of Cultural History and Museum Studies, and head of the Focus Gallery Project at the Bard Graduate Center, New York City. Gaskell taught history and curated collections at Harvard for twenty years before assuming his current position. His work addresses intersections among history, art history, anthropology, museology, and philosophy. His many publications include *Vermeer's Wager: Speculations on Art History, Theory, and Art Museums* (2000) and six co-edited books in the series *Cambridge Studies in Philosophy and the Arts*. He has made numerous contributions to journals and edited volumes and has curated many experimental exhibitions at Harvard and, of late, in New York.

Sara J. Schechner is the David P. Wheatland Curator of the Collection of Historical Scientific Instruments at Harvard University, where is she is a member of the History of Science Department and has taught museum studies. Recent honors include the Joseph H. Hazen Education Prize of the History of Science Society for a career of innovative and diverse object-based teaching. Schechner has curated nearly thirty exhibitions and is the author of numerous articles on material culture, early modern astronomy, and colonial American science. Her books include *Comets, Popular Culture, and the Birth of Modern Cosmology* (1997), *Western Astrolabes* (1998), and the forthcoming *Time and Time Again*, which explores through objects how science and culture have shaped our sense of past, present, and future. Her current research focuses on sundials, science, and social change.

Sarah Anne Carter is the Curator and Director of Research of the Chipstone Foundation and the Chipstone Fellow in Material Culture at the University of Wisconsin-Madison. She was previously a lecturer on History and Literature at Harvard University. She earned a Ph.D. at Harvard in the History of American Civilization and an M.A. from the Winterthur Program in American Material Culture at the University of Delaware. She is the author of the forthcoming book *Object Lessons*, a nineteenth-century practice that shaped the ways Americans understood their material worlds and learned to talk about race and citizenship. Her research has been supported by several grants, and she has published essays in *The History of Photography*, *The History of Childhood and Youth*, and *The Museum History Journal*.

Samantha S. B. van Gerbig is Exhibition Designer and Photographer at the Collection of Historical Scientific Instruments at Harvard University. Deeply interested in the intersection between art and science, she earned a B.A. from Harvard University in Visual and Environmental Studies and an M.Sc. in the History of Science from Oxford University. Her recently designed exhibits include *Body of Knowledge: A History of Anatomy (in Three Parts), Tangible Things, Paper Worlds: Printing Knowledge in Early Modern Europe, Wireless World: Marconi & the Making of Radio*, and *The Astrolabe: East and West*. A skilled museum photographer, she has shot thousands of objects for documentation, research, and publication over the last decade.

Picture Credits

18. Unidentified artist, dagger, ca. 1840s (handle detail), cast bronze with gilded silver and engraved steel; 34.3 cm (13 ½ in.) Harvard Art Museums/Fogg Museum, purchased through the generosity of Mariot Fraser Solomon in memory of Arthur K. Solomon, 2003.240. Photo: Imaging Department © President and Fellows of Harvard College.

19. Plaster cast of an arthritic hand, USA, ca. 1904–06, Warren Anatomical Museum, Francis A. Countway Library of Medicine, WAM 20466.

20. Tiger cranium and jaw, *Felis tigris tigris*, Mammalogy Collection, Museum of Comparative Zoology.

21. Unidentified text written on palm leaves and bound accordion-style between wood, Indonesia, Houghton Library, MS Indo 2.

22. *Tangible Things* gallery view, "muddle" case at the Collection of Historical Scientific Instruments, Harvard University, spring 2011.

23. Armillary ring sundial, Lucca, 1764, Collection of Historical Scientific Instruments, 7166.

24. Prepared skin of a pink fairy armadillo, *Chlamyphorus truncatus*, collected by Louis Agassiz, Mendoza, Argentina, 1872, Mammalogy Collection, Museum of Comparative Zoology, 3207.

25. Courtesy of the Mineralogical and Geological Museum at Harvard University, Vesuvianite, MGMH ID# 136534. © 2012 President and Fellows of Harvard College. All rights reserved.

26. Fragments of textile (mounted between glass), Spiro Mounds, Muscogee people, Spiro, Oklahoma, USA, before ca. 1450, courtesy of the Peabody Museum of Archaeology and Ethnology, Harvard University, 39-21-10/13077.

27. Two cuneiform tablets with clay envelopes, Nuzi, Mesopotamia, ca. 1500 BCE, Semitic Museum, 1899.2.355 and 1899.2.70.

28. Fragmentary oracle bones, Henan Province, China, gift of Langdon Warner, courtesy of the Peabody Museum of Archaeology and Ethnology, Harvard University, 15-44-60/D836.40.

29. Letter employing cross-hatching, to "my dear sister Bessie," November 4, 1855, Huntting-Rudd Family Papers, Arthur and Elizabeth Schlesinger Library on the History of Women in America, MC284.

30. Silkscreen poster, *Women Are Not Chicks*, Chicago Women's Graphics Collective, 1972, Arthur and Elizabeth Schlesinger Library on the History of Women in America, GR-15 2002-M130.

31. Hiram Powers, *Loulie's Hand*, 1839, carved marble; 7.3 x 14 cm (2 7/8 x 5 1/2 in.), Harvard Art Museums/Fogg Museum, gift of Professor James Hardy Ropes, 1928.115. Photo: Imaging Department © President and Fellows of Harvard College.

32. Conical tea bowl with *Yōhen*-type glaze, Kimura Moriyasu, Kyoto, Heisei period, dated 1999,

Temmoku-type ware: light gray stoneware with slate gray glaze mottled with blue overglaze; with impressed seal mark reading "Moriyasu" on the exterior wall above the foot ring; 6.8 x 14.6 cm (2 11/16 x 5 3/4 in.), Harvard Art Museums/Arthur M. Sackler Museum, gift of Moriyasu Kimura, 2000.23. Photo: Imaging Department © President and Fellows of Harvard College.

33. Cenotaph cover, seventeenth-century lampas (detail), silk lampas on satin foundation; 138 x 67.5 cm (54 5/16 x 26 9/16 in.), Harvard Art Museums/Arthur M. Sackler Museum, Stuart Cary Welch Collection, gift of Edith I. Welch in memory of Stuart Cary Welch, 2009.202.48. Photo: Imaging Department © President and Fellows of Harvard College.

34. Unidentified artist, *Blolo Bla* (spirit partner), nineteenth–twentieth century Iroko wood; 41 x 7.3 x 9 cm (16 1/8 x 2 7/8 x 3 9/16 in.); with base: 43.3 x 10 x 9 cm (17 1/16 x 3 15/16 x 3 9/16 in.), Harvard Art Museums/Fogg Museum, Lois Orswell Collection, 1998.311. Photo: Imaging Department © President and Fellows of Harvard College.

35. Edward Weston, *Cabbage Leaf*, 1931, printed later, gelatin silver print; 18.2 x 22.9 cm (7 3/16 x 9 in.); sheet: 20.4 x 25.2 cm (8 1/16 x 9 15/16 in.) Harvard Art Museums/Fogg Museum, gift of Sam Pratt, P2003.250. Photo: Imaging Department © President and Fellows of Harvard College.

36. "Mondrian," Edwin H. Land, Cambridge, ca. 1975–85, Collection of Historical Scientific Instruments, 2004-1-0255.

37. Plaster casts from the Boston Phrenological Society: Dr. Johann Gaspar Spurzheim (1776–1832), Anne-Josèphe Théroigne de Méricourt (1762–1817), and René Descartes (1596–1650), USA, before 1835, Warren Anatomical Museum in the Francis A. Countway Library of Medicine, WAM 03562.001, 03364, 03499.

38. Armillary sphere, USSR, ca. 1960, Collection of Historical Scientific Instruments, 2006-1-0109.

39. Armillary sphere, USSR, ca. 1960 (detail), Collection of Historical Scientific Instruments, 2006-1-0109.

40. Anni Albers, bedspread (black, white, and red) for Harvard Graduate Center, 1949 (detail), woven cotton, plain weave plaid; 241.2 x 143.3 cm (94 15/16 x 56 7/16 in.), Harvard Art Museums/Busch-Reisinger Museum, gift of Anni Albers, BR67.20 © 2003 The Josef and Anni Albers Foundation / Artists Rights Society (ARS), New York. Photo: Imaging Department © President and Fellows of Harvard College.

41. Sash of watered blue grosgrain ribbon formerly worn by George Washington, ca. 1775–83, gift of the heirs of David Kimball, courtesy of the Peabody Museum of Archaeology and Ethnology, Harvard University 979-13-10/58761 60742960.

42. Framed military epaulette, France(?), ca. 1780, General Artemas Ward House Museum, HU1695.

43. Framed military epaulette, France(?), ca. 1780 (detail), General Artemas Ward House Museum, HU1695.

44. Parasitic tapeworms, *Taenia* sp., Boston, 1893 (detail), Department of Invertebrates, Museum of Comparative Zoology, 37376.

45. Orchid, *Epidendrum lorifolium*, with watercolor drawing by Blanche Ames Ames, 1923, Orchid Herbarium of Oakes Ames, Harvard University Herbaria, 00070528.

46. Orchid, *Epidendrum lorifolium*, with watercolor drawing by Blanche Ames Ames, 1923 (detail), Orchid Herbarium of Oakes Ames, Harvard University Herbaria, 00070528.

47. Blanche Ames Ames, *Dendrochilum Foxworthyi Ames*, in Oakes Ames, *Orchidaceae: Illustrations of the Family Orchidaceae, issuing from the Ames Botanical Library, North Easton, Massachusetts*, seven fascicles (Boston: Merrymount Press, 1905–22), Fascicle 3 (1908), plate 26 [Seq. 574], Harvard University Herbaria.

48. Four-handled glass jar, Roman, fourth–fifth century, Semitic Museum, 1936.2.98.

49. Four-handled glass jar, Roman, fourth–fifth century (detail), Semitic Museum, 1936.2.98.

50. Interior view of Maximilian Kellner's study, Scrapbook of Maximilian L. Kellner, Harvard University Archives, HUA 885.44 f.

51. Fragment of *Plato's Republic* on papyrus, Oxyrhynchus, Egypt, ca. 250–300, Houghton Library, MS Gr SM3740.

52. Fragment of *Plato's Republic* on papyrus, Oxyrhynchus, Egypt, ca. 250–300 (reverse side), Houghton Library, MS Gr SM3740.

53. Excavation of Oxyrhynchus, Egypt, courtesy of the Egyptian Exploration Society, London.

54. Mold for casting openwork ornaments, 550–800 AD, carved limestone; 2.2 x 6.9 x 4.7 cm (7/8 x 2 11/16 x 1 7/8 in.), Harvard Art Museums/Arthur M. Sackler Museum, gift of Bruce Ferrini, 2001.270.59. Photo: Imaging Department © President and Fellows of Harvard College.

55. Bottles of chemicals marked "Medical College of Alabama," Rousseau Frères, Paris, ca. 1862, Collection of Historical Scientific Instruments, 4516, 4529, 4609, 4618, 4654, 4661, 4671.

56. Bottle of chromic oxide marked "Medical College of Alabama," Rousseau Frères, Paris, ca. 1862 (detail), Collection of Historical Scientific Instruments, 4609.

57. Crimson field-hockey dress, Radcliffe College, ca. 1925, Elizabeth Wright Plimpton Papers, Arthur and Elizabeth Schlesinger Library on the History of Women in America, SC 98.

58. Gym suit worn by Edith Hall Plimpton for basketball and gymnastics, 1896–97, Radcliffe College Archives, SC 13, Arthur and Elizabeth Schlesinger Library on the History of Women in America.

59. Crimson field-hockey dress, Radcliffe College, ca. 1925 (detail), Elizabeth Wright Plimpton Papers, Arthur and Elizabeth Schlesinger Library on the History of Women in America, SC 98.

60. *Tangible Things* gallery view, "müddle" case at the Collection of Historical Scientific Instruments, Harvard University, spring 2011.

61. Enju-school short sword (from Higo Province, Kyushu), cut down from longer blade, Muromachi period, ca. 1530 (detail), metal with mixed-media scabbard; total (including hilt): L. 61.5 x W. 7.2 x D. 7.7 cm (2 13/16 x 3 1/16 x 24 3/16 in.), Harvard Art Museums/Arthur M. Sackler Museum, gift of Professor Albert Bushnell Hart, class of 1880, 1936.126.B. Photo: Imaging Department © President and Fellows of Harvard College.

62. Medal of Livio I Odescalchi, designed by Giovanni Martino Hamerani, Rome, 1689. Harvard Art Museums/Fogg Museum, gift of Edward W. Forbes, by exchange, 1996.220.

63. Ostracon concerning textiles, vicinity of the First Cataract of the Nile, Egypt, ca. 100–200, Houghton Library (transferred from the Fogg Art Museum), MS Ostraca 3152.

64. Chops from the silk industry, China, late nineteenth century, Kress Collection, Baker Library, Harvard Business School.

65. Bird's-head pestle found by Henry David Thoreau, Concord, Massachusetts, USA, courtesy of the Peabody Museum of Archaeology and Ethnology, Harvard University, 69-34-10/2382.

66. Blanding's turtle, *Emydoidea blandingi*, Herpetology Collection, Museum of Comparative Zoology, Z111.

67. Vellum manuscript with watercolor drawings and inscriptions, bound in quilted satin, with a letter to the recipient of the gift, Frances Lady Douglas, by Sarah Ponsonby and Eleanor Butler, Wales, 1788, Houghton Library, MS Eng 1225.

68. Reticule purse associated with the vellum manuscript with watercolor drawings and inscriptions, bound in quilted satin, with a letter to the recipient of the gift, Frances Lady Douglas, by Sarah Ponsonby and Eleanor Butler, Wales, 1788, Houghton Library, MS Eng 1225.

69. Vellum manuscript with watercolor drawings and inscriptions, bound in quilted satin, with a letter to the recipient of the gift, Frances Lady Douglas, by Sarah Ponsonby and Eleanor Butler, Wales, 1788 (detail), Houghton Library, MS Eng 1225.

70. Vellum manuscript with watercolor drawings and inscriptions, bound in quilted satin, with a letter to the recipient of the gift, Frances Lady Douglas, by Sarah Ponsonby and Eleanor Butler, Wales, 1788 (detail), Houghton Library, MS Eng 1225.

71. Galapagos giant tortoise, *Testudo nigra* holotype, marked "Ship Abigail," Galapagos, Ecuador, 1834, Herpetology Collection, Museum of Comparative Zoology, R-11064.

72. Galapagos giant tortoise, *Testudo nigra* holotype, marked "Ship Abigail," Galapagos, Ecuador, 1834 (detail), Herpetology Collection, Museum of Comparative Zoology, R-11064.
73. Galapagos giant tortoise hunted by English whaler, *Illustrated London News*, July 13, 1850, Widener Library, Harvard Library.
74. Ship *Abigail* logbook, 1831–35, open to the days in May 1834 when the sailors hunted tortoises in the Galapagos (detail), courtesy of the Trustees of the New Bedford Free Public Library.
75. Spoon carved with a human hand, Luanda, Angola, 1857 or before, gift of Mrs. John B. Sparhawk, courtesy of the Peabody Museum of Archaeology and Ethnology, Harvard University, 83-14-50/30212.
76. Spoon carved with a human hand, Luanda, Angola, 1857 or before (detail), gift of Mrs. John B. Sparhawk, courtesy of the Peabody Museum of Archaeology and Ethnology, Harvard University, 83-14-50/30212.
77. Tortilla made from flour corn, *Zea mays*, Mexico, 1897, Economic Botany Herbarium of Oakes Ames, Harvard University Herbaria, Cat. 8535.
78. Tortilla made from flour corn, *Zea mays*, Mexico, 1897 (detail), Economic Botany Herbarium of Oakes Ames, Harvard University Herbaria, Cat. 8535.
79. Tortillas collected by Edward Palmer in San Luis, Potosí, Mexico, 1878, Harvard University Herbaria, 17643.
80. Woman preparing tortillas, courtesy of the Peabody Museum of Archaeology and Ethnology, Harvard University, 79-14-00/1.1 99080007.
81. Beetle necklace or bracelet, Naga people, India or Myanmar, 1913 or before, courtesy of the Peabody Museum of Archaeology and Ethnology, Harvard University, 13-24-60/D2145.
82. Beetle necklace or bracelet, Naga people, India or Myanmar, 1913 or before (detail), courtesy of the Peabody Museum of Archaeology and Ethnology, Harvard University, 13-24-60/D2145.
83. "Blondie goes to Leisureland: a Westinghouse game," USA, ca. 1940, Baker Old Class Collection, Baker Library, Harvard Business School.
84. "Blondie goes to Leisureland: a Westinghouse game," USA, ca. 1940 (detail), Baker Old Class Collection, Baker Library, Harvard Business School.
85. "Blondie goes to Leisureland: a Westinghouse game," USA, ca. 1940 (detail), Baker Old Class Collection, Baker Library, Harvard Business School.
86. Three sheep or goat knucklebones, West Asia, Iron Age, Semitic Museum, on deposit from the Department of Archaeology, University of Edinburgh, L3657, L5059, and L4507.
87. Vesical calculus on display in the Mineralogical Hall of the Harvard Museum of Natural History as part of the *Tangible Things* installation, Harvard University, spring 2011.
88. Vesical calculus formed from oxalate of lime, uric acid, and phosphate of lime, USA, 1809. Warren Anatomical Museum in the Francis A. Countway Library of Medicine, WAM 04089.
89. Pencil that belonged to Henry David Thoreau, Concord, Massachusetts, ca. 1850s, along with a note and mailing container, ca. 1948, Houghton Library, *47Z-7.
90. Pencil that belonged to Henry David Thoreau, Concord, Massachusetts, ca. 1850s (detail), Houghton Library, *47Z-7.
91. Patent medicine bottle, "Macamoose, The Great Indian Tonic," containing the desiccated body of a house mouse, *Mus musculus*, USA, ca. 1865, General Artemas Ward House Museum, HU 2072, on display in the Mammal Hall in the Harvard Museum of Natural History as part of the *Tangible Things* installation, Harvard University, spring 2011.
92. Dog paw print in a mud brick, Nuzi, Mesopotamia, 1500–1300 BCE, Semitic Museum, 1930.13B.2, on display in the Mammal Hall in the Harvard Museum of Natural History as part of the *Tangible Things* installation, Harvard University, spring 2011.
93. Louis Comfort Tiffany, floriform vase, ca. 1900, glass; 40.6 x 15.9 cm (16 x 6 1/4 in.), Harvard Art Museums/Fogg Museum, gift of Murray Anthony and Bessie Lincoln Potter, 1957.43, on display in the Glass Flowers gallery in the Harvard Museum of Natural History as part of the *Tangible Things* installation, Harvard University, spring 2011.
94. Louis Comfort Tiffany, floriform vase, ca. 1900, glass; 40.6 x 15.9 cm (16 x 6 1/4 in.), Harvard Art Museums/Fogg Museum, gift of Murray Anthony and Bessie Lincoln Potter, 1957.43. Photo: Imaging Department © President and Fellows of Harvard College.
95. Pocket globe, James Ferguson, ca. 1757, the Ebenezer Storer Collection, Harvard University Archives, HUG 1808.1000.1, on display in the Peabody Museum of Archaeology and Ethnology as part of the *Tangible Things* installation, Harvard University, spring 2011.
96. Pocket globe, James Ferguson, ca. 1757, the Ebenezer Storer Collection, Harvard University Archives, HUG 1808.1000.1.
97. Camp Fire Girls-style dress, belt, and beads, by Sarah Jenney Gilbert Kerlin, 1947–50, Arthur and Elizabeth Schlesinger Library on the History of Women in America, gift of Catherine Wilder Guiles (Radcliffe, 1959), 2006-M88, as displayed in the Peabody Museum of Archaeology and Ethnology as part of the *Tangible Things* installation, Harvard University, spring 2011.
98. Camp Fire Girls-style beads, by Sarah Jenney Gilbert Kerlin, 1947–50, Arthur and Elizabeth Schlesinger Library.

99. Silver band for a Passamaquoddy (Peskotomuhkati) woman's hat, Maine, USA, or New Brunswick, Canada, ca. 1875, courtesy of the Peabody Museum of Archaeology and Ethnology, Harvard University 985-27-10/60273A, as displayed in the Arthur M. Sackler Museum of the Harvard Art Museums as part of the *Tangible Things* installation, Harvard University, spring 2011.

100. Silver band for a Passamaquoddy (Peskotomuhkati) woman's hat, Maine, USA, or New Brunswick, Canada, ca. 1875, courtesy of the Peabody Museum of Archaeology and Ethnology, Harvard University 985-27-10/60273A.

101. Hans Peter Müller, mounted carved coconut goblet decorated with scenes from the story of Samson (with lid), ca. 1600, coconut and gilt silver; 30.2 x 8.2 cm (11 7/8 x 3 1/4 in.), Harvard Art Museums/Busch-Reisinger Museum, purchased in memory of Eda K. Loeb, BR61.58.A-B, as installed in Houghton Library as part of the *Tangible Things* installation, Harvard University, spring 2011. Photo: Imaging Department © President and Fellows of Harvard College.

102. Hans Peter Müller, mounted carved coconut goblet decorated with scenes from the story of Samson (with lid), ca. 1600, coconut and gilt silver; 30.2 x 8.2 cm (11 7/8 x 3 1/4 in.), Harvard Art Museums/Busch-Reisinger Museum, purchased in memory of Eda K. Loeb, BR61.58.A-B. Photo: Imaging Department © President and Fellows of Harvard College.

103. Framed dress fragment, said to have belonged to Priscilla Mullins, seventeenth century, Radcliffe Picture Collection, Arthur and Elizabeth Schlesinger Library on the History of Women in America, as displayed in Houghton Library as part of the *Tangible Things* installation, Harvard University, spring 2011.

104. Framed dress fragment, said to have belonged to Priscilla Mullins, seventeenth century, Radcliffe Picture Collection, Arthur and Elizabeth Schlesinger Library on the History of Women in America.

105. Unidentified artist, President's Chair, turned great chair, ca. 1550–1600, European ash with later American oak handgrips; 118.1 x 82.6 x 53.3 cm (46 1/2 x 32 1/2 x 21 in.), Harvard Art Museums/Fogg Museum, loan from the President and Fellows of Harvard College, 979.1933.

106. President's Chair (detail of back). For complete credit information, see credit 105.

107. President's Chair (detail of needlepoint seat cushion). For complete credit information, see credit 105.

108. Meerschaum corncob pipe, Missouri, 1919, Economic Botany Herbarium of Oakes Ames, Harvard University Herbaria, #00200162, as displayed at the Harvard Mark I computer belonging to the Collection of Historical Scientific Instruments, 1997-1-0963a, situated in the Science Center, as part of the *Tangible Things* installation, Harvard University, spring 2011.

109. Meerschaum corncob pipe, Missouri, 1919, Economic Botany Herbarium of Oakes Ames, Harvard University Herbaria, #00200162.

110. Robert L. Hawkins, a Harvard technician, smoking a corncob pipe while working on the multiply-divide unit of the IBM Automatic Sequence Controlled Calculator (known as the Harvard Mark I computer) during its installation in the Cruft Laboratory at Harvard University, Feb. 1, 1944, Collection of Historical Scientific Instruments, Lib.1964-049.

111. Palette used by John Singer Sargent, nineteenth–twentieth century, oil on wood; 56.5 x 38 cm (22 1/4 x 14 15/16 in.), Harvard Art Museums/Fogg Museum, gift of Miss Emily Sargent and Mrs. Francis Ormond in memory of their brother, John Singer Sargent (through Thomas A. Fox, Esq.), 1933.49, as displayed in the Putnam Gallery of the Collection of Historical Scientific Instruments as part of the *Tangible Things* installation, Harvard University, spring 2011.

112. Palette used by John Singer Sargent, nineteenth–twentieth century, oil on wood; 56.5 x 38 cm (22 1/4 x 14 15/16 in.), Harvard Art Museums/Fogg Museum, gift of Miss Emily Sargent and Mrs. Francis Ormond in memory of their brother, John Singer Sargent (through Thomas A. Fox, Esq.), 1933.49. Photo: Imaging Department © President and Fellows of Harvard College.

113. Palette used by John Singer Sargent, nineteenth–twentieth century (detail), oil on wood; 56.5 x 38 cm (22 1/4 x 14 15/16 in.), Harvard Art Museums/Fogg Museum, gift of Miss Emily Sargent and Mrs. Francis Ormond in memory of their brother, John Singer Sargent (through Thomas A. Fox, Esq.), 1933.49. Photo: Imaging Department © President and Fellows of Harvard College.

114. Palette used by John Singer Sargent, nineteenth–twentieth century, oil on wood; 56.5 x 38 cm (22 1/4 x 14 15/16 in.), Harvard Art Museums/Fogg Museum, gift of Miss Emily Sargent and Mrs. Francis Ormond in memory of their brother, John Singer Sargent (through Thomas A. Fox, Esq.), 1933.49, as displayed in the Putnam Gallery of the Collection of Historical Scientific Instruments as part of the *Tangible Things* installation, Harvard University, spring 2011.

115. Die-cut tin bluebird sign, Massachusetts, 1915, Women's Rights Collection, Arthur and Elizabeth Schlesinger Library on the History of Women in America, as displayed in the Harvard Museum of Natural History as part of the *Tangible Things* installation, Harvard University, spring 2011.

116. Die-cut tin bluebird sign, Massachusetts, 1915, Women's Rights Collection, Arthur and Elizabeth

Schlesinger Library on the History of Women in America, as displayed in the Harvard Museum of Natural History as part of the *Tangible Things* installation, Harvard University, spring 2011.

117. "Bluebird" in Chester A. Reed, *Bird Guide: Land Birds East of the Rockies from Parrots to Bluebirds*, rev. ed. (Garden City, NY, 1909), Ernst Mayer Library, Museum of Comparative Zoology.

118. Portrait of Katharine Lane Weems as a young woman, ca. 1918, Arthur and Elizabeth Schlesinger Library on the History of Women in America, W379205.

119. Walking plow, Massachusetts(?), late eighteenth century, General Artemas Ward House Museum, HU 4070, as displayed in the Semitic Museum as part of the *Tangible Things* installation, Harvard University, spring 2011.

120. Walking plow, Massachusetts(?), late eighteenth century, General Artemas Ward House Museum, HU 4070, as displayed in the Semitic Museum as part of the *Tangible Things* installation, Harvard University, spring 2011.

121. The Ward House attic, ca. 1890s, General Artemas Ward House Museum, Harvard University, HU4093.4.

122. Jean-Baptiste Oudry, avian album, eighteenth century, parchment-covered album with ninety-six bird studies executed in black ink and watercolor on eighty-three leaves of off-white antique laid paper (43 x 34.5 cm). Some drawings have been pasted into the album; others were drawn directly on the album leaves; 44 x 35 x 5 cm (17 5/16 x 13 3/4 x 1 15/16 in.), Harvard Art Museums/Fogg Museum, anonymous gift, 1953.75. With skull of a helmeted hornbill, *Rhinoplax vigil*, Sumatra, Borneo, or the Malay Peninsula, the casque carved in China, nineteenth century, Ornithology, Museum of Comparative Zoology. Both as displayed in the Arthur M. Sackler Museum of the Harvard Art Museums, as part of the *Tangible Things* exhibition in spring of 2011.

123. Skull of a helmeted hornbill, *Rhinoplax vigil*, Sumatra, Borneo, or the Malay Peninsula, the casque carved in China, nineteenth century, Ornithology, Museum of Comparative Zoology.

124. Skull of a helmeted hornbill, *Rhinoplax vigil*, Sumatra, Borneo, or the Malay Peninsula, the casque carved in China, nineteenth century (detail), Ornithology, Museum of Comparative Zoology.

125. Skull of a helmeted hornbill, *Rhinoplax vigil*, Sumatra, Borneo, or the Malay Peninsula, the casque carved in China, nineteenth century (detail), Ornithology, Museum of Comparative Zoology.

126. Jean-Baptiste Oudry, avan album, eighteenth century, parchment-covered album with ninety-six bird studies executed in black ink and watercolor on eighty-three leaves of off-white antique laid paper (43 x 34.5 cm.). Some drawings have been

pasted into the album; others were drawn directly on the album leaves; 44 x 35 x 5 cm (17 5/16 x 13 3/4 x 1 15/16 in.), Harvard Art Museums/Fogg Museum, anonymous gift, 1953.75. Photo: Imaging Department © President and Fellows of Harvard College.

127. Jean-Baptiste Oudry, avian album, eighteenth century, parchment-covered album with ninety-six bird studies executed in black ink and watercolor on eighty-three leaves of off-white antique laid paper (43 x 34.5 cm.). Some drawings have been pasted into the album; others were drawn directly on the album leaves; 44 x 35 x 5 cm (17 5/16 x 13 3/4 x 1 15/16 in.), Harvard Art Museums/Fogg Museum, anonymous gift, 1953.75. Photo: Imaging Department © President and Fellows of Harvard College.

128. Quirt handle, Omaha or Ponca peoples, Nebraska, ca. 1870–90, General Artemas Ward House Museum, HU 4175.

129. John Cocks, *Algarum Fasciculi; or A Collection of British Sea-weeds, Carefully Dried and Preserved, and correctly named after Dr. Harvey's "Phycologia Britannica,"* Fascicle 1 (Dublin: M. H. Gill, 1855) (detail), Farlow Herbarium of Cryptogamic Botany, Harvard University Herbaria.

130. Slate with "spirit writing," Herrick-Chapman Family Papers, Arthur and Elizabeth Schlesinger Library on the History of Women in America, 2007-M7.

131. Slate with "spirit writing" (detail), Herrick-Chapman Family Papers, Arthur and Elizabeth Schlesinger Library on the History of Women in America, 2007-M7.

132. *Clasped Hands of Robert and Elizabeth Barrett Browning*, Harriet Hosmer, Rome, original cast 1853, Harriet Hosmer Papers, Arthur and Elizabeth Schlesinger Library on the History of Women in America, A-162.

133. *Clasped Hands of Robert and Elizabeth Barrett Browning*, Harriet Hosmer, Rome, original cast 1853 (detail), Harriet Hosmer Papers, Arthur and Elizabeth Schlesinger Library on the History of Women in America, A-162.

134. Divination basket on a gourd base containing fifty-four items of assorted materials, Chokwe people, Benguela Highlands, Angola, twentieth century, courtesy of the Peabody Museum of Archaeology and Ethnology, Harvard University, 39-64-50/3459 60741220.

135. Two figurines from the divination basket, Chokwe people, Benguela Highlands, Angola, twentieth century (detail), courtesy of the Peabody Museum of Archaeology and Ethnology, Harvard University, 39-64-50/3459 60741220.

136. A spotted cloth bundle tied to sticks, taken from the divination basket containing fifty-four items of assorted materials, Chokwe people, Benguela Highlands, Angola, twentieth century (detail), courtesy of the Peabody Museum of Archaeology

and Ethnology, Harvard University, 39-64-50/3459 60741220.

137. Edward Lamson Henry, *The Message*, 1893, oil on board; 23.5 x 30.5 cm (9 1/4 x 12 in.), Harvard Art Museums/Fogg Museum, gift of Theodore E. Stebbins Jr., 2003.279. Photo: Imaging Department © President and Fellows of Harvard College.

138. *The Republic*, statue by Daniel Chester French, *Harper's Weekly*, 1893, Widener Library, Harvard Library.

139. "Life of Aunt Jemima," promotional pamphlet published by R. T. Davis Mill, ca. 1895 (cover), Arthur and Elizabeth Schlesinger Library on the History of Women in America.

140. Abby Fisher, *What Mrs. Fisher Knows About Old Southern Cooking* (San Francisco, 1881) (cover detail), Arthur and Elizabeth Schlesinger Library on the History of Women in America, 641.613 F533w.

141. Octant, Benjamin Martin, London. Gift to Harvard College by Ezekial Goldthwait in 1764 to replace a similar one given by him in 1760 for the Transit of Venus, 1761, Collection of Historical Scientific Instruments, 0007.

142. Reflecting telescope, Benjamin Martin, London, 1761. Gift to Harvard College by Thomas Hancock, 1761. On long-term loan to the Collection of Historical Scientific Instruments from the Science Museum, London, SM-1911-283.

143. John Singleton Copley, *John Winthrop* (1714/15–1779), 1771–73, oil on canvas; 127.5 x 102.1 cm (50 3/16 x 40 3/16 in.); framed: 155.6 x 121.3 x 11.4 cm (61 1/4 x 47 3/4 x 4 1/2 in.), Harvard Art Museums/Fogg Museum, Harvard University Portrait Collection, gift to Harvard College by the executors of the estate of John Winthrop and heirs of Mrs. Andrews, 1894, H113. Photo: Imaging Department © President and Fellows of Harvard College.

144. British ships of war landing their troops in Boston, 1768. Engraved, printed, and sold by Paul Revere, Boston, with hand-coloring by Christian Remick, ca. 1770, American Antiquarian Society Revere Collection, box 2, folder 1, courtesy of the American Antiquarian Society.

145. Pottery plate painted by Nock-ko-ist (Bear's Heart), Cheyenne people, ca. 1878–82, courtesy of the Peabody Museum of Archaeology and Ethnology, Harvard University, 44-25-10/27481.

146. Harvard student summer garment, USA, ca. 1834–35, Harvard University Archives, HUD 837.87.

147. Harvard student summer garment (rear view). For complete credit information, see credit 146.

148. Harvard student summer garment (detail of fringe). For complete credit information, see credit 146.

149. Harvard student summer garment (detail of shirring). For complete credit information, see credit 146.

150. Harvard student summer garment (detail of repair). For complete credit information, see credit 146.

151. Harvard student summer garment (detail of sleeve hook). For complete credit information, see credit 146.

152. Harvard student summer garment (detail of button). For complete credit information, see credit 146.

153. Harvard student summer garment (detail of weave). For complete credit information, see credit 146.

154. John Cocks, *Algarum Fasciculi; or A Collection of British Sea-weeds, Carefully Dried and Preserved, and correctly named after Dr. Harvey's "Phycologia Britannica,"* Fascicle 1 (Dublin: M. H. Gill, 1855), Farlow Herbarium of Cryptogamic Botany, Harvard University Herbaria.

155. John Cocks, *Algarum Fasciculi* (page opening for *Chrondrus crispus*). For complete credit information, see credit 154.

156. John Cocks, *Algarum Fasciculi* (detail of page with *Chrondrus crispus* specimen). For complete credit information, see credit 154.

157. John Cocks, *Algarum Fasciculi* (detail of glued *Chrondrus crispus* specimen). For complete credit information, see credit 154.

158. John Cocks, *Algarum Fasciculi* (detail of page with *Cladostephus verticillatus* specimen). For complete credit information, see credit 154.

159. John Cocks, *Algarum Fasciculi; or A Collection of British Sea-weeds, Carefully Dried and Preserved, and correctly named after Dr. Harvey's "Phycologia Britannica,"* Fascicle 1 (Dublin: M. H. Gill, 1855) (detail of page with *Delesseria sinuosa* specimen), Farlow Herbarium of Cryptogamic Botany, Harvard University Herbaria.

160. John Cocks, *Algarum Fasciculi; or A Collection of British Sea-weeds, Carefully Dried and Preserved, and correctly named after Dr. Harvey's "Phycologia Britannica,"* Fascicle 1 (Dublin: M. H. Gill, 1855) (detail of glued *Delesseria sinuosa* specimen), Farlow Herbarium of Cryptogamic Botany, Harvard University Herbaria.

161. Patent medicine bottle, "Macamoose, The Great Indian Tonic," containing the desiccated body of a house mouse, *Mus musculus*, USA, ca. 1865 (detail), General Artemas Ward House Museum, HU 2072.

162. Four-handled glass jar, Roman, fourth–fifth century (detail), Semitic Museum, 1936.2.98.

163. Blanding's turtle, *Emydoidea blandingi* (detail), Herpetology Collection, Museum of Comparative Zoology, Z111.

164. Burmese amber, pine, *Pinaceae*, Myanmar, Archives of the Economic Botany Herbarium of Oakes Ames, Harvard University Herbaria, 00201028.

165. Walrus ivory carving of a dog-sled team, Netsilik Inuit people, Kugaaruk, Nunavut, Canada, twentieth century, courtesy of the Peabody Museum of Archaeology and Ethnology, Harvard University, 64-34-10/43938.

Index

Printed in the USA/Agawam, MA
September 25, 2017